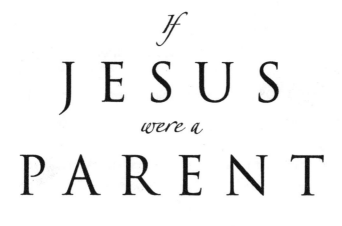

# *If*
# JESUS
## *were a*
# PARENT

### COACHING YOUR CHILD
### TO FOLLOW JESUS

# HAL PERKINS

If Jesus Were a Parent: Coaching Your Child to Follow Jesus

Copyright © 2006 by Hal Perkins

Printed in the United States of America

ISBN: 978-0-9787698-0-2

# For Debbi

Without you as mother and wife, we both know this book would never have been written. It was your typical, persistent encouragement that ultimately persuaded me that perhaps God wanted me to write.

But of infinitely greater significance was your life: your prayer, your partnership, your loyalty, your hospitality, your optimism, your spontaneity, your enthusiasm, your playfulness balancing my intensity, your faith, your laughter, your affirmation, your parties, your songs, your persistently positive words to our children—about God, about them, about church, about even me. Without you, what this book celebrates would not have happened. Only eternity will thank you appropriately.

I want to encourage and challenge you now to write your own book. Every mother needs to know what you know, to do what you do, and to reap the benefits you are now enjoying. "Her children will rise up and call her blessed."

In the meantime, I affectionately and thankfully dedicate this book and any eternal benefits derived from it to you. I love and honor you.

# ACKNOWLEDGEMENTS

♦The Grandview Church of the Nazarene Church Board for a month to begin the project and patience for the completion

♦Denise Culver for editing

♦Communication team Joy Mount, Cathy Jackson, Nicole Ammerman for caring assistance with the project

♦Pastoral team, church members, and other friends for reading and giving valuable feedback; especially Ruth Todd and Craig Rench

♦Debbi for giving the most time and best editing suggestions of all

# CONTENTS

# INTRODUCTION

In a generation more broken and wounded than any other in all history, there is an alarming deficiency of parents taking their God-given place in the lives of their children, resolutely leading them in love, truth, and wisdom. Parents are overwhelmed and ill-equipped, leaving them unable to untangle the web of circumstantial complexities and emotional complications in the lives of their kids.

We need a revelation of how *Jesus Himself* would parent. This is the subject that Hal addresses in *If Jesus Were a Parent*, giving understanding and extremely practical equipping of how to disciple your children according to Jesus' most excellent example, as portrayed in the gospels.

I'll never forget the first time I met my friend Hal Perkins at a pastors' conference about twenty years ago. In our first conversation I asked him to tell me about his church and his pastoral strategies. Instead of telling me about his demanding life as a senior pastor, he got out his wallet and introduced me to his family, his *first* ministry. I was struck by the depth and wisdom of this father, recognizing the unique grace that the Lord had given him in doing what Christian parents all over the earth want to know how to do—bring up kids who voluntarily choose to love and follow Jesus through all of life's struggles and difficulties. Since before their children were born, Hal and Debbi laid out a very purposeful parenting plan of how to bring forth strong hearts after God in their four children. They carried through with that plan throughout their children's lives, from birth to leaving home, and this is the disciple-making plan that they have published in this book.

Through the years, I have had the privilege of knowing Hal and Debbi's four children very well, even laboring side by side in ministry with several of them. They are some of my dear friends, and comrades, each pursuing Jesus in wholehearted lifestyles and marking many lives by leading others into loving abandonment to God. Hal's two daughters, Deborah and Dana, have been a part of the leadership team of the International House of Prayer since its beginning in 1999 and are both invaluable to me in who they are as persons, leaders, and examples among our staff here at IHOP. The fruit of Hal and Debbi's lives are clearly seen in their children by their deep confidence in God, their commitment and zeal to live the lifestyle described in the Sermon on the Mount, their great people skills, and their revelation of the greatness of the family dimension of God's kingdom. Their lives are characterized by teachability and humility, both fruits of confidence, and that confidence flowing largely from the parenting they received throughout their lives.

I wholeheartedly recommend *If Jesus Were a Parent* as a crucial resource to you both as parents and as leaders. I believe that as parents today begin to receive this God-given role at the deep level that God desires we will begin to witness a most essential transformation to the face of parenting across our Christian culture today.

*Mike Bickle*
Director of the International House of Prayer of Kansas City

# PREFACE

## Our Story

This book is really a story. It is the story of a young couple whose first pregnancy resulted in triplets. They were shocked. They quickly came to believe that the way to raise the triplets would be to attempt to disciple them in the ways that Jesus discipled His men. The process started by understanding and implementing parental authority. It continued by systematically helping the children logically yet freely choose to follow Jesus while simultaneously diminishing parental government. The ultimate goal was for the children to be fully devoted followers of Jesus who would be equipped to lead others to know and similarly follow Jesus. The story began considerably before the triplets were born.

I was a coach and math teacher before I became the father of triplets. In my second year of teaching, I sensed God's call into professional ministry. Immediately I decided to study all the accounts of Jesus' life in the gospels. My reason: to study and take notes on everything I could observe about His ministry. My intent was to learn all that I could from Him and, as much as possible, make His ministry pattern my ministry pattern.

I launched into the study. I observed Jesus' preaching ministry to the masses. I noted Jesus' care for the temporary needs of people. In the midst of all this, a dominant theme was emerging: Jesus spent a great deal of time with a very small group of His followers who later became leaders in His world-serving cause. When Jesus went to the lost, helped the hurting, or preached to the masses, a few men were almost always with Him. Toward the end of His time on earth, Jesus spent much of His time with this small group. They were called His disciples. They became His family (Matthew 12:48-50). Through them, Jesus turned the world upside down (Acts 17:6).

I believed the Holy Spirit spoke to me. I responded—in the midst of other pastoral activity, an indispensable strategy in my ministry would be making disciples. I studied Jesus' pattern for disciple-making in the gospels. While I was a youth pastor and then a student at seminary, a strategy for making disciples was evolving.

Then, in my first full-time pastoral responsibility, I finalized the strategy. Yellow pads of paper were filled with notes from the biblical record of Jesus' ministry. The ultimate mission was to lead as many as possible to Jesus in my lifetime. The immediate strategy was based on Jesus' example and command to make disciples. It took into account the limitations of both laymen and pastors. I was pleased, believing that I had found Jesus' strategy for me to lead the church I pastored into effective service with Him.

Then a vision began to emerge. I did the math. If, through me, Jesus made one disciple per year, each empowered by Jesus to make one disciple per year who made one disciple, etc., in 40 years the whole world would be discipled. I knew then—and even more so now—that visions and dreams are seldom fully realized. However, the vision and dream dramatically help to keep one going in the challenges of life's drudgeries, victories, and disappointments. If we are to be faithful to a God-given vision and strategy, we will need God-given empowerment and human resolve, or as it is often called—mission.

In January 1978, a mind-transforming event occurred in my life. Late one night I was reading a book written by a former Communist party leader who had become a Christian. It was written neither to refute nor support the ideologies or purposes of the Communists. It was written to reveal the strategies that enabled the Communists to grow. They multiplied from a small band of 17 men in the early part of the twentieth century to a powerful world force that would dominate one-third of the world and intimidate the other two-thirds by the middle of that same century.

As I read the book, zeal and passion welled up in my mind and emotions. The core strategies (not values or world view) that the Communists employed were virtually identical to those I had discovered in Jesus' making of disciples. The Communists employed the very same concepts, applications, and even words I had written down in my yellow pads as I observed Jesus' disciple-making ministry.

As I continued to read, I would occasionally set the book down and pace, tears streaming down my face. My heart was broken that Jesus' church had not taken seriously enough His disciple-making mandate and ministry (Matthew 28:18-20). I saw clearly what the Communists had accomplished in just a few decades by employing Jesus' disciple-making strategies—and without God's Word and Spirit for direction and power.

As I continued to read, a vision began to emerge in my mind and spirit. The Communists, without the message of the Cross, the Word of God, or the Holy Spirit, were able to capture the heart (mind, emotions, desires, and will) of at least one-third of the world in a short time. They made disciples of their thinking, values, purposes, and practices.

What would happen if Jesus' people—the Church around the world—were to take seriously their Master's mandate to go into the world and make disciples? What if Christians became *leaders* in the cause of Christ instead of remaining nominal, confused, half-hearted followers? (Their confusion and half-heartedness were understandable because they had not been discipled to authentically know and follow Jesus; no one had lived with them as Jesus lived with His disciples.) What would happen if the leaders in Christ's church would make it the top priority of their ministry to invest in a few, who would then be equipped to influence and lead others, and so on?

The vision was getting clearer. What would happen if each congregation had just one person committed not only to being a leader in Christ's cause but to making leaders for Christ? What would happen if a ministry of disciple-making were to spring up in every church?

The vision was now burning in my heart. What would happen if there were just one person committed to making leaders in every town and city? One pastor could not reach the world, but all of the world could be reached if there were leaders in every church committed to multiplying other leaders.

I dreamed of what should and could be. I wondered how I could bring others to see the necessity of following Jesus' model of disciple-making. I decided I could do very little, except work faithfully where I was.

Interestingly, about five years after my experience, Christian books about disciple-making flooded the church. Sadly, the concept of making disciples and disciple-makers got watered down in most churches to classroom teaching. We changed the name of our Sunday school classes from "Christian Education" to "Discipleship" but basically kept things as they had previously been. We thought we were making disciples by merely informing those who came to class once a week. We were "teaching them," but without significant relationship and accountability, we were not "teaching them to *obey everything.*" Most leaders did not take time to disciple a few people to be actual disciples of Jesus and to influence them to disciple others. The good news is that there have been and continue to be some churches and movements that are faithful in making disciples.

It is God's call for our children to become purposeful, strategic world visionaries who live daily on a mission—a mission to make disciples that is called, guided, and empowered by Christ. The key is that they be discipled to make disciples. Whether they become mothers, business owners, accountants, car mechanics, teachers, or wherever else God may place them, He wills that they be discipled and become disciple-makers.

What about your child? Has it occurred to you to teach your child to *obey everything* Jesus taught? Does this include teaching him to make disciples?

Is it reasonable in our culture to think that someone from your church will spend enough time with your child to truly disciple him to be Jesus' disciple and to make disciples of Jesus? How much time would be required per week? Per day? Can a Sunday school teacher, children's pastor, or youth pastor disciple your child's heart and life in Christlikeness? The best hope for your child to become a discipled disciple-maker of Jesus is for his family—especially his parents—to disciple him to do so.

My conclusion: Jesus would disciple His child to be and to make disciples. To help you help your child to be His disciple is the aim of this book.

# FOREWORD

I was afraid to become a parent. Most of the parents of teens I knew were struggling with resentful, rebellious teenagers. My fears escalated when my wife and I received the news that we were having triplets. Even during her labor, I began to groan in anticipation of three teenagers who would—among other things—all get their driver's licenses the same day and all go to college in the same year.

For a few days, I caught myself crying out in prayer, "Jesus, what shall I do?" Gradually, I realized that Jesus Himself had demonstrated the answer to my question. My desperate meditation led to this answer: "Parent as I, Jesus, would parent." This book is the story of Debbi's and my attempt to discover and parent as Jesus would.

What do you desire for your son or daughter? Dream for him? For her?[1]

This book will detail for you how to win the great war for the *heart* of your child. Myriads of books have been written describing various viewpoints on parenting. This book is all about helping you understand how to cooperate with God in positively influencing and winning your child's *heart*. By heart, I mean the interplay of thoughts, emotions, motives, desires, and will. You will learn how to know and work with the root of your child's need (the cause of behavior), not just the fruit (the visible behavior). A foundational thesis of the book is that "man looks on the outward appearance, but God sees the heart." (1 Samuel 16:7) The book empowers you, the parent, to effectively serve your child's highest good by discovering and working with his heart.

There are many other books that offer easier plans for parenting. This book starts with Parenting 101, and then leads you step by step into the more challenging aspects of parenting, coaching, and discipling your child to know

---

1 For ease of reading, throughout the book I will speak of one *child* using the pronouns *him, his,* or *her* to simplify the more inclusive but cumbersome use of *sons and daughters, him and her, his and her,* etc.

and authentically follow Jesus. Remember, Jesus does not command the impossible; what He commands, He empowers (Matthew 28:16-20; Philippians 1:6; 1 Thessalonians 5:23-24).

No matter where you are in relationship to your child, this book will give you essential understandings and practical tools to go from here. Our dream and prayer is that the Holy Spirit will use this book to empower you to parent as Jesus would if He were a parent. In reality, we pray and dream that Jesus Himself will parent your child—through you.

The stories in this book are mostly stories of our family. They are the fruit of what we dreamed, prayed, implemented, and experienced as a family. Sometimes we succeeded. Sometimes we failed. The stories are intended to illustrate concepts, mostly around disciple-making, that I studied and found in Jesus' ministry. We do not try to tell other parents' stories, which would in many cases be far more remarkable. We don't try to cover or document the best of family research on the market. We simply try to recount what happened in our family and why.

We purposefully discipled our children as we observed Jesus discipling His disciples. Today we are the parents of four adult children, all of whom are in full time, professional ministry—two at the International House of Prayer in Kansas City and two on staff at New Life Community Church in Colorado Springs. Each is an authentic follower of Jesus. Each spends many hours per week meeting with Jesus. Each is making disciples of Jesus. Debbi and I had no idea of how God would develop and use them as preachers, teachers, writers, and leaders. I tell a few of their accomplishments in the book. I write of these things fearful that you may consider it boastful. However, God knows what the intention and passion of my motives are:

- To exalt Him, our great God, who gives guidance to parents and then supernaturally blesses small faith and stumbling obedience
- To inspire and empower every parent possible—regardless of age—to parent as Jesus would: with the optimistic expectation that their children will become devoted followers and reproducers of Jesus

- To secure understanding of, commitment to, and accountability for a parenting process called disciple-making

Let's quickly get to the bottom line. Either God exists or not. Either there is eternity or not. Do you believe in God and eternity? If you do, then surely your desire and dream would be that, at *any* cost, your child is rightly related to God for eternity. This book is all about parenting your sons and daughters to be with God in heaven for eternity. Love for your children easily embraces this cost.

Further, because you love your children, you will give yourself to preparing them for what is best in this life: in relationships, in lifestyle, in vocational preparation, etc., in order to reach their highest potential. By following Jesus' teaching and example, this book reveals how you can successfully parent your children for their highest potential in this life.

It's really about *you* reaching your highest potential as a parent. I pray this for you.

# CHAPTER ONE

# Parent Power— Used, Abused, or Abandoned

**If Jesus were a parent, where would He start?**

Every Sunday when I was a kid, my parents took me to church. As the years passed, most of those church services disappeared into a crowd of childhood memories, but one Sunday will always stand out.

I was seven years old. That Sunday, when the pastor had been into the message for a while, I fidgeted in boredom and thought about the marbles I'd stashed in my pocket earlier that day. I reached in and pulled out a handful to admire. Realizing my best marbles were still in my pocket, I got greedy and tried to pull out more. Within a moment, all of the marbles spilled out onto the floor. There was no carpet to muffle their landing.

Bang, bang, bang! Can you hear the marbles hitting the hardwood floor? Can you hear them rolling down to the front of the church and slamming into the altar? Can you see the pastor halting his message to lean over the pulpit and glare his disapproval while the congregation all focused their attention on "the kid"? I slouched in my seat, certain that I was in for the worst whipping any kid ever got for bad behavior in church.

Suddenly, I felt a big hand on my shoulder. In the midst of my fear and embarrassment, my dad had slipped his arm around my shoulders and was patting my arm. I looked up to find him staring straight ahead, his expression declaring, "This is my son and I love him. Yes, he drops his marbles sometimes and everyone else wonders about him. But I am well pleased with him. I know he was a problem, but he didn't mean to be. I stick by him. I'll speak with him and help him understand. When it's all over, he'll do better than any of you realize. I'll see to it."

I would do almost anything with and for my dad. Even now as I write this memory, tears well up in my eyes. Why? I loved him. I easily submitted to his authority. Why? He parented me with grace. He was kind, patient, not rude, not easily angered. He forgave me and stood with me. He spent time with me. This gave him _relational_ authority with me. He explained things to me gently. He instructed and corrected me kindly. He explained things so they made sense to me. This gave him _rational_ authority. To be sure, he gave me specific directions and disciplined me firmly when I failed to obey. This is _positional_ authority. In brief, in all the above ways, he parented me as Jesus would.

The authority of the parent(s) is the essential key to having a functional, healthy home. If the child is not raised with appropriate authority, every kind of chaos and disaster can easily be bred. How does a parent get and maintain the appropriate authority for the child's first eighteen years? Each season in life seems to call for different kinds of authority. What are they? How can they be implemented so the child grows up not only healthy, but holy and happy?

If Jesus were a parent, where would He start?
"For the law was given through Moses; grace and truth came through Jesus Christ." _John 1:17_
"Do not think that I have come to abolish the Law ..." _Matthew 5:17_

## Jesus would parent His child with three kinds of authority.

What are the three kinds of authority that Jesus used with His disciples?

* Relational authority – think _grace_
* Rational authority – think _truth_
* Positional authority – think _law and government_

Parents are bigger, stronger, smarter, and richer than their children—at least for a while. Compared to their little children, parents have great power.

Some abuse their power. Some abandon it. God intends that parents use it with love that leads to relational authority, logic that leads to rational authority, and law which leads to positional authority.

My dad used all three kinds of authority in raising me. We begin the discussion of parenting seeking to understand and implement Christlike authority. My dad inadvertently mimicked Jesus, Who clearly articulated and demonstrated each of these kinds of authority in discipling His closest followers. Seeking to understand and implement effective authority into our parenting process is the focus of this chapter. It majors on relational authority. Positional authority is the topic of Chapter 2. Rational authority is the major focus of Chapters 5, 6, 7, and 11.

## Relational Authority—Grace

Relational authority means having a sufficiently caring relationship with your child so as to naturally and significantly influence him.

To illustrate relational authority, here is a picture of how it looked from the perspective of our daughter, Deborah, as she grew up experiencing relational authority. She recently spoke at our church and shared the following story:

> When I was very young, something constantly happened between my dad and me. I was kind of the strong one of the triplets, they say. I was the feisty one. It seemed to me that my brother and sister could always do everything right. I was the one that always messed up. I would say to myself, "Oh, Deborah, can you just do it right for once?" I seemed always to get in trouble. I would do something wrong.
>
> I still remember hearing my dad's voice after I would mess up. He would say, "Honey, come here." And I would think, "Oh, Deborah, why did you blow it again?" The last thing that I wanted was, once again, to walk to my father as a failure. Now I was going to have to stand in front of him ... again em-

barrassed that I had messed up. I would feel so much shame. From my childish mind I would think, "My dad is mad at me." I assumed he would reject me because once again I didn't measure up. So I would drag myself over to my dad. He would be on his knees. He would look at me eye to eye. He always put his arms around me. This happened over and over, and every time the same thing would happen. My dad would be holding me, but I would pull away. His arms were around me, but I would resist his embrace … pulling back. I could not look at him. I would look over this way and that way. Then, every time, he would open his arms, and I would fall down. Every time I would be totally embarrassed, because I had again fallen down. He would just ask me questions. "Honey, why are you pulling away from me?" I would get back up, and now we are eye to eye again. "I've got to get this over," I would think, "so I'd better just look him straight in his eyes." So now I'm looking at his eyes. And I remember that every time the first thing out of his mouth was, "I love you. I love you." And I would think, "No Dad, you can't love me now. I just messed up again. I can't receive your love right now. You are supposed to punish me. I'll do my punishment. I'll do my time. Then I will come back when I'm all cleaned up, and then you can hug me and then you can tell me that you love me. Don't tell me you love me right now. I can't accept it." This is a battle that some have with God's grace for us …

Deborah then went on to make the point that Jesus comes to us, in our weakness and failures, first with grace. Returning to the illustration from our relationship:

My behavior was changed because of receiving grace in my weakness. One time — I remember it very clearly — we were right beside the green and gold sofa. I had again done the wrong thing. Again my dad called me to come to him. Again I dreaded facing my failure. Again my dad held me. But this time, I did not resist his embrace. This time, when he let go, I did not fall backward. This time I simply relaxed in his embrace. Dad said, "Look! I am holding you and you are not pulling away." I saw it. I was relaxing in dad's embrace ... even though I had just failed ... again. That day I realized that I actually believed that my dad loved me ... even liked me ... in spite of my stumbling and weakness ... in spite of my failures. That day I realized that the lie was broken. The lie: *Dad will love me if I am good enough.* The lie expands: *God—the holy, righteous God—will love me if I am ever good enough.* This lie seems to inevitably get in, and must be broken. This is what we need to know and feel about our heavenly Father: He loves us. He knows us and likes us, even in our failures. In a world that focuses on and rewards success, and that rejects or even punishes imperfection, we all find it nearly impossible to believe that our heavenly Father is gracious. Let's review grace: God is love. He loves me and wants to hold me even though I just messed up. Because He loves me, He wants what is best for me. He dies for my best even while I am a rebellious sinner. But He experiences great pleasure ... great enjoyment ... He likes me, in spite of immature performance. He sees my heart and sees that I intend to be responding to Him ... to please Him. This results in my having severe pain when I fail Him, and imagining that He is equally pained as He looks at my failure. But He is looking at my heart that truly wants to do what He wants. My Heavenly Father likes me ... enjoys me ... is pleased with me even when I mess up ... even in my immaturity ... even in my brokenness ... because my intent to do what He wants is infinitely greater to Him than my ability to do it.

Jesus comes to all of us as Deborah described, first with love and grace. He is the ultimate example of creating relational authority. Crosses adorn necks and buildings the world over, a tribute to relational authority. Jesus governs with grace. Grace is the face that love wears as it looks at failure and imperfections. In love, Jesus left heaven and came all the way to where we are … while we were yet sinners (Romans 5:8). Jesus spent time with His "family" at campfires, in fishing boats, in synagogues, at parties. He served and blessed them. He graciously suffered on a terrible cross for us in spite of our indifference and rebellion and perpetual marble-dropping. He demonstrates His heart of grace toward us and then invites all to come to Him and enter His family and kingdom. Because we trust this God of grace, we follow Him. As we follow Him, He transforms us.

Like an ideal parent, Jesus initiates relationship with goodness and grace. He served, sacrificed, and suffered for us. Our hearts are warmed as we increasingly realize the depths of His grace and goodness. His love ultimately influences us to live for Him who died for us (2 Corinthians 5:15). This is relational authority.

—∿—

*Grace is the face that love wears as it looks at failure and imperfections.*

—∿—

## To parent as Jesus would, we establish relational authority.

How can parents build relational authority with their children? A few of the foundational concepts include:

+ **Experiencing the grace of God personally**

To say that God is gracious toward me means that He does good toward me even though I do not deserve it. The grace of Jesus for us, revealed supremely in the cross, changes how we view ourselves and others. When we receive the grace of God, we see ourselves as wanted and valued, in spite of our imperfections and weaknesses. We are not compulsively focused on our performance as the means to acquire value. Because we think this way about God's valuing of us, we are inclined to feel and give value to others, especially our children, in spite of their imperfections and weaknesses.

The grace of Jesus in us, by the indwelling presence of His Holy Spirit, provides the inclination and the reminder to be gracious (Romans 5:8; John 14:26; 16:13-14). Therefore, we have the spiritual ability to lead our families with grace, if we will. We are empowered by the Holy Spirit to initiate love. We can value, serve, bless, accept, and forgive. We can suffer with and for our children when they "drop their marbles." This gracious lifestyle will give us influence, authority, and government just because our children love and respect us. We are thus empowered to manage our families well (1 Timothy 3:4).

### ✦ Being proactively kind and sensitive

Love does what it believes to be the best for the one loved. My dad's love for me did not mean that he gave me whatever I wanted. It did mean that he was kind and sensitive, even when I did not deserve it. His kindness opened my heart to him very early in my life. Our "big adventures" included walking to the Dairy Queen for a soft ice cream cone and driving to the airport to see the planes take off and land. When my dad had to drive across the state on business, he often asked me to go. He listened to me before reacting to my behavior. It was easy to obey my dad because he loved me. It was easy to believe whatever he told me, because I trusted the one who was good to me. My immature, uneducated mind unconsciously assumed whatever he said to be correct. This is relational authority. For better or for worse, it is powerful.

### ✦ Revealing your value, pleasure, and delight in your child to your child

Many of my earliest memories involve spending time with my dad. He asked me to do things with him and in the process I felt important to him. It seemed to me (and I believe it was true) that he enjoyed being with me. He was excited about my interests and progress. I felt his pleasure in me. He took me to his work and to company events. As he introduced his five-year-old son to the executives in his company, I felt his delight and pride in me. As he casually poured his thoughts into my childlike, non-critical mind, my ways of thinking and values were shaped, thus my life was shaped. Initially, it was not his logic, but his love that caused me to listen to him. I believed him because I liked him because he first loved me. He had developed relational authority.

### ✦ Revealing the grace of God when your children "drop their marbles"

God makes possible our being gracious to our families. It is our opportunity and responsibility to cooperate with the Holy Spirit by working out the grace He has worked in (Philippians 2:12-13). This may initially require self-control and self-discipline. Over time, it becomes a way of life.

Like Jesus, my father responded to my immaturity with grace. Revisit my father's response after I dropped my marbles: my dad was gracious to me in my foolishness and weakness. He was caring and kind, though I had just dropped my marbles. He chose to stand with me in my weakness, rather than abandon or condemn me. When others glared at me for my external failure (dropping marbles), my dad chose to put his arm around me. He did not condone my errors, but he responded first with grace before teaching or chastising. Note: He did talk with me about my errors, and he did discipline me when I needed it, but always with love and kindness, not anger and rejection. It was easy to obey him because I loved him (John 14:15). He had relational authority.

If you struggle in being gracious to your child, remember that God truly is working in you to will and to do His gracious purposes (Philippians 2:13). Your kids drop their marbles … consistently. Even if it requires an act of your will, work out what God has worked in: put your arm around them. There is more to do, but not until you have genuinely revealed grace. When immediate control or discipline is required, do it, but don't excuse yourself from being gentle and kind in the process.

Relational authority is a powerful influence. Love leads to trust, which leads to influence. The Communists reportedly said that if they had a child up to age six, they had him for life. I knew that my human father was for me, whether I was perfect in church or dropped my marbles. He valued me when I hit a single and when I struck out. I was loved by him and I felt it. Feeling his love when I failed dramatically influenced me to love him and do what he wanted. This is relational authority.

If your child tries to do what you want because he feels your love, you have relational authority. Jesus said that, "If you love me, you will obey what I command." (John 14:15) We love Him because He first loved us (1 John 4:19).

## Rational Authority—Truth

Rational authority is the ability to reason and persuade resulting in your child agreeing and being influenced.

Very early our children ask many questions, including "why" questions. "Daddy, why do you put pepper on the meat?" Questions are raised repeatedly with respect to required behavior. "Why do I have to go to bed now?"

Be assured of this: as soon as a child is able to communicate and ask questions, you are well into the time to start working on rational authority.

Jesus governs with truth. He reveals the truth about God (John 1:18; 14:9). His truth—known, believed, and obeyed—sets us free. His truth enlightens what is dark and confusing. This allows us to see truth and right so that we don't stub our toes in the dark or fall off a cliff to our destruction. He is the truth and the light (John 1:4, 14).

Jesus has powerful authority in our lives when He speaks; for we know that what He, the God of infinite knowledge and wisdom, says is absolute truth and reality. If He tells us the way things are or will be, we know it is true. It is easy to choose to live from that perspective. If He tells us what to do, we unhesitatingly set out to obey because we have faith in Him. He knows what

He is talking about. As His truth becomes ingrained in our minds, we unconsciously live more like the way He lived because His mind is now our mind and governs internally without external control.

Like Jesus, parents have influence with their children. From the start, I unquestioningly adopted my dad's ways of thinking because I felt his love (relational authority). From then on, most of what he said made sense because I had already unquestioningly accepted his basic ideas. My mind was shaped by what he said. New things that he said further dovetailed into my little mind because I already thought much the way he thought. When my dad spoke, I listened. What he said made sense to me. What made sense, I believed. What I believed determined how I behaved. He had rational authority. It is powerful!

The openness that results from relational authority is almost always a prerequisite for parents to influence their children rationally. Without a strong relationship, many children will not believe their parents, regardless of how logical their parents' teaching is. Why?

If you have negative thoughts and feelings about me—no matter how logical I may be—it is hard for you, especially if you are a child, to receive and respond to my logic. Relational authority opens the door to rational authority. Because of my dad's relationship with me, he could reason with me. Where grace exists (relationship), truth is heard. Recognizing and receiving a parent's logic (rationale) is far more possible when love and grace are felt by the child. If I know you love me, I am far more likely to consider your logic. My dad explained his perspective, giving me reasons for what I might think and do. His truth, mingled with his love, powerfully influenced me. I agreed with him—his values, his dreams, his plan for surviving life. I accepted his world view. When I did not understand, or even disagreed, my dad's graciousness allowed discussion. He had many more years of experience, and in gracious conversational give-and-take, he could easily persuade me. Unknowingly, I thought like and thus became very much like my dad. I was his little disciple.

Cults are able to brainwash their victims because they initiate and establish relationships with care and kindness. They secure rational power by first establishing relational authority.

Rational authority is a dramatically powerful force. It empowers good or evil, depending on the world view of the one with rational authority. Jesus identified Himself as the truth, and said His truth would set us free. Satan rules much of this world, primarily through lies (Ephesians 2:2). My dad did not have to pressure me to see his way. My heart was open to his thinking. He did not have to impose external government on me. Independent of my dad's supervision, I did what he would do because I thought the way he thought. This is rational authority.

―∿∿―

## *I was not afraid of my dad, but I was afraid to disobey him.*

―∿∿―

To parent as Jesus would, we establish rational authority. We can engage our children in a constant search for truth. God's word says, "Come, now, let us reason together." (Isaiah 1:18) When children are very young, we must simply expect them to do what we say without giving them an explanation. However, as children develop the ability to communicate, our position changes. Our style changes from *No!* and *Go!* to *What should we do?* or *Here is why I think this*, or *How should we handle this?* or *What do you think?* or *Do you have a better idea?* or *What would you do if you were a parent? Why?* Before we issue ultimatums, we can engage in mutual conversation to find the best solution. We listen, show that we understand, explain our thinking, and find out if our children understand us. When our child agrees with us and believes accordingly because we have truly persuaded him, we have rational authority. How to plant truth into your child's heart is the topic of Chapters 5, 6, 7 and 11.

## Positional Authority—Law and Government

Positional authority is the delegated responsibility by God to care for others, including the responsibility to benevolently govern behavior (Romans 13:1).

A policeman pulls up behind you, lights flashing. If you don't pull over, he has the authority to make you pay—financially and otherwise. His position gives him *authority*. The government that gives him position has the power to judge, impose fines, require community service, even imprison. Out of respect for—even fear of—the authority and power of the government, you do what the policeman says. God has given parents a similar position of authority.

To parent as Jesus would, we establish positional authority. As parents, we have been given a title and position of authority. Jesus directs children to obey parents (Ephesians 6:1-3). He directs parents to teach children to obey (Deuteronomy 6:4-9; Ephesians 6:4; Matthew 28:18-20).

During my childhood, my dad was "the policeman," the law, the one with authority. He had power and would use it if necessary. I respected and honored his right and ability to govern my behavior. If he looked at me and shook his head no, or pointed and quietly but firmly said go, I did not hesitate to obey. I was not afraid of my dad, but I was afraid to disobey him. In his position, he had the power to make me pay if I ignored his will. Positional authority must be established very early. (Chapter 2 explains how to do this.) However, positional authority must be established and implemented kindly (grace) and wisely (truth). Thus, even the implementation of parental governance is an opportunity to—like Jesus—be full of grace and truth.

---

### *The child's interests and preferences are not to be "lord" of schedules.*

---

Jesus is Lord and has all authority and power to govern as He wills (Matthew 28:18). All those who have authentic faith in Him (that is, who believe He is King, Lord, God) will "pull over when His lights are flashing." He is the ultimate in positional authority. Ideally, we desire to obey Him because we experience His love (relational authority). We may desire to obey Him because we believe that what He commands is what is best for us (rational authority). At the very least, Christians are committed to obey Him because we recognize His position as King of kings with all authority and power. We have faith that He—and He alone—is God.

One way that Jesus' kingdom and government is made tangible on earth is through those who obey Him. Their will is set to obey Him because they actually believe that He is God. What He directs through scripture, they intend to obey because they believe Him to be their Lord, Master, and God. As God, obviously He can and does act independently and with power any time He deems best. However, He does not have to overpower or overrule believers. Jesus has positional authority for those who authentically believe Him to be God. A heart to obey is the only logical response of those who believe that Jesus was and is God (Romans 1:6; 16:26).

At this point, I want to caution parents. Any parent (at least for a while) has the power to intimidate, dominate, or manipulate because of superior size and strength. It is tempting to govern a family entirely or primarily out of position backed by power. It is a common but grave mistake for parents to rely solely on power. Sadly, some parents follow this pattern because it was the only one modeled during their childhoods.

Parenting with only positional authority often results in radical rebellion. If our child obeys us only because we have the power to make him sorry if he does not, we have much work to do in helping him understand and submit to God and others with positional authority. He often will rebel against all authority.

The other extreme is for parents to abdicate governing, usually excusing it as "love." There are many parents who have abandoned or neglected teaching their children to obey. They then have a child-oriented home where the child's desires and whims control and govern the family priorities and activities. The child's interests and preferences are not to be "lord" of schedules ("I want to go to the game!"), of finances ("But Mom, I just have to have it."), or of values ("But everyone else is doing it.").

13

The solution is to use parental authority to govern with grace and guidance, using power only as a last measure. This is how Jesus governs ... grace and truth, with ultimate accountability for response to His grace and truth. If Jesus were a parent, He would consistently care, including thoughtful, clear direction with appropriate reward or discipline. This is the kind of parenting our children desperately need.

---

*This is how Jesus governs ... grace and truth,*
*with ultimate accountability.*

---

The order of parental authority needs always to be consistent:

*Grace*—Gracious love needs to be constant, from beginning to end. This leads to relational authority.

*Truth*—Logical explanation (parental perception of truth and right) is given for the benefit of all being governed, including the child. Initially, logic and explanation cannot be employed because the child is incapable of communication. In the child's early years, logical explanations are given without dialogue. Gradually, the child is purposefully included in the process of thinking and determining direction. To the degree that a parent has the ability to have his perspective make sense to and influence the child, the parent has rational authority.

*Law and Government*—Governing (securing compliance to direction, usually with reward for obedience or penalty for disobedience) is almost always required to train children in righteousness. The nature and extent of government is based on the child's response to love and truth. The transfer from parental government to a child's self-government (with the goal of Jesus' government) can occur strategically and gradually. This strategic transfer is the topic of Chapter 3.

Think with me. Who will establish an obedient heart in your child? Will the TV? Movies? Friends? Children's ministry at your church? If they won't, who will? In the next chapter specific and strategic steps are given to teach your child to obey.

# CHAPTER TWO

# Teach Them to Obey— or Else

" … teaching them to obey everything I have commanded you …" *Matthew 28:20*

## Jesus would teach them to obey.

Jesus required that His disciples obey Him (Matthew 7:21; 10:5; 14:22; Luke 6:46-49). Further, He commanded that His disciples teach their disciples to obey everything He commanded (Matthew 28:18-20). To parent as Jesus would, parents must teach their children to obey.

This chapter will greatly help you establish heart obedience in your child. For an armload of reasons, including the salvation of your child, you must teach and train your child in heart obedience. Many reasons are listed at the end of this chapter.

What is the true essence of obedience that God expects of His children? Understanding this will clarify how to lead our child into God's will regarding obedience. Imagine the following dinnertime scenario: A family is sitting at the table. The father reminds his children that there was a problem the night before when one family member spilled his milk. He tells them to be careful tonight to not spill their milk. Dinner goes smoothly until the doorbell rings. The four-year-old jumps out of his chair. In his excitement, he unintentionally knocks over his glass of milk. It spills across the table and onto the floor. The father helps his son quickly clean up the milk while the mother welcomes their guests into the living room. A few minutes later, while the family visits

17

with their company, the older brother sees an opportunity. He dislikes milk. He knows his parents expect him to drink his milk, but as they visit, off to the kitchen he goes to deposit his milk in the sink. He delights in watching it go down the drain.

Let's analyze this simple story. Both boys spilled their milk. Were both sons disobedient? The younger brother didn't mean to spill his milk. It was an accident. But by some parents' way of judging, the four-year-old was guilty of disobedience because he did, in fact, spill the very milk he was told not to spill. Technically, the older brother didn't "spill" his milk. He purposefully poured it in the sink. Did either or both boys disobey their father's direction to not spill the milk? If only one disobeyed, which one was it?

## God does not judge primarily by external appearances.

God does not judge primarily by external appearances (John 7:24). He observes the heart (1 Samuel 16:7). If Jesus were the human father, how would He respond to the two boys?

I believe that a father like Jesus would pull the four-year-old on his lap, hug him, and then help him clean up the mess. I think he would talk to the younger son about what happened and why, and what he needed to learn and change in the future. Aren't you glad that the Lord treats us graciously when we are weak and make mistakes?

What about the older boy? A father like Jesus would, I think, ask the older boy to sit down and talk. He would gently and graciously expose or confront the disobedient behavior. Suppose that the older boy was truly repentant, confirming that he knew how his self-rule violated the father's rule. Suppose he showed resolve to submit to the father's rule in the future. The father would be pleased and express his delight appropriately. He would also respond with wisdom by talking about what happened, why it happened, and the immediate and long-term cost of willful disobedience. Appropriate consequences would need to be implemented. For example, the father may require that the boy buy two gallons of milk with his own money, or do the dishes for three nights, or drink three glasses of milk right then, or something the father determined to be meaningful consequence commensurate with the wrong behavior. The real issue was settled: the honest intention of the boy to obey his father. This is heart obedience.

What if the older boy responded with excuses, blaming, or arguing? In that case, I think a father who is like Jesus would kindly but firmly say something like: "What you did is no longer the issue. The issue is your thinking and attitude. The issue is your position toward me, your father. It is your heart. Am I the father here—the head of this home—or are you free to live in my home but ignore me and my government? Do you trust that I am for you and our family? Do you trust my wisdom? If not, do you at least recognize that I am the head, governor, and father of this family?"

If the boy said that he believed from his heart the right and responsibility of the father to rule, the father could easily test the boy's heart. "What about the milk? Next time, will you drink it or throw it away?" If the older boy were uncertain about the issue of authority, the father would point out that they need to go back to the relationship issue. To the father, the milk is not the issue. Whether the boy drinks or does not drink milk is small.

The essential issue is the father-son *relationship*. From the boy's point of view, who is his father? A good buddy? A housemate? Santa Claus? Or a father with authority? If the father cannot depend on the boy to choose to submit and sincerely seek to obey the father's rules, then the father will have to put penalties for disobedience into place. This is control by force because of an unsubmissive—even rebellious—heart in the son.

The father's deep desire is to have a son who knows and trusts him. He desires a son who knows that his father is for him and would only call for what is best. If the son had that kind of faith in his father, he would always be willing to obey and there would be harmony in the home. If the son did not have faith in the father, the father's only recourse would be to set laws, including penalties for violation of the law. The father has the power to make the son obey. This is far from the ideal father-son relationship. The father wants a relationship based on his love and wisdom for the boy, and the boy's trust in the father. If the boy does not love the father enough to freely submit, or trust the father enough to freely submit, the boy must finally be required to submit to the father's position and power.

Jesus, like our heavenly Father, is full of grace and truth. For those who refuse to respond to Him, He will ultimately resort to judgment based on their performance. He will exercise His right and power to punish. Our heavenly Father does not want that kind of relationship or its result. Immature children who sincerely intend to obey God but accidentally spill their milk will be in God's eternal Kingdom. Those who refuse to trust the heavenly Father's love and wisdom, as demonstrated by unwillingness to bend their knee to His authority, will not be allowed to destroy heaven with sinful pride and selfishness.

Children must be taught to submit to parental authority so that they understand and have experience in submitting to authority when they come to realize who their heavenly Father-King is (Ephesians 6:1-3).

---

*I have an obedient heart when my spirit is willing,*
*even though my body is weak.*

---

## What is an obedient heart?

Earlier, it was noted that Jesus required obedient hearts in His disciples. Children are not born with obedient hearts. Parents *must instill* a heart to obey. What does an obedient heart look like?

I have an obedient heart when my *will is set* to obey God and others in authority over me. I may not know what to obey, or feel like obeying, or have the ability to obey. My motive for obeying may be less than perfect. Regardless of all of those factors, when my will is set to obey, I have an obedient heart.

Jesus said, "The spirit is willing, but the body is weak." (Matthew 26:41) I have an obedient heart when my spirit is willing, even though my body is weak.

Think with me a moment about what the Bible calls our "heart." We think in our hearts (Genesis 6:5). We feel in our hearts (Genesis 6:6). We have inclinations in our hearts (Genesis 8:21). We pray in our hearts (Genesis 24:45). We have desires in our hearts (Genesis 34:3). We can have glad hearts (Exodus 4:14). And the list goes on. As if in a crock pot, all of these varied heart functions simmer together in our hearts.

Return with me to Chapter 1. Did the little boy who dropped his marbles have a "bad heart"? He did not *intend* to be bad. He did not intend to disrupt the service or even to disobey his parents' direction to "be good." In his immaturity, he simply lacked wisdom and skill. Children allow their immediate desires and emotions to govern them. Thoughts, feelings, inclinations, desires, etc., all influence each other. When a child is aware of a good reason to behave counter to his desires or emotions, and chooses this behavior, it is an impressive act of the will. Think of a child who has been trained so that his will is set to obey those in authority over him. His desires, emotions, and logic may pull him to oppose the direction given by a parent. But if the child genuinely *tries* to obey, in spite of his desires and regardless of the outcome, he has an obedient heart. He may not know what to obey or how to obey. He may not be able to obey. But if he *intends* to obey, he has a "heart to obey"; an obedient heart.

Sometimes a child's willpower is overcome by conditions of confusion, weakness, bad judgment, forgetfulness, overwhelming external pressures, etc. Jesus, however, knows and values the commitment of the child's heart—the will. He knows without question when a child is *willing* to do right yet is overcome by weakness. He also knows without question when a child has not set his will to do right. To follow Jesus in parenting, parents must teach and train the heart of their child to obey.

If I do not successfully coach my child in obedience, who will? If I do not successfully train my child to submit to authority—including God's—who will?

My family is my first and highest responsibility. As a disciple of Christ and a Christian parent, I must teach my child to obey everything Jesus taught (Matthew 28:20). Therefore, I must first help him to develop a willingness to obey from the heart. How?

## Steps to train an obedient heart

The following training needs to begin immediately for any child who is not trained to submit to parental authority:

### Step 1: Affection

Consistently communicate deep, profound affection for each family member. A few ways of communicating affection include personal attention—time alone, sensitive hugs, encouraging e-mail notes, phone calls, gifts, etc. These unconditional expressions of affection are called grace. Unless they are ignored or misinterpreted, they strengthen relational authority.

### Step 2: Communication

Well before children can speak, they can understand. Further, they can be trained. They can be taught "no" by using gentle negative reinforcement, and "go" by using positive reinforcement. When these children throw food on the floor, or take pictures from the coffee table, a consistent, gentle but firm "no" associated with an appropriate thump on the hand jolts most children into stopping and gradually learning that "no" means something. They learn to obey; some quickly, some gradually. Our children were trained to obey "no" and "go" before they could walk or talk.

A tasty piece of soft cookie can be placed strategically so that a crawling child can be shown where the cookie is. The child can be told to go get it. The reward for obedience is the cookie. To further strengthen the training, put the cookie within reach of the child. Say, "No." When the child reaches for the cookie, say, "No," and give an appropriate thump. They can early learn they don't always get what they want. The child can, very early, be trained to obey.

Through careful, consistent training, obedience can be learned very early.

As early as possible, *communicate* that Jesus expects parents to represent Him by loving and leading their children. Your child needs to know that his parent is under authority to do what is best from God's perspective. One way to communicate this is by saying something like: "Jesus calls me to love you and all our family by doing His will for our family. I need to lead us by finding out what He wants for our family and leading us to do it."

Parents need to lovingly and clearly *communicate* what their children are to do. As children grow in ability to understand and communicate, it is very important that parents explain *why* obedience is absolutely necessary. Over and over, in many different ways, the reasons for obeying should be talked about until children can explain why to their parents' satisfaction. Five of these reasons are listed at the end of this chapter. Explain the benefits of happily obeying and the cost of disobeying parents, teachers, policemen, and God. Far more important than the particular issue at stake is developing submissiveness to authority.

When our son Dan was four, he was having a problem. He wouldn't leave his shoes and socks on. Debbi had her hands very full with three nine-year-olds and one four-year-old. It became exasperating to her for Dan to always be barefoot when she was ready to go, to say nothing of being unable to guess where the shoes and socks may be located. So I very clearly directed him to take his shoes and socks off only when his mother gave him permission. I also told him that something very bad would happen if he took them off without permission. This was the communication phase. My great threat didn't faze him. I got word the next day that, once again, he took off shoes and socks without permission. So Dan and I had a talk about his disobedience and the penalty. His penalty that night was to come to me, take off his shoes and socks, run through the living room, into the kitchen, through the family room, and back to me (it made a nice running track). Then he would put his shoes and socks back on, fasten them perfectly, show me, and then take off the shoes and socks again, go run around the house again, come back to me, and repeat the process—20 times. It was a long night, but he did remember to not take off his shoes without permission. More importantly, the heart issue of obeying parental positional authority was getting in. Someone called this "Bootie Camp."

As parents, our motive is not to be the "dictators" of our families. Our motive is to know and sensitively do God's will for each family member. This will ultimately include helping our children seek and find God's will for themselves independently of us.

For now, you must be committed to *communicating* exactly what each child is to know and to do, including the rewards for obedience and the consequences for disobedience. *Communicate* clearly your expectations, such as boundaries, rules, expected behaviors, etc. Don't forget character standards from passages of scripture like 1 Corinthians 13. Carefully *communicate* these as family standards.

Communication is unsatisfactory until it is fully understood by all parties involved. Ask your child to repeat back exactly how you expect him to behave and the rewards for obedience and the consequences for disobedience. Some families write out their expectations and have children sign this list. Accountability includes the process of supervision, along with positive or negative rewards.

---

## Share God's delight in your child's willing heart.

---

*Communicate* the reasons for your expectations. Explain why you are creating a boundary, rule, or family policy. Help your family to know your heart—the reasons you are creating government in this area. It is best to initially seek understanding, agreement, and commitment based on understanding instead of reward or threat of punishment.

Ask your child if he understands the reasons for your expectation. This helps him respect or "stand under" your understanding. If your child cannot explain your reasons to your satisfaction, ask if he needs to hear the reasons again or if he would like another chance to explain the reasons to you.

## Step 3: Affirmation

Encourage and affirm your child every time you see him obeying (Hebrews 10:25). Remind him of the expectations you have established when you think it will help. Be the voice of the Lord to encourage. Share God's delight in your child's willing heart and any progress. Reward good intentions and good actions spontaneously or as you have promised.

## Step 4: Caution

Warn your child when he fails to obey (1 Thessalonians 4:6). How many warnings are appropriate? Too many will spoil the process. When a child begins to assume that a warning will be given, it is past time to quit giving warnings. If you choose to be merciful by not punishing wrong behavior, explain that you are being merciful (not giving the disobedient one what he deserves), and explain exactly why.

Sometimes a warning is not in order. Failure to obey an immediate, specific directive is a problem of rebellion not habit or memory. Children need to be taught to obey and to know that correction without warning is to be expected for disobedience. However, new expectations may be forgotten in a moment of weakness. When the parent discerns that the child accidentally "spilled the milk" a warning and mercy are in order.

## Step 5: Correction

Keep your promise to penalize disobedience (Proverbs 19:15; 13:24) Carry out the previously communicated penalty for stepping over a boundary or failing to obey a directive.

Colossians 3:21 says, "Fathers, do not embitter your children." Are you focused on lovingly doing what is best for your child or are you reacting to his behavior? You are not ready to correct your child until your negative thoughts and emotions are under the control of the Holy Spirit. If you need to, walk away from your child to bring your own emotions and thoughts into alignment with what Jesus thinks and feels. Lead yourself to Jesus and His truth. Pray.

As you correct your child, be kind and compassionate (Ephesians 4:32). Your facial expression, tone, and volume of voice are crucial. Test your feelings and motives. Many a parent is unaware of the hurt, anger, and rejection his child feels because of the parent's body language. This can dramatically hurt any attempt to discipline effectively. Do your best to speak softly and gently.

Also, do your best to never embarrass your child by correcting him in front of others. The opinion of others rather than the violation usually becomes the issue. It also communicates insensitivity and lack of concern for your child's feelings. As inconspicuously as possible, pull your child aside for a private response to the wrong behavior.

---

## You would obediently submit to a coach, supervisor, or police officer. Why not Jesus?

---

Establish responsibility. When you talk to your child, ask, "What did you do?" (Matthew 12:36) Focus on the facts. At this point, the issue is not *why* your child violated your expectations, but the fact that he did. The child's behavior is revealing. As well as you can tell, his behavior shows indifference to your expectation, or worse—defiance. When a child disobeys, he exerts his own will over the parent's will, whether he thinks of it that way or not.

Next ask your child to explain why you are going to discipline him. You have already communicated your expectation and the consequences for violating this expectation. Affirm your love credibly. Assure your child that you care and that you want what is the best for him, which includes a heart to obey authority. Review the seriousness of ignoring or rebelling against parental authority and learning habits of indifference to authority—especially God's.

Finally, carry out the discipline you have promised.

Our children learned that unacceptable behavior would often result in a serious talk, probably with Dad. I would ask them questions like: "What happened? Why? What was your responsibility? What do you think you should have done? Why? What do you think you will do next time? Do you need anything to help you remember? Do I love you? Does Jesus love you? What do you think Jesus would like you to do? Why?"

These talks served two purposes. First, Debbi and I used problems and conflicts to bring grace and truth to our children. Second, the talks somewhat motivated our children to not behave inappropriately in the future, partly because of the "punishment" of the loving but sometimes long talk with a parent about wrong behavior. This takes time, but it consistently turned a problem into a positive time to experience love and truth. Whenever possible, use creative discipline to tie the behavior to the discipline (like fastening and unfastening shoes). Hebrews 12:4-11 will help your child understand that our heavenly Father disciplines us with love.

**Step 6: Restitution**

Any person or group that has been hurt by your child's behavior must be contacted and restitution made. It was a hard moment for one of my children when we had to go into a local store and explain that a candy bar had been stolen. But it was the right thing. Further, it was most memorable and most impacting. Train your child (by your example and instruction) to say, "I was wrong," without blaming others or excusing himself. Responsibility for actions, regardless of circumstances, must be learned.

**Step 7: Reflection**

After correction and restitution have been accomplished, there is still more work to do. Reflect on—talk together about—the experience. Carefully demonstrate love and sensitivity to your child. After taking disciplinary action, sensitively tell your child that you care and desire what is best for him. It may mean asking if he thinks you have been unfair or unloving. You might want to pray to celebrate God's love for the child and all others involved, to request wisdom, and to show your faith in God to bring good for all who love Him. Be careful not to "blame" God for the child being disciplined. Make sure that your child understands that the discipline was because of his choice based on thoroughly communicated expectations.

## Becoming the picture of obedience

Parent, you can be the *picture* of a willing heart that will train your child far better than a thousand words. Show your child your will to obey whatever Jesus says. In order to teach and train your child in an obedient heart, be sure the following issues are settled in your heart:

*Set your will to be obedient.* "Follow me as I follow Christ." (1 Corinthians 11:1) Renew or establish your absolute allegiance to Jesus as your King. Through faith in Him, you have entered His Kingdom. You are a loyal subject of the King. You would obediently submit to a coach, supervisor, or police officer. Why not Jesus? You believe that Jesus created everything, came to redeem us by dying for sin, was resurrected, and lives now as King of kings. He is the King. You trust and love Him. Therefore, it is natural for you to bow your knee to Him and His will. Whatever you know to be His will for you to do, you will seek to obey. Tell your family of your commitment to obey Jesus, including specific biblical areas He is speaking to you about.

When Jesus says, "Quit gossiping," we commit to quitting. When the Holy Spirit convicts us of resentment, we willingly repent and get it right. Our example is one of willing obedience to anything Jesus speaks to us about— swearing, serving, harshness, tithing, alcohol, criticalness, encouraging, movies, fear, self-pity, pornography, exaggeration, unkindness, complaining, selfishness, etc. Christians do not knowingly say "No" to Jesus. Your example of a will set to obey Jesus will greatly influence your child to a similar set of his will.

*Confess unChristlike behavior to any family members who may observe or suspect unChristlikeness—disobedience—in you the parent.* "Confess your

sins to each other and pray for each so that you may be healed." (James 5:16)
One great way to demonstrate heart obedience and loyalty to Jesus in a positive, non-threatening way is when you confess your own unChristlikeness to your family. You have a chance to teach a great deal in that moment. You teach them that when Christians make errors (drop their marbles, spill their milk), they are honest about these errors. You teach that Christians are saved by God's grace through Christ's death on the cross—not by performing perfectly without error. You teach that Christians hate and repent of their errors. They do not compromise. They don't get discouraged and quit because they fail. They don't make excuses or blame others. They try to make right what they have done wrong.

—⁓—

## Don't underestimate the power of opening your imperfect heart to your family.

—⁓—

When you have messed up, consider saying something like the following to your children: "My words [or tone, motive, attitude, etc.] were wrong. You know I am committed to following Jesus. He showed me how wrong I was. I agreed with Him that I don't want to be that way. He has forgiven me. I trust Him to help me be better. I'll do my best to not let this happen anymore. Is there anything that you and I need to do about this situation?"

Don't underestimate the power of opening your imperfect heart to your family. Let them see that followers of Jesus are far from perfect, that they are honest, and they know what to do when they "drop their marbles." Teach them clearly from your own imperfections about walking with Jesus, and getting up when you fall down. Your honest confession to your child of falling will be of utmost value in his grasping the Christian walk. Your child will learn greatly as you explain what you learn from your experience of falling and learning how to get up and go again.

*Demonstrate for your child how to handle failure.* Your child will be tempted to be discouraged or devastated when he slips and falls while committed to obeying you and Jesus. Be prepared to pick him up. When your child first tries to walk, you coach him to not give up when he falls. Similarly, you want to prepare him to walk with Jesus. When he comes to know Jesus enough to trust Him, he will, quite naturally, try to do what Jesus says. If Jesus says to be kind or to forgive enemies or to serve others, he will try. Often, for many legitimate reasons, he will fall. He will come short of God's will. He will fail Jesus and be disappointed with himself. You must teach him how to get up when he falls.

A big part of having an obedient heart is simply being *unwilling to quit.* We must decide to get up again and again, no matter how many times we have fallen. The key is to run to Jesus instead of from Him. He is on our side, infinitely more than even we are for ourselves. He is not surprised that we fall. He died because we fall and for our falls. I invite you to learn and use the following steps to be an example to your child when he "spills his milk" and is condemning himself or being condemned.

Be sure to help your child avoid the following responses:

+Condemning and rejecting himself

+Blaming others, like brothers or sisters, or kids at school, or teachers, or parents, etc.

+Excusing or justifying himself

+Giving up

+Denying that a problem exits

+Trivializing behavior that is unChristlike

+Assuming that God is "OK" with this unChristlikeness or He would have prevented it

Carefully prepare yourself to teach your child the following steps to respond to failures:

### 1. Confess

"If we confess our sins, He is faithful and just and will forgive us our sins and purify us from all unrighteousness." (1 John 1:9) Confession is agreement with God. Confession is thinking the same thing God thinks about the issue. It is authentic agreement with God about sin. God hates sin, and when I actually agree with God about sin, I will feel about it as He does.

Don't stop by confessing your sin. Confess—agree with God—about His genuine love for all ... including you, even when you fail. Authentic confession agrees with His delight in you as one who is seeking Him (2 Chronicles 16:9; Jeremiah 29:13-14). Our core identity will be strengthened if we are truly confessing God's true thoughts and feelings about us, His sincere but immature children. Also confess God's love for you even before you repented and became His child (Romans 5:8)."Lord, I agree with You. You are right. You still love me even though I just 'spilled my milk.'"

Confession also includes agreeing about Christ's suffering for your weakness, forgetfulness, confusion, pride, selfishness, even temporary indifference. Whatever issue you are struggling with, Jesus died that you could be forgiven, accepted, and included by grace into God's great family (Ephesians 2:8). Confession also includes agreeing with God about His indwelling presence to cleanse you and to empower you to be more than conqueror over your character and behavioral challenges.

### 2. Celebrate

Celebrate that Christ is with you, as promised, even though you fell down (Isaiah 41:10). When you fell, He did not abandon you. It is Jesus in you Who revealed that you fell down (John 16:13)."Thank You, Lord, for showing me. This reveals You are still with me."

Celebrate that you are a new creation (2 Corinthians 5:17). Before we repented and received the Holy Spirit into our lives, we did not hate sin like we do now. In fact, sometimes we were proud and even bragged about it, remember? The pain we now feel about unChrist-likeness—behavior or heart issues—demonstrates that we hate sin as Jesus does, that we have repented and want to walk in the light, and that we truly are changed, new persons.

Celebrate that you are a child of God. You are His child in spite of your errors. You are adopted into God's family not by your own goodness but because of God's love and Jesus' sacrificial death, resurrection, and life for you and in you. Celebrate communion on the spot! (Romans 8:1)

3. *Correct* (Luke 19:8-10; Matthew 5:23-24)

Humbly seek to make right any pain, problems, or other kinds of unChristlikeness that have occurred because of your heart condition or behavior. Any absence of good that you should have done, seek to make right (James 4:17).

**Ask your family to watch over you and to speak the truth in love to you whenever they see unChristlikeness in your life** (Galatians 6:1; Ephesians 4:15). Take your child through passages such as Matthew 5-7, Romans 12, 1 Corinthians 13, etc., to show him what you want to be. Ask him to pray for your progress and to give you feedback about how you're doing.

You might say something like: "I passionately desire to follow and obey Jesus. I don't ever want to miss His will. I am often blind to the effect of my behavior and words. When you see unChristlikeness in me, you will be a friend by helping me see it."

When your child gives you feedback, do not defend or excuse yourself or blame others. Thank him sincerely and demonstrate in every way possible the steps listed above in how to get up when we fall down.

## Why obedient hearts matter

How important is it to instill an obedient heart into your child? Have you thought about what will happen to him if you do not teach him to obey? What are the reasons to teach your child to obey you?

*Reason 1:* **To prepare your child for eternity.** By far the most important reason is this: it is abundantly clear in God's Word that an obedient heart as defined above is essential to eternal salvation. "Once made perfect, He [Jesus] became the source of eternal salvation for all who obey Him." (Hebrews 5:9; see also Romans 2:13; 2 Thessalonians 1:8; 1 John 2:3; 3:24; Matthew 7:19-21) If for no other reason, children must develop a willingness to submit to authority to prepare them to submit to the authority of Jesus and be in His Kingdom.

To help your child be authentically Christian, it is of great significance that you understand what follows. Many well-intentioned parents did not understand. The results have been, in too many cases, disastrous.

Imagine that the idea of *heart* obedience is a narrow road with a ditch on each side. Some slide into a ditch on one side, assuming that inability to obey the commandments of God results in rejection by God, and the ability to perfectly obey earns rightness with God. This ditch is often called legalism: trying to earn relationship with God by keeping His law. This group includes those we call Pharisees—the self-righteous, the finger-pointers, the dishonest, the discouraged, and those who have given up on Jesus because they cannot be good enough. This terrible ditch is also called "salvation by works."

Many, perhaps most, Christians have rightly reacted to this satanic lie by stating that no one can be saved by acts of obedience. This is absolutely true. We rightly understand that salvation is a gift from God through Jesus. Salvation is not given because of our own righteousness. Nor is it withheld because we are imperfect. Tragically, many of this group reacts to the above described legalism by sliding into a ditch on the other side. This ditch has been called "cheap grace." Those in this ditch assume that their only necessary response to God's love expressed through Christ is to believe that their sins have been forgiven. They do not really have faith in Jesus, the Person, but in a partially true but inadequate doctrine of forgiveness. Their faith is more in the "doctrine" than in the person of Jesus. They have not repented. Repentance—turning from spiritual rebellion or indifference to the faith that follows Jesus—is necessary for the forgiveness of sin (Acts 2:38). Having faith in Jesus involves far more than just believing in the few hours in His life when He died on the cross. Christians have faith in the *person* of Jesus Christ, revealed as the (1) uncreated, world-creating Word, (2) Who became flesh and revealed His Father for thirty-three years, (3) Who was crucified and resurrected, and (4) Who has ever since and will forevermore reign as King of kings and Lord of lords in all the universe.

If you fear that talk about obedience makes Christianity another form of salvation by human works, I would ask you to consider the middle ground, the narrow road between the two ditches. Our tension and struggle comes from looking on the *outward* behavior and performance. God repeatedly says that He observes and judges the *heart* (1 Samuel 16:7). He judges the heart in his conclusions about a person's behavior. The Lord searches every thought and understands every motive behind the thoughts (1 Chronicles 28:9). The Lord knows the thoughts of a man. He knows us and tests our thoughts about Him (Jeremiah 12:3). We justify ourselves, but God knows our hearts (Luke 16:15; Acts 1:24; 15:8). He searches our hearts (Romans 8:27; 1 Corinthians 3:20; Revelation 2:23).

Remember: the heart is the sum of our mind, emotions, desires, and motives. Add these all together and you get THE WILL. When we view obedience as God does, through the lens of the heart or will, we eliminate the perceived tension between salvation through grace and salvation by works. A person with a willing heart can be at any level of ability in external obedience. He or she is not saved based on good performance, nor lost based on poor performance. This person is saved through Jesus' sacrifice for sin, if he has faith in Jesus. Faith in Jesus includes a *will* to submit to Jesus as Lord. To ignore Jesus' Word is to not have faith in Him. Heart obedience reflects a faith relationship in Jesus based on Who Jesus is. It is not a work to merit forgiveness of sin or inclusion in God's family. Outward obedience will occur, sooner or later, in the life of one who has an obedient, *willing* heart (Matthew 3:8). It is not the outward obedience that saves us.

———

*Parents must train their child to avoid both "legalism" and "cheap grace." They dare not tolerate willful disobedience nor create a "you're loved if you perform well" mindset*

———

These issues are crucial to your parenting strategy. Parents must train their child to avoid both "legalism" and "cheap grace." They dare not tolerate willful disobedience nor create a "you're loved if you perform well" mindset. This, again, is why it is imperative that you work with your child's heart (Chapters 5-7).

**Reason 2: To prepare your child for success in this life.** Children who obey their parents receive great God-given benefits and success (Exodus 20:12; Deuteronomy 5:16; Ephesians 5:23-6:4). Children will be terribly frustrated, angry, and troubled in life if they do not learn to obey and submit from the heart to God-ordained authority. They will have conflict with their parents, teachers, employers, law enforcement agencies, maybe their prison officers.

Conversely, if children learn to humbly submit to authority, they will experience favor from their family, school, work, and government. They will learn to cooperate, work with people, and appreciate structures that strengthen society. They will be richly rewarded. Children who learn heart obedience and are submitted to authority are a significant blessing, even benefit, to their parents, family, school, employer, and community. Faith in Jesus requires a *willingness* to submit to human authorities. Jesus, through His Word, teaches us to obey those in authority.

♦"Everyone must *submit* himself to the governing authorities, for there is no authority except that which God has established."

(Romans 13:1)

+"Children, *obey* your parents in the Lord, for this is right." (Ephesians 6:1)

+"*Obey* your leaders and submit to their authority. They keep watch over you as men who must give an account. Obey them ..." (Hebrews 13:17)

+Every Christian is to be *taught to obey* everything Jesus taught in the disciple-making process (Matthew 28:20).

Jesus served and blessed those with whom He lived. This included leaving no confusion about the requirements for being His disciple: to be His disciple one was required to say "No" to himself and "Yes" to Jesus; that is, to come under Jesus' authority (Matthew 11:29; 16:24; Luke 9:23; 14:26). Loving parents will do the same for their children. They must establish in their child the will to obey God and His delegated authorities.

*Reason 3:* **Parents are expected by God to teach their children to obey.** "Children, obey your parents in the Lord, for this is right. Honor your father and mother—which is the first commandment with a promise—that it may go well with you and that you may enjoy long life on the earth. Fathers, do not exasperate your children, instead bring them up in the training and instruction of the Lord." (Ephesians 6:1-4)

"Take to heart all the words I have solemnly declared to you this day, so that you may command your children to obey carefully all the words of this law." (Deuteronomy 32:46; see also Deuteronomy 6:4-9; Matthew 28:18-20)

*Reason 4:* **Jesus is the example for Christians.** Christians follow Jesus. Note that Jesus obeyed His parents (Luke 2:51). He learned to obey through suffering (Hebrews 5:8). We must help our children learn to obey us because, among other reasons, Jesus was obedient to His earthly parents. Jesus was able to become the sacrifice for our sins because He perfectly obeyed His heavenly Father (Philippians 2:5-9; John 14:31; 15:10).

*Reason 5:* **Parents are commanded to make disciples.** As followers of Jesus, parents are called by Jesus to make disciples ... to disciple someone ... to teach someone to obey everything that Jesus taught His disciples (Matthew 28:19-20). Who will it be? Is there any person you should disciple who is of greater priority than your child?

If parents don't disciple their child to honor, be aware of, and follow Jesus, who will? My family is my first and highest responsibility. As a disciple of Christ and a Christian parent, I must *teach my child to obey everything* Jesus taught. Therefore, I must develop in them a willingness to obey ... from the heart.

Where from here? Can you transition your child from your parental authority to living freely and fully under God's gracious government? Yes—with God's help. The next chapter outlines four processes and stages to accomplish this.

# CHAPTER THREE

# Authority—From All to None

"Come to Me ... take My yoke and learn of Me ..." *Matthew 11:28*

Shortly after our triplets were born, Debbi and I knew we needed a parenting plan. Every Monday morning we secured a baby sitter so we could go to a McDonald's in Cherry Hill, New Jersey. There we prayed and planned how to parent our new family. This chapter records a highly valuable "big picture" plan that was scratched out when the triplets were infants. Parents must be leaders, and leaders must make plans. Leaders think about the best possible future for those entrusted to their leadership, and how to get there. Debbi and I conceived of a plan. The plan worked well. The plan was prompted by Jesus' process of developing His disciples. The plan was to prayerfully, strategically, and gradually transfer our parental authority and control over them from us to Jesus in four specific phases. The plan covered from birth until our children would leave home. The transitions were not based on age, but on demonstrated readiness for the next phase.

+Phase 1: I (the parent) decide
+Phase 2: We (parent and child) talk; I (the parent) decide
+Phase 3: We talk; you decide (If your decision is too dangerous, I decide.)
+Phase 4: You decide; we talk only if you ask to talk (This phase is to be reached before each child's last year at home.)

The unsung hero of this book is my wife, Debbi. She magnificently partnered with me in implementing our plans for our four children. We knew that our children must be trained to obey from the heart. We understood that for a few years we could insist on obedience. We wanted them to willingly obey, even desire to obey. We knew that if they were "sitting down on the outside" (externally compliant) but "standing up on the inside" (internally resistant) they would sooner or later not only run from our authority but from all that we value and want to pass on to them. In short, parents must do much more than control external behavior. Therefore, we developed the following plan.

## Guiding children from parental authority to Jesus' authority: Four Phases

Our primary mission for our children was to establish faith in, submission to, and love for Jesus. We taught our children the following four phases of family government early. The end result should be independence from parents, full dependence on God, and inter-dependence with adult Christian friends, including Mom and Dad.

Each of the following four phases are to be initiated when the child is "almost" ready for them:

### *Phase 1 of Authority:* I decide.

In Phase 1, parents communicate specific rules and require obedience through positive and negative rewards. Parents must establish the will to obey authority. Human authorities will reward our children positively for obeying or negatively for disobeying. Very early on, repeatedly explain to children that obeying Jesus, because He is the One we put our faith in, will benefit them now and will save them eternally. If your child has not learned yet to obey, regardless of his age, lovingly establish boundaries and consequences. Lovingly and resolutely carry them out. The old proverb said it this way: "My roof, my rules." Parents must teach obedience (Ephesians 6:1-3; Deuteronomy 32:46). All of Chapter 2 was given to establishing this phase of authority.

### *Phase 2 of Authority:* **We talk—if we disagree, I decide.**

As soon as children are able to ask and answer questions, parents need to include the child in dialogue about direction, decisions, and directives. As soon as the child starts to ask "Why?" explain gently that he must learn to submit to parental authority. Further, because he must learn to submit to all kinds of authority, you are helping him learn the hard but essential attitude of submission to authority. But don't just stop there. Take advantage of his questions to demonstrate your wisdom. Tell him exactly *why* you are telling him what to do. This is the time to begin a crucial process where, instead of giving your child answers, you ask him questions to help him learn how to come to wise, godly conclusions while exposed to your supervision.

Parents could have something like the following understanding between themselves about their son: Somewhere between ages two to four, instead of always telling our son what to do or not to do, we will often ask him what he thinks would be best, and why. For example: "What do you think will happen if you run out into the street?" "What do you think you should do?" "Why is it good to not hit your brother?" We must help each other give our son plenty of opportunity to answer us before we tell him.

If your son does not know what to say, you might ask him this question: "What do you think I think?" As soon as possible, you want to help him to start thinking about including Jesus in his decision making process. So you sometimes ask: "Do you have any idea what Jesus thinks or wants?" If you agree with his decision, you'll celebrate his maturity and, of course, let him do it. If you disagree with him, you will explain why and expect him to obey your direction.

---

### *A major goal is to train your child very early not to leave Jesus out of the decision-making process.*

---

A major goal is to train your child very early not to leave Jesus out of the decision-making process. Because **we are** Christians, we believe that what

Jesus wants is what is best for our child. So more and more we'll ask him if he knows what Jesus wants. If he decides to become a Christian (and we will do everything in our power to help him make life's most important commitment), we will then assume he wants to know what Jesus wants. We will then aggressively help him seek and discover what Jesus thinks and wants. If our son does not agree or want what we think Jesus wants, we'll reserve the right to tell him what to do, with all the benefits or consequences as stated in Phase 1 above.

---

### *A child must be given freedom in order for the parent to coach the child in how to handle freedom.*

---

In short, in the second phase we will less and less directly tell him what to do and more and more ask him what he thinks is best. We want to help him learn to think from Jesus' and others' point of view about what is best for him. If we agree with his choice, he obviously has our support. If we disagree, we will decide for him just as we did when he was very young. We will seek to help him understand, but we will make the final decision and expect him to respectfully obey. The goal is to train him to think with Jesus in his choices.

Soon after your son or daughter is asking and answering questions, this concept can be implemented. Not long after that it can be explained.

### *Phase 3 of Authority:*  We talk—you decide.

As soon as possible, and in the context of consistent dialogue with their child (see Chapters 7 and 11), parents can give their child *responsibility* to make more and more decisions. What we do with our freedom is one of life's biggest challenges. A child must be given freedom in order for the parent to coach the child in how to handle freedom. This begins in minor areas with minimally significant consequences or risk. When a child knows he has to make the decision, he is much more likely to seriously listen to his parents' perspective. The child must be told that he is being trained for life. His parents are requiring him to think about his own conclusions in light of his parents' perspectives. He will talk with his parents, make the decision, and live with its outcomes. This process prepares the child/teen for life as an adult. The goal is not for the child to get his way, or for the parents to get their way, but together to find God's way.

The parent might explain as follows: "You are developing in your own ways of seeing life. You occasionally disagree with us about some things. We will let you make more and more of your own decisions. We'll do the second step above, except that when we disagree, if it is not too big an issue, we'll let you decide if to do it your way or our way. If you do it our way, we'll support you strongly in the outcome. If you do it your way, we may or may not support the outcome of this particular choice. We want you to learn that there are real consequences for choices. We must not give positive reinforcement to negative choices and behavior. Of course, we will continue to profoundly care for your well being. (Example: We have taught you to obey those in authority over you. If you get a speeding ticket, we may pay all, some, or none of the ticket, depending on the circumstances.) Our goal is to have you making all your decisions (with Jesus, we hope) long before you graduate from high school. In this way, you'll be fully on your own while still in our home, rather than making decisions on your own for the first time in a college dorm or apartment somewhere."

Let me illustrate this from an experience with David. David was ten when he was selected to play on the city's soccer team. We were excited with him. It was a significant accomplishment and honor to be chosen for the "town team." One tournament two hours away was going to be an overnighter with the finals on Sunday. Our conversation went something like this:

*Dad (Hal):* Are the games on Sunday morning?

*David:* Well, if we win both Saturday games, the first playoff game is on Sunday morning.

*Dad:* What do you think would be best to do if you have a Sunday morning game?

*David:* I think it would be best to go to church.

*Dad*: Why?

*David*: Because that is what you want me to do.

*Dad*: What do you want? What do you think would be best?

*David*: I'm not sure.

*Dad*: I will give you a name of someone you can call if you need a ride, but what you do is up to you.

It was a tough test to give him this kind of freedom. His understanding and only experience was that nothing kept us from going to church on Sunday.

David went to the tournament. His team won the first two games. He went to the coach and said that he thought that he should go to church on Sunday morning. He told his decision to a teammate, who decided that he, too, would go to church on Sunday morning. Really tough choices. At the church they attended, the pastor heard the story and called both boys to the platform. The boys told their story, and in the process preached a very, very powerful message—especially by their lives. Can you imagine the impact on all who saw and heard the story of two boys, who had freely chosen to attend church instead of playing soccer in the semi-finals? It's my opinion, as a former coach, that their coach allowed them to play in the championship game as a re-ward for their tough choices. They lost. But they won a much bigger "game." In honor of his choices, Debbi purchased a trophy for David and had the plaque engraved with the words: MAN OF INTEGRITY. He had made his decision as well as he could determine from Jesus' point of view. He was growing in integrity—living out what he was inwardly committed to—doing what he thought Jesus wanted even when it greatly opposed his personal preferences. There was much to sort: "keeping the Sabbath"; church attendance; loyalty to team; peer pressure; parental preferences; personal preferences, etc. His motives may have been somewhat mixed, knowing we would probably ask what happened. But are not many of our motives mixed? And our heavenly Father knows, and delights in us, for He understands the mixture in our hearts, and is thrilled that more and more we sincerely desire more and more of His will.

At age ten, Dana and Deborah came to our family meeting with a request. They were both committed to our church's lay pastor ministry. The lay pastors had a quarterly conference coming on Friday night and Saturday morning. The girls had been invited to go to an overnight party with eight friends from school. The rationale given was that they would be able to minister more to these eight girls through the all night party than the good they would receive from attending the lay pastors' conference. They were questioned: *What are the other up sides of going to the party? What are the down sides? What will it say to the other lay pastors if you are not there? What will you miss at the conference? What will you do about that?* They were given freedom to make the decision. They went to the party. Good discussion. Was it good to let them decide? What do you think?

The following situation from Deborah's life is an extreme application of Phase 3 ("We talk—you decide."). Many years of relating, meeting, and discipling preceded the following offer I made to Deborah. Deborah and I were out on our weekly appointment (my time to listen to her, to know her. I call it a "listening structure." See Chapter 7.). It was 4:00 Wednesday afternoon. We were driving on one of Oklahoma City's straight, wide major thoroughfares. I was being "fatherish"—asking probing questions about what was going on. I could sense the stress—even irritation—in her heart by the way she was sitting, by the look on her face, and by the struggle we were having in communicating. The questions I was asking were about the young men who were taking great interest in her. The current one was a very popular guy; very good looking, first team all-city football player.

It wouldn't take Einstein to observe that Deborah had suddenly blossomed into a very attractive young lady. For whatever reasons, she had not received nearly the favorable attention from her peers that her triplet siblings had as they grew up. To suddenly be the center of attention, especially from one of the "big men on campus," was heady stuff. I knew that Deborah's heart resolve was to follow Jesus. I was concerned that the pressures she would face from dating these guys would push her commitments to Jesus to the limit. I sensed that the attention she was getting was tantalizing and capturing her heart. Our heavenly Father effortlessly sees and knows the heart: attitudes, emotions, motives. Earthly parents must work hard to discover the heart.

When I attempted to "open her heart" (to be discussed in Chapters 5 through 7), it was very difficult for both Deborah and for me. I was not able to get the deepest issues out in the open for consideration. I understood that it was too "dangerous" for Deborah to expose what she was truly feeling—maybe thinking—probably wanting. If she did open up, I might not agree or approve. She wanted my approval. Worse yet, I might do what parents often do. I might try to separate her from this tantalizing, thrilling, new adventure she was delightfully experiencing. No matter how carefully I probed, it felt to me that she was dodging the core issues for which I was searching. For several weeks I had been trying to open her heart with respect to her male friend. No real progress.

I believe I was led by the Holy Spirit to make a bold move. I credit the Holy Spirit because, in retrospect, what was a very great "gamble" on my part resulted in her being saved from what appeared to be a very negative direction. Here is my best memory of what happened.

We stopped at one of her favorite eating places—Chili's—for one of her favorite nutritious meals—Diet Coke with lime and chips and salsa. I can see myself leaning across the table. I was about to make Deborah an offer. "I am very aware of the pressures you are facing with Joe [not his name]. I know you want me to be excited about your relationship with him. You can sense that I'm a little leery. I could forbid you to see him, and I know you would obey me—with your will." (For 15 years Deborah had been taught to obey. The one universal rule we had at our house was that if Mom or Dad gave a directive, it was to be obeyed. There were a few basic housekeeping rules, but we liked helping our kids think with Jesus about what He wanted in each unique situation. We were, therefore, willing to take many issues on a case-by-case study. But we had the final say. The kids had been taught and trained to submit to our authority. Back to the date and my "dangerous offer.") "I know you would obey me with your will. But your thoughts about him, your feelings for him, and your desires regarding him would live on in your heart, for at least a while. If I directed you to break up, you may or may not be willing to share your heart with me. It seems like you are closing your heart to me now. At this point in your development, I believe I would be of the most help to you by being a friend with whom you can without fear freely share your desires and thoughts. I think that would be more helpful than retaining control over your external behavior as your 'dad.'"

It is important to restate that Deborah's willingness to submit to parental authority was firmly in place. It is very important for us, as children of God, to be committed to obeying God even when we don't understand and don't want to obey. God does some of His very best work in our hearts when we are obeying Him, in spite of what we think and want.

---

*I believed that if I had access to her heart, and she would seriously consider my response to her heart, I would have more influence on her future than if I controlled her behavior.*

---

Several points were at stake. I want to raise just one. I wanted to be of the most help possible to Deborah. Because we had had a date almost every week for many years (plus our normal family life), I had a "feel" for her heart. I believed at this time in her development it would be best to make a gamble, an offer. So I did. "Deborah, I will make you an offer. It is based on my confidence in you that if you make a promise to me that you will keep it. Here's the offer: I will, from this moment on, never again tell you what you have to do, or cannot do. In exchange for this freedom, you must promise me that you will do your very best to be absolutely open with me about everything in your heart—what you feel, what you think, what you want, and why—and you will let me ask you anything. Further, you will carefully listen to my counsel and ask the Lord to show you if my input to your situation is best for you. If you take my counsel, I will support you in the consequence. If you ignore my counsel, I will love you and determine how much to help you when you experience the consequences of your choices."

This may seem like a dangerous position for a parent of a sophomore. I knew Deborah's good history with Jesus. I knew that soon she would be on her own—making big decisions based on her emotions, thoughts, desires—without her parents. *I believed that if I had access to her heart, and she would seriously consider my response to her heart, I would have more influence on her future than if I controlled her behavior.* I was willing to give up my positional authority to strengthen my relational and rational authority. I did it earlier than I had planned, but I was sensing this would be my best hope to help her. I believed I could disciple her far better by influencing her heart than by temporarily modifying her behavior with a rule but risk shutting her down and losing input to her heart.

Now a young adult, as Deborah recalls this time, she says,

"My dad extended my boundary lines and honored me and gave me dignity and freedom of choice which saved me a thousand deaths. I know that if he would have come down on me and out of fear enclosed me any more than he did, then I would have made choices that would have hurt me far worse than giving me freedom and letting me make very significant choices on my own. There were still boundary lines, but they were extended. Because of that, I was able to make more decisions and learn. I ended up never rebelling. Just like in Psalm 18:35, 'Your gentleness has made me great.' (NLT) God allowed King David to come forth in voluntary love, which takes such great maturity and wisdom. My dad did that for me, and I think that is one of the greatest principles of making disciples. He showed me great mercy. His gentleness and the way he led me helped me through some deep waters. But it was not out of fear; it was out of his confidence in God's mercy. Therefore, he could be merciful with me. That was the greatest thing that he did in a very slippery time. I'm using biblical language. In a slippery time in my life, he gave me a greater boundary line. It is just the opposite of what a human should do. When something is slippery, you should increase the control and not give more freedom. But my dad gave more freedom in a time when I was in a slippery way and that saved my life. Of course, there were a lot of years of making progress up to this point, but in the teenage years, this is critical. If the parents have worked hard to keep relationship, they can be huge on mercy, on tenderness and gentleness. It is so important they don't operate out of fear, but out of confidence and mercy. They have to experience this from God or they won't be able to feel it for their children. They need to be like Jesus to their children. Every time that I went out with my dad, I was so aware of letting him know my heart and of trying to articulate the real depths of my heart so that we could stay friends even though I knew he didn't agree with the guy I was dating."

Was the decision good or bad? Parents can require rebellious teens to come in at midnight, but they cannot control their thoughts, emotions, and desires. If the heart is independent, rebellious, confused, angry, hostile, arrogant, etc., sooner or later bad choices with terrible consequences will occur.

## Phase 4 of Authority: You decide.

Debbi's and my goal was that sometime before our children's senior year in high school, we would give them complete freedom to make all their personal decisions.

Children early on desire to make their own decisions. Parents need to explain that it is the desire of the parents, not just the child, to give the child freedom as soon as possible. Further explain that early freedom can be earned contingent on trust being earned. The message sounds something like this: "Sometime before your senior year in high school, you will no longer be required to obey us. It is our responsibility and goal to get you ready for life without us. Our goal is that you will have at least one full year of complete freedom before you leave our home instead of experiencing full freedom for the first time in a dorm or apartment. We will always 'be there' for you any time you want to talk. If you want to share your thoughts, or if you want to dialogue, or if you want to ask our perspective, we will be there. But from that time on, we want you to make all your decisions and to be responsible for the consequences. We will have given you our best by then."

―⁓―

## *It is our responsibility and goal to get you ready for life without us.*

―⁓―

All of our children ended up being free long before their senior year in high school. They were *required* to make their own decisions. We would dialogue with them about anything they requested, but we would not decide.

Following is the rest of the attitude and message we tried to send to our children: "As the years go by, you will have many, many experiences that are well beyond us. You will be facing far more difficult challenges than we have faced in the increasingly complex world we live in. You are always welcome to come to us. But we will less and less have adequate information to wisely help you. However, we have tried to connect you to Jesus. He knows all. You are in the best of hands.

"Sometime we will need to ask a favor of you. Our desire is that you will let us (your parents) come to you for perspective, for you will be far wiser than us in this new, changing world we will live in. As we get older and more childish, the roles will reverse. We pray we will have given you a very good model for helping children, particularly yours. There will be two more children in your life, for your parents will become more childish and will need your grace and truth more than any of us now realize. Prayerfully, we will become more child-like—like Him who came to us and as a Child grew in wisdom and stature and favor with God and man.

"In the meantime, we are disciples of Jesus. We obey Jesus. Therefore, we must obey Him by seeking to lead you, our children, into being disciples of Christ. We must lead you to Him (by our lives and words), baptizing you in the name of the Father, Son, and Holy Spirit (totally and continually immersing you, by our lives and words, in the character and activity of the Triune God), and then (with Jesus as our model disciple-maker) teach you to obey *everything* He taught us through His Word, His Spirit, and His people."

We pray that these four phases will be helpful to you as you seek to teach your sons and daughters to respond well to positional authority. This starts with heart obedience to you, grows to heart obedience to other human authorities, and as quickly as possible, moves to heart obedience to King Jesus as ultimate authority and basis for submission to all other authorities.

In the next chapter, we look carefully at one of the greatest obstacles for parents to overcome in purposefully discipling their children: fear of failure.

# CHAPTER FOUR

# Your Child Will Believe—
# In Something

*"Believe in God, believe also in Me." John 14:1b*

Faith is quite easy for a parent to pass on. Our children are quite naturally capable of developing faith. With little planning by the parent, children come to believe what they see and hear. For example, they somewhere hear that a big, overly pudgy, white-bearded, red-suited grandfatherly fellow will go down every chimney in the world on Christmas Eve to give presents to everyone. Can you believe that many children believe it? They do. Faith, for the young, comes easily. How great is our opportunity to speak of the true Savior of the world. We must flood the air with truth. The big question: How do we as parents demonstrate our faith in our Creator? Our Redeemer? Our Counselor? Our King? Does our faith show through our lives? How can we help our children come to saving and living faith in Jesus? How can we disciple our children?

---

## *We must flood the air with truth.*

---

There is a rumble I can hear, coming from knotted stomachs of parents who say, "I just don't have what it takes to help my child know and follow Jesus. I am not a counselor or a youth pastor." This chapter will help you overcome one of the greatest obstacles to proactively disciple your child: the fear of inadequacy and failure.

## Jesus would disciple His child in faith

Jesus' invitation for His disciples to "do life" with Him resulted in their watching Him deal with food shortages, sickness, storms at sea, financial crunch, death threats, etc. These challenging circumstances led to discussions about having faith in His Father.

- "I tell you the truth, I have not found anyone in Israel with such great faith." *Matthew 8:10*
- "You of little faith, why are you so afraid?" *Matthew 8: 26*
- "According to your faith will it be done to you." *Matthew 9:29*

Our children desperately need—must have—the same faith example, instruction, and supervision.

## Leading your child to saving faith

Seth was three. He and his mother, Tanya, sat down to eat some macaroni and cheese for lunch. Tanya prayed as usual. After prayer, Seth started asking questions about Jesus. (This is normal when Jesus is the object of prayer and conversation.) When asked where Jesus lives, Tanya answered, "Jesus lives in my heart." Seth said, "I want Jesus in my heart." Tanya, not a Bible school graduate but an authentic Christian, helped Seth understand what Jesus did on the cross and why. She helped Seth come to believe the truth about Jesus and commit to Jesus as his Lord and Leader. Simultaneously, the most important calling for Tanya as a mother and the most important issue in Seth's life were occurring. Interestingly, Seth immediately turned to his eighteen-month-old brother and began to explain what had just happened to him.

Before we talk about training your family in faith for day-to-day life, let's think about leading them to Jesus and the faith that sets them on the road to eternal salvation.

You can start, at a good moment, by asking your child what he knows about Jesus. If he responds positively, continue on. Even with a very young child, you can ask if he wants to be a Christian. If your child answers "Yes," it is extremely important to celebrate. Then ask questions to discern what your child understands about Jesus, the cross, grace, faith for forgiveness of sins, repentance, heart and life obedience, etc. If these words or concepts feel foreign to you, study them in a Bible dictionary. This information is infinitely more important than studying about a car or a computer. You can and need to gain this basic knowledge of how to enter into authentic relationship with Jesus. There are many books and printed resources available to help you. Ask your pastor or spiritual coach for help. Through a sincere, brief study of these terms and their meanings, you will be able to guide a valuable discussion with your child.

If your child resists the question, thank him for his honesty. Relax, and continue to pray and obey. If he receives the question with willingness but ambiguity, now is a wonderful time to ask questions about the above-listed topics. Clarify his understanding and ask if he desires to become a follower of Jesus. Millions of people have come into saving relationship with Jesus through "The Four Spiritual Laws" or other similar tools. You can study one of these to assist your child into faith in Jesus as his Savior for eternal life.

---

### *Responding to Jesus' offer of eternal life is the greatest commitment of life.*

---

Please note that you could ask a "professional" like a pastor or children's pastor to lead your child to Jesus. However, I strongly encourage you to ask the "professional" to coach *you* in how to do it instead. Responding to Jesus' offer of eternal life is the greatest commitment of life. You are the one for the task! To be instrumental in helping your child start and sustain a life-long commitment to follow Jesus is your highest privilege and call as a parent. Regardless of who leads your child into relationship with Jesus, celebrate your child's commitment dramatically and do it again on every anniversary of your child's conversion. It is good to buy a special, new Bible for your child. Emboss his name on the cover. Write the date and story of his conversion process inside.

## Steps to train in faith

The remaining portion of this chapter examines three ways to parent your children in developing faith in Jesus.

### 1. Use _formal_ teaching and training.

‣Commit to the purposeful discipling discussed throughout this book (planned times with your child and as a family for teaching and training).

‣Be deeply determined to have your child grow in faith through being involved in a strong, biblically balanced church. Speak about the leaders and people of your church with thanksgiving, loyalty, and confidence. Criticism of your church and its leaders very often undoes much of the church's positive influence in a child's life. If you have any type of problem with people in your church, particularly influencers, pray for them. If the problem is not resolved, go to them in private to resolve any issues (Matthew 18:15-17). To speak negatively of your leaders in front of your family is not only destructive but disobedient. It discredits the ones who teach God's Word, the very instrument God uses to build faith in your child. There is a time for candor, but only after an appropriate process and in the right way.

### 2. Use _informal_ but conscious faith teaching and training.

Freely and naturally talk about the Lord in the regular routine of life. This is a most powerful training tool. The purposeful discussion of God's presence, promises, and power that arise from the fears, frustrations, and struggles of life teach your child to include God and His truth into life. This is illustrated in Chapter 6 through our son's junior high battle. It is explained in Chapter 11, which focuses in detail on purposeful, informal faith development. To not include God informally inclines your child to exclude God from life.

Your informal conversation is a dramatically powerful way to train your child in faith. Faith comes by hearing, and hearing by the Word of God (Romans 10:17). Purposely, routinely, and regularly include Jesus in everyday conversation. Your child will catch your faith. Conversely, the absence of speaking about Jesus will powerfully influence your child to leave God out of his life. I beg you: talk naturally and positively about Jesus.

What do you say to your child about Jesus? Speak about Jesus' involvement in creation and nature (Romans 1:18-32; Hebrews 1:2; Colossians 1:16; John1:3). Talk about His involvement in every good relationship, experience, and thing (James 1:17). Speak of His activity even though you don't see it or understand circumstances. He is at work for those who love Him (Romans 8:28). Celebrate His grace when you or others fall down. Proclaim His promises for every kind of need (Philippians 4:19). Do all of this naturally, honestly, and diligently. If the words are not sincerely from your heart, look at Jesus and God's Word until you do believe. What you overcome through your fight for faith will be useful in training your child. Don't beat yourself up if this seems difficult. Be patient and remember that it is a fight. One in one hundred Christian parents may talk too much about Jesus; many, if not most, are more likely to talk too little about Jesus and His Word.

—⁓—

### *Your informal words are powerful— for better or worse.*

—⁓—

Your informal words are powerful—for better or worse. Stop yourself immediately whenever you are tempted to complain, express fear, or communicate anger or discontent. All of these, and many more negative words, communicate your "faith" that something is wrong, and your "faith" that God is absent, ignorant, cruel, or weak. In no way am I advocating dishonesty or pretense. If you cannot speak positively and persistently about God, go to Him or to someone you trust to find out why. Those who experience true heart faith in Jesus naturally talk about what they truly believe to those with whom they live. We behave our beliefs. Talk with your child consistently about Jesus, even before your child can speak.

- "Jesus made us."
- "Jesus owns us."
- "Jesus died for us and saved us from being rejected because of our failures."
- "Jesus knows everything."
- "Jesus wants to help us. Let's ask Him for help."
- "We run to Jesus when we fall because He loves us."
- "We trust Jesus and know that His will is best."
- "Let's find out what Jesus thinks and wants."
- "Jesus is Lord and King of the universe. He is in authority over us and has total power to bless or discipline us."
- "We need not be afraid of Jesus because He is for us. We need only be afraid if we ignore or rebel against Jesus. He is our King."

---

*Your child does not know the reasons for your good life or your good choices unless you tell him.*

---

Your child needs to know the reasons for your peace and purpose. Tell him often why you have peace. Tell him consistently why you seek to be kind. Your child does not know the reasons for your good life or your good choices unless you tell him. We reflect our faith in Jesus by the choices we make regarding time, money, entertainment, church attendance, behavior, words, etc.

When your child hears that Jesus is the reason for your behavior, it will greatly strengthen his faith that Jesus exists and that Jesus is a good Lord to be trusted and obeyed.

*3. Demonstrate faith by your life.* "Let your light shine before men, that they may see your good deeds and praise your Father in Heaven." (Matthew 5:16) If faith comes by hearing the Word of God, and one picture is worth a thousand words, imagine the power the picture of your life is painting day by day because of your faith in Jesus. When your family sees your good works and they ask why you do what you do, you will open your heart and tell of your faith in Jesus. This will plant powerful seeds in their open hearts to increase their faith that Jesus is the One to follow. The rest of the chapter will be given to...

## How to become the picture of faith

When our son Dan was about eight, he was playing basketball in a local YMCA league. One Saturday he accidentally left his basketball at the gym. He didn't mention it to Debbi until the following Saturday on the way to practice. As they pulled into the parking spot, Debbi turned to Dan and said, "Let's stop right now and pray that God helps us find your ball." They prayed. As they entered, the two gyms and the halls were packed with people. They went to the front desk and asked about the ball. Of course, it was not there. As they walked into the first gym, the referee blew the whistle to stop the game for a time out. Immediately, a little five year old boy on the sidelines jumped up to shoot during the time out—with Dan's ball. Dan saw it and kindly asked the little boy if he had found that ball at the gym. He gave the ball to Dan. God answered prayer!

Routinely, Debbi would draw our children around her for prayer—be it about sickness, car malfunctions, lost articles, or whatever. These demonstrations—not only of faith, but of answers to prayer—planted powerful seeds in our children to increase their faith that Jesus does interact in our lives and is worthy of being trusted wholeheartedly.

When you get bumped by life, what spills out? What does your child see? The bump may be small, like the air conditioning going out of your car. The bump might be large, like losing your job. The bump might be a disaster, like a family member being stricken with cancer. Will your child see authentic faith in the hard times? Will he be able to grasp the value and power of walking by faith in God? We all pray so.

There is one arena in which many Christian parents do not have faith. The mention of this arena of parenting sends shivers up and down their spinal cord. The arena? Being the person to disciple their child to know and follow Jesus, like I have been asking of you in this book.

I desire, with as much sensitivity as possible, to caringly engage you in an "open-hearted" talk about becoming a picture of faith in the "scary" arena of discipling your child.

Do you, like most parents, feel seriously inadequate to disciple your child? I hope you do not feel this way, but if you do, I have great news. You are squarely in the middle of a *Divine opportunity*. You are in a position to dramatically grow in faith. Faith is the very asset you must acquire to be an example to your family of faith. You are positioned to become the picture of faith that your child needs to see in order to become a person with faith. Let me illustrate: During the first few months after our triplets were born, I remember being and feeling overwhelmed. As a new parent, I felt an enormous sense of responsibility. Parenting three babies all at once seemed way beyond too much. I pictured three two-year-olds bouncing off the walls, three sixteen-year-olds learning to drive, and three students going to college at the same time. Sometimes I was filled with joy and excitement. Other times I was overwhelmed with the fear of inadequacy and responsibility. I could never have dreamed that what felt so impossible would become a blessing beyond description.

I have shared my fear of failing as a parent in several arenas. Maybe you are a parent who is reading this book precisely because you have felt inadequate to lead your family in this most crucial arena—faith. You hear me (and I pray the Holy Spirit through me) asking you to disciple your family. The idea is so foreign or difficult that you may feel like you are being called to jump out of a boat and walk on a turbulent, raging sea. Your mind and senses make it abundantly clear that you are going to sink. The fact is this: You do have faith—you are quite confident—that you will fail. You believe—you "have faith"—that you cannot disciple your family to have authentic faith in Jesus and become one of His followers.

If this is how you feel, you do have faith—*for failure.* Maybe you are uncertain about what a modern-day disciple is, or maybe you do not know if you are one. One thing is certain: You believe (have faith) that you don't have what it takes to make a disciple. In your mind, this issue is settled. This task seems impossible. In short, you do not have specific faith in Jesus that He will work through you to make your child His disciple.

---

### *We grow most in faith when we have courageously jumped out of our "boat of security."*

---

We grow most in faith when we have courageously jumped out of our "boat of security." If we perceive that we can do a task on our own, we do not consciously depend on God. When we perceive that we cannot accomplish the task, we are faced with either not trying or very deliberately seeking help—in this case I am speaking of help from God. If we can come to believe that God wants us to attempt something over our heads, and through courageous faith in Him we "jump out of our boat," the "jumping" puts us into the risky and terrifying waters called possible "drowning." If we jump out of the boat, and don't drown, and in fact even have a little success, and realize that is God who helped us, the result is that we grow in faith in God.

Your family desperately needs an example of faith. Faith is spelled "R-I-S-K." You cannot develop faith while sitting in the boat. Jesus is calling you out of the boat into the water to disciple your family. What He calls you to do He promises to empower you to do. If you jump out of the boat and don't sink, you will experience the delight of being held up by Jesus. You will leap forward in faith.

However, if you stay in the boat, you actually will be placing your faith in the boat instead of Jesus to hold you up. Excuses will lead you to try to get someone else to care for your child's spiritual well-being. In this scenario, you will have allowed your fear of failure to overrule Jesus' call to disciple your child. Your heart of unbelief and fear will be reinforced and strengthened. Instead of becoming a wonderful picture of faith, your example—at least in the arena of discipling your child—will be a picture of fear of failure.

---

### *If you stay in the boat, you actually will be placing your faith in the boat instead of Jesus.*

---

Conversely, your faith will be stronger if you trust Jesus enough to obediently jump out of your boat of comfort and convenience to start discipling your family. Your family will see your faith—shaky though it may be. They will begin to be discipled in risky faith, a little or a lot, by your example of taking a risk and living by faith.

Our raw faith in Jesus to follow Him in the circumstances of our life is dramatically powerful. Let me illustrate negatively from my personal experience: I do not want to dishonor my dad or his memory; however, I think he would want me to share our story in this situation, for he highly valued truth. My dad was a very good man; in fact, he was my hero. Like all parents, he was a disciple-maker, even though he did not know it. He unconsciously discipled me to be just like him in some crucial areas. One of these areas was "self-reliance," resulting from his belief in functional deism (that is, God made everything and then functionally left us to figure things out on our own and run things by ourselves). By his word to me, he didn't become a genuine believer and follower of Jesus until age 65, although he had attended church and served in many significant capacities prior to that time. While I was growing up, my dad's faith was in himself to figure out how to survive, and his faith was in himself to work hard to actually survive. He openly doubted the Bible to be God's inspired Word. He did not really conceive of being guided into truth by the Holy Spirit. He did not believe that God would involve Himself in our lives. It was up to us.

My dad's unbelief in God's activity became deeply ingrained in my heart, even though neither of us made that conscious choice. I simply assumed that life worked without God. My dad did not speak about God's presence or activity, because in his heart he did not believe enough in God's activity to value it. Instead, he gave himself ulcers through worry. He seemed to fear the worst in every situation and talked about it to me. I assumed that he was right. I didn't know any differently. After all, he was my hero.

Had my dad believed that the Holy Spirit would guide us into all truth, I would have believed it. Had my dad believed that God would, in answer to prayer, intervene in relational, physical, and moral issues, I would have believed it. I needed my role model to believe in an imminent, active God.

I do not fault my dad. Based on the circumstances in which he grew up, it is shocking, phenomenal, and explainable only as an act of God that he did all the good he did. The point is that throughout my childhood, my dad's lack of faith influenced me powerfully.

For years, even into being a senior pastor, I did not recognize the extent of my unbelief. I was committed to believing, but in the core of my world view, I was not boldly assured of God's imminent activity. I have some regrets as a parent, and at the top of the list is that my children did not have a better model of enthusiastic, bold, verbal faith in God through me. God's great gift to them in this arena has been Debbi, with her unabashed boldness concerning God's care and involvement in every circumstance. One of my current challenges is to boldly believe and proclaim that God will empower parents by the hundreds in the church I pastor to become disciplers of their own families. This book is one way I am jumping out of my secure boat and seeking to build an army of parent-disciplers.

God is calling us to lead and influence our families. If we think, "I can't; it's impossible," we are really saying, "I do not have faith that the God of the universe is able to do through me what He has directed me to do." We need to reject that faithless thought. When we are weak, we can become very strong, for we look to God who is our strength (2 Corinthians 12:10). We can see ourselves jumping out of our boat by meeting with our children as an initial step of confidence in God to empower us to disciple them to follow Jesus. Though we feel weak and immature, as we faithfully cling to Jesus, we will see Him working in and through our weakness. Gradually, our faith in God grows. We will experience His power at work through our obedience—our willingness. Our faith will grow—and show (2 Corinthians 12:9).

---

## Our self-perceptions of inadequacy are not to rule our lives.

We will grow as God-praisers. Our children will see and hear their parents celebrating God. The faith that God is building into our hearts—in spite of our weakness—becomes one of the greatest gifts we give our families. We are now discipling our children to follow us in walking by faith in Jesus through our very example of jumping out of our boat in response to Jesus' call to disciple our children.

Do you recognize any fear to lead your family spiritually as an expression of unbelief in Jesus to empower you? Do you think that influencing your child to be a disciple of Jesus is impossible for you to do, so why try? If so, you are in an "impossible" situation, which can turn out to be a good place because only God can deliver from "impossible" situations. I challenge you to rejoice in your sense of inadequacy! It is your inadequacy that will drive you to Jesus. Rejoice in this gift.

I fight feelings of failure and inadequacy. I experience the "fight for faith" and the "battle to believe." Our self-perceptions of inadequacy are not to rule our lives. Jesus is to govern our lives. If we have looked at Jesus and His promises long enough to establish authentic, heart faith in Him, our feelings of inadequacy did exactly what they should do. They served us by driving us right where we want to go as Jesus' disciple—to Jesus.

Dare we jump out of our boats? Faith is not the absence of fear. Faith is the bold courage to obey God in the face of fear. Dare we depend on Jesus to hold us up? To empower us to make disciples? To create in us great faith in Him in the process?

## Don't be deceived. Faith is a fight.

Faith is more precious than gold (1 Peter 1:6-7). Our faith lasts forever. Our faith increases God's power in and through us. Our faith allows our children to see their role models walk by faith in a great God. Our faith influences our children to have authentic faith in Christ. Our honesty in revealing our weakness influences our children to "jump out of their boat" in spite of their uncertainties, fears and inadequacies. An environment of faith generates faith. Don't be deceived. Faith is a fight (1 Timothy 6:12). When our unbelieving, un-renewed mind is confronted by God's truth, a fight begins. When truth wins, faith is the result.

The apostle Paul celebrated his weakness because he had learned that when he was weak, then he was strong through Christ Jesus (2 Corinthians 12:9-10; 1 Corinthians 2:3-5). Paul said that, in spite of his weakness, he could do all things through Christ's indwelling power, which strengthened him (Philippians 4:13; 2:13; 1 Corinthians 12:6; 15:10; Galatians 2:8). He prays for the same power for us. "I pray that out of His glorious riches, He may strengthen you with power through His Spirit in your inner being, so that Christ may dwell in your hearts through faith ... that you may be filled to the measure of all the fullness of God. Now to Him who is able to do immeasurably more than all we ask or imagine, according to His power that is at work within us...." (Ephesians 3:16-17, 19-20)

Can you delight in the weakness you feel about discipling your children to be disciples of Jesus? You can do it through Christ. Even when you feel absolutely inadequate, you will be fine because you are obeying Jesus and constantly deciding that He can do all things through you. Your faith in Jesus will be growing and showing.

I have watched big, tough fathers of teenagers weep as they repented for failing to be an example to their nearly adult children. But by repenting and following Jesus, these fathers showed authentic change to their children. Imagine the impact on the children and teens who watched their parents repent and change life direction. It's never too late to start.

Jesus said, "I tell you the truth, anyone who has faith in Me will do what I have been doing...." (John 14:12) You will be made adequate to make disciples like Jesus did when you always cling to Him regardless of outward circumstances.

Remember, faith is a frequent fight (1 Timothy 6:12). Faith results when our un-renewed minds collide with the truth of God and truth wins out.

## What does faith look like?

A heart with faith in Jesus looks like a spectrum ranging from rest and peace to jubilation, depending on the nature of the circumstance. Faith in Christ overcomes depression, anxiety, and fear. It looks like peace. Faith in Christ battles hurt, resentment, anger, and rage. It looks like acceptance, forgiveness, and love. Faith in Christ can look as docile as rest and as dynamic as celebration.

Many of our negative emotions reveal a faithless heart. Jesus said that if we come to Him He will give us rest, peace, and joy (Matthew 11:28; John 16:33; 15:11). Can you see yourself restful, peaceful, joyous, happy, and even celebrative? This is what faith in Jesus normally looks like to our family. This picture is worth a thousand words.

With God's help and your deep resolve, you can be the picture of faith your child needs!

In the next three chapters we consider very practical skills to disciple your child and to win the war for his heart. These chapters will help you establish and enhance your relational and rational authority as you grow in parenting Jesus' way.

## CHAPTER FIVE

---

# Who Can Know the Heart?

" ... for the Lord searches every heart and understands every motive behind the thoughts." *1 Chronicles 28:9*

"Above all else, guard you heart, for it is the wellspring of life." *Proverbs 4:23*

Monday was my day off. It was "family day"; the day each week that Debbi and I devoted to doing something special with our family. One Monday the six of us were driving to Spokane, Washington. We stopped at a restaurant for lunch. The dining area of the restaurant had the normal booths extending from the walls of the room. But the center of the dining room was completely filled with round tables. The six of us sat down, and immediately I knew that what Debbi and I had casually talked about had to become a reality.

We needed one of those round tables. We needed an eating and a meeting place where each family member could be equally seen and heard, where thoughts and desires would be most likely to be freely expressed, where mutual eye-to-eye conversation could occur. Since the "eyes are the windows to the heart," we wanted daily times to look into the eyes and hearts of each family member. Each one needed to feel personally valued. The family as a unit had to have a way of making decisions that would be best for all. As father of the family, I was held responsible by God to positively guide the behaviors and choices of our little family unit toward Jesus. I greatly needed to make very sure that I had ways of knowing the heart of our family unit—what each was thinking and feeling, and why. The round table would help with all of this. We bought one.

## A round table in every heart

Just as our family has a round table around which we gather and meet, every child has something like a "round table" inside him, even though he is not aware of it. The "round table" is his heart—the *gathering and meeting place* of his thoughts, his motives, his emotions, and several other "heart members." These "members" scream to be heard and to get their way. As the father of my family, I had to listen to each family member but I was finally responsible for making the best choice for the whole family. In the same way, every child must be taught to make the best choices for his "whole" life through being sensitive to but not governed by all these "voices" in his heart.

This heart reality can be pictured well through an analogy based on King Arthur and his round table. In this chapter, I will use this analogy to explain how every "heart" works, and how to work with your child's heart. The chapter's purpose is to help you understand how your child's heart works so you can work in his heart.

Think with me about the legend of Camelot with King Arthur and his advisors of the round table. Picture the pomp and dignity as each member enters and places his sword at precisely the right position on the round table. Every member of the round table gave input to King Arthur about governing the kingdom, but none of these advisors were the final decision-maker. The advisors had influence, and Arthur listened carefully. But Arthur was king. He made the decisions. Whatever his decision, the total will and resources of Camelot could be used to implement that decision.

What follows will surprise some Christ-followers. There is a kingdom in your heart, and you, as a truly born-again Christ-follower, are *still* the king. You are the *little* king. We may invite Jesus to come into our lives, capture our hearts, and govern and rule and reign. He will graciously serve and help us, even in ways totally unknown to us. But He will very, very seldom overpower and control our wills. We are the little kings of our lives. We have no choice but to make choices that determine our destiny. Jesus won't take over and unilaterally rule our lives. He did not create us to control us.

He will guide and empower, but not make us robots.

King Arthur's round table is a wonderful picture of the meeting table in every heart. The meeting in your heart occurs continually. You, the little king, are seated at the table with ultimate responsibility for all decisions that are made.

---

## *We have no choice but to make choices that determine our destiny.*

---

Since you are a Christian, King Jesus is seated at the table in your heart. He sits at your table to serve rather than control you. He normally serves you through His Word to you. He seldom—if ever—rules by overpowering you. Jesus is the King and He intends you to relate to Him as your King. But at your table, He has taken off His crown. When you invited Him into your heart, He wrapped a towel around His waist. He is present to serve you, the little king, by sitting on your advisory board. *Jesus has sovereignly determined that you have no choice but to make choices.* You are made in His image. You have dignity, potential, personality. He won't strip you of these qualities. He wants to prepare you for an eternity of love relationship with Him and for reigning in His Kingdom. Loving relationships by nature require freedom.

Jesus treats you with dignity as a free, sovereign, independent little king. He could easily overpower you and get His way in your heart, or shout so loud that you have no choice but to hear Him. But that's not how He relates. He, King Jesus, has come into your life at your invitation and He is seated next to you at your round table. King Jesus often whispers in the midst of all the noise and shouting at the table. You have a very hard time hearing Him unless you tell everyone else to be very quiet. Often, the others are so unruly and unaccustomed to being disciplined that it is a battle to quiet them. The Spirit of King Jesus lovingly, patiently, and persistently keeps serving you, whether you recognize His voice or not.

King Jesus is not the only one at your round table. Other advisors are also present. Some truly love you and will loyally and doggedly tell you what they think you should do. There are also beggars at your table. They are consistently begging you to give them what they want. Some of these beggars creatively disguise themselves as friends, even counselors. There are others present who are also cleverly disguised. They intend to sound and look like friends to you, but in fact they are liars, thieves, murderers, and destroyers. Your inner circle has been invaded by some treacherous traitors. Because they are your desperate enemies, you must be on the alert for them.

The advisors at the round table in your heart do not wait for you to call a meeting. They talk to you all the time. In fact, they talk so much that you can hardly get away from them. If you don't respond, they holler. By now, you may realize who your advisors are. Let's talk about them.

### Desire

Desire is a loud and persistent beggar, often disguised as a counselor. More and more he comes to the meetings telling you that his name is Need. This confuses you. Some things that he wants are very good. King Jesus has had a big influence on him and he actually wants some of what Jesus wants. Many times Desire truly believes that what he wants is best for you. He is really quite compelling. He often talks to other members of the round table before the meeting to get their support.

---

*You must learn to consistently turn to King Jesus and ask, "My King, is this desire Your desire?"*

---

Desire is quite pushy. Be very careful about giving in to him (Ephesians 4:22). The problem is that most of the time he wants things that, though enjoyable, last only a few hours, days, or years, but not forever. When King Jesus gets him to truly desire eternal pleasures instead of temporal pleasures, you have an unbelievable ally at your table. But that will probably take awhile. Regardless, in spite of the strength and persistency of Desire, don't let him get his way. He is not your King. You must learn to consistently turn to King Jesus and ask, "My King, is this desire Your desire?"

## Mind

The guy sitting to Desire's left is Mind. This guy is complicated. He has an amazing past and he has not forgotten anything that ever happened to him. However, some things are so deeply buried that Mind himself does not realize when those things affect him. He brings things up at the strangest times.

Mind is usually of maximum help to you, but you have to watch him. He comes to every discussion with all kinds of ideas already in place. He then analyzes each discussion based on the ideas and conclusions he brought to the table. King Jesus is helping him to re-think some of his positions, but he still brings to the table many assumptions and conclusions from before the time that Jesus came into your heart (Romans 12:2). Even now, Mind gathers all kinds of new information and he often forgets to check with King Jesus to see if this new information is true. Mind is a trusted and loyal friend. He works tirelessly to bring you data. But remember that some of his ideas are wrong or simply unwise. Mind has inadvertently received many lies and partial truths— the trickiest kind of lie—from Satan. You have listened to him so completely that you don't realize how much power he has on your decisions, little king. In fact, you would never knowingly go against his recommendation. To go against his counsel seems insane. Still, do not let mind rule your final decision (2 Corinthians 10:5). Remember, Mind is not your King. Determine to constantly turn to King Jesus and ask, "My King, do You agree with what Mind just said?" (2 Corinthians 10:5)

## Emotion

Emotion does not look or sound much like Mind, but almost everything about Emotion comes directly from Mind. If Mind thinks something, Emotion feels it. Both Desire and Emotion have explosive, immediate energy, and both are powerful. Emotion will raise the biggest fuss at meetings, but Desire will persistently and powerfully keep after you for his way. In most cases, you should get past the first rush of Emotion's pressure. Make him calm down. Ask Mind what in the world Emotion is hollering about. Mind can probably help you understand, since Emotion is almost always the by-product of what Mind has just told Emotion.

Emotion is an honest friend; he tells you how things really are in your heart. He is something of the tattletale of your advisors. He is for you, but he can get you into a mess if you give in to him. On the other hand, when Mind gets the eternal picture from King Jesus of your importance to Jesus as His lover and soldier, then Emotion gets set on fire in a very good way. In this way, Emotion will greatly help you become very strong in your commitments.

Like Desire, Emotion can be self-serving, so watch him. When he is afraid, he forgets that King Jesus is greater than whatever caused his fear. When he is angry, he is usually—not always—being selfish and needs Jesus, you, or Mind to slow him down. Emotion feels many things for a real reason, and you need to listen to him. Let him tell you that something is wrong or needs to be done. Often when he has a problem, it is because Mind has a problem. You can't help but hear Emotion. He's loud and persistent. Listen to him, go through Mind to King Jesus to figure out what Emotion is excited or discouraged about, but do not let Emotion make the decision. He will get you into much trouble. More importantly, he is not your King.

### Body

Right across from you, looking you in the eye all the time, is Body. When he is young, he serves your decisions quite well, at least to the extent that he has been trained. As he gets older, he will increasingly start screaming during meetings. Many times you will be about to make a difficult but good decision when Body suddenly gets the picture and sounds like a rebel. If he thinks that the decision will threaten him, he'll even throw a tantrum. He influences Desire very much. You'll often see them talking between meetings. Check with Jesus through Mind very carefully to see if Body is legitimate. You have to listen to Body, but he can't rule.

## *People*

Next to Body is a guy called People. He has all kinds of opinions, especially about you. You may or may not have invited him to the table of your kingdom. Somehow he always seems to get in. Mind usually invites him without asking your permission. Desire and Emotion often invite him as well. They do not intend People to mess up the meeting. Since they can't seem to help inviting him, you may as well get used to him being at your table.

The fact is, King Jesus tells you to invite People to your table. However, you better get a good recommendation from King Jesus so you invite only the right People. People can be your spouse, parents, or prayer partner. (By reading this book, you have invited the author to sit at your table.) Even when you carefully choose to invite People, remember that he has a round table in his heart and he brings his own set of advisors to your table. I would encourage you to find People as mature in the Lord as you can to sit at your table. People will serve you in ways that your other advisors can't or won't. Still, don't let him control you because he is not your King (Galatians 1:10). When People talks, turn to King Jesus and ask, "My King, do You agree?"

## *Evil Powers*

I hate to include this part of your heart, but I have to tell you. There is a terrible, wretched, evil, vile being who hates your King. Because you are so precious and valuable to King Jesus, this terrible enemy wants to destroy you. If he can't just come out and persuade you to leave King Jesus, he must either deceive you or destroy you. He can do great damage at your table. His method is to somehow seduce you, often through deceiving Desire, or by getting Mind to think and come to conclusions without checking with Jesus. If that doesn't work, he will seek to cause direct problems for you, like attacking Body with pain or Mind with accusations or—watch this one—compliments. This is dangerous, for he knows it might drive you more fervently to King Jesus. Finally, if he can't kill your trust in and loyalty to your King, he'll try to slander you so that he can kill your influence.

The enemy has access to your table. He even showed up at your King's table several times. Do you remember? He seldom comes to your table personally; he commissions his evil spirits with fiery darts to attack Mind, Emotion, Desire, Body, or People. He can get at you many ways. He wants to seduce you into forgetting that Jesus is your King. All he has to do is somehow get you to act like the king, to put on King Jesus' crown and make the decisions alone. King Jesus is sitting next to you by your invitation to lead your life. If the enemy can keep you habitually calling the shots, regardless of who counsels you, he can keep your life in turmoil, preventing your healing and happiness and holiness. With sinister intent, he seeks to destroy—if possible—your relationship with your King. If he cannot destroy you, he with rage seeks to minimize your effectiveness in the King's purposes. One way or another, He is determined to create havoc in your loyalty and service to your King. There cannot be two acting kings: King Jesus and any other king. Sooner or later a house divided will fall.

*Sometimes representatives of your enemy boldly show up without much cover, screaming at you through Desire, Mind, or Emotion.*

Enemies are coming at you, even through your trusted advisors. Watch out. "Be self-controlled and alert. Your enemy, the devil, prowls around like a roaring lion, looking for someone to devour." (1 Peter 5:8) Sometimes representatives of your enemy boldly show up without much cover, screaming at you through Desire, Mind, or Emotion. They have many aliases: Lust, Rejection, Unloved, Unimportant, Success, Appetite, Wealth, Beauty, and Power. Some of what they say sounds like truth, so you are tempted to agree. There are many more liars waiting to infiltrate your table. Watch for them. These enemies attack through the darkness of any at your table. Like their father the devil, they are cunning and evil.

### Will

Of course, you, little King Will, are also seated at your table. You are the little king. You decided to invite King Jesus into your life to be your King. He sits at the table with you, but you still have to decide to whom, of all your counselors, you will give the last word. You will. In fact, that is your name— Will. Others have named you Spirit or Soul. I just like to call you Will.

---

## As little king, your single role in governing is to make sure Jesus alone is governing.

---

You are not as strong as some say you are. Some tell you to not be ruled by Mind or Emotion. The fact is that Mind and Emotion are so powerful that, unless carefully governed, they overpower you in most situations. Without realizing it, you easily give in to Emotion, who feels deeply what Mind assumes to be true. You must make Mind find out the truth from King Jesus, who is the Truth. If you don't, Mind will be influenced by others. What Mind thinks Emotion feels. You will have a hard time overcoming Mind and Emotion. On the upside, when they get their way and things don't go well, they at least tell you they are sorry. At that reflective moment, you are strong enough to tell Mind to learn from the King Jesus, your Master Teacher. One reason why Mind recommended inviting King Jesus to the table in the first place is that Mind recognized that King Jesus is brilliant. You must be strong enough to constantly send Mind to King Jesus so that Mind has the habit of being sensitive to King Jesus in everything.

You made the best choice possible of your government and for your kingdom when you chose King Jesus to be your King. He is The King of all the little kings. As you listen to all your counselors and try to discern the deceivers, you need to make Mind, Desire, Emotion, Body, and even People submit their counsel to King Jesus. Ask them: "Did you ask our King?" As little king, your single role in governing is to make sure Jesus alone is governing. Do not tell your counselors, family, friends, and Jesus that He is King and then let someone else rule. It is your job, Will, to see that King Jesus is included in the discussions and that everyone agrees to His thoughts and His desires.

The purpose of this lengthy parable was to dramatize how your child's heart works ... and yours. Do you see the absolute necessity of guarding your heart and parenting your child to guard his? (Proverbs 4:23)

## How to conduct the meeting in my heart

I am responsible for my heart. Jesus (by His Spirit) is in my heart to serve me. Remember, He took off His crown and came as a servant with a towel. He will seldom, if ever, force His thoughts or desires or emotions on me. From my naïve perspective, I often wish He would. But He wants a relationship, not a robot.

—◦◦—

*Examine yourself—not just what you do but why you do it*

—◦◦—

Jesus sits with me at the round table called my heart, always available, always listening, and often speaking, seeking to lovingly guide me. If He knows I won't respond, He may just be silent until something hard enough happens to make me recognize that I need to pay attention to Him. As the little king of my heart and life, I must guard and govern the continuous meeting which occurs in my heart. This starts with trusting King Jesus to help me move His provisional government into actual reality in my heart and life. To do this requires three general steps:

1. Examine the components of my heart with Jesus' help

2. Search for and discern the components of Jesus' heart

3. Embrace the heart of Jesus, repenting of heart issues unlike Jesus

### 1. *Examine the components of my heart*

When a thought, emotion, or desire is running through my mind, I must grab it. Examine it. Evaluate it. Get it out in the open where I can see it for what it is. One of the critically important processes in becoming like Jesus is this simple but challenging practice of recognizing and examining the contents of my heart. If I do this, I will be taking a big step in preparing to influence my family to know and follow Jesus. Many Christians do not learn to do this, and it costs them greatly. The "quiet time" we often speak about must include healthy introspection, getting quiet enough to observe and examine my thoughts, motives, desires, and emotions. By learning to purposefully do this in a "quiet time," I can do it more and more in "noisy" times—like when I am afraid, or angry, or depressed, or bored, or feel worthless or alone. All those negative experiences are the result of something in my heart that needs to be recognized and dealt with. If I do this well, I am on my way to becoming a changed person. Examine yourself—not just what you do but why you do it (1 Corinthians 11:28).

### 2. *Search for and discern the components of Jesus' heart*

When I capture the thought—or emotion—or desire, I must ask if that component of my heart is like Jesus'. I must ask Jesus by His Word and Spirit to show me if this heart area is like His. Does my heart seem to violate, in any way, the intent or the "feel" of scripture? The Kingdom of God is righteousness, peace, and joy in the Holy Spirit (Romans 14:17). Does this thought seem right? Does the emotion bring peace? Joy? The thoughts that Jesus desires to celebrate, create, or correct are the truths proclaimed in scripture. I seek to know His thoughts and ways with respect to His Kingdom—relationship with God, righteousness, ministering in Jesus' name, right relationships, and right management of time, money, and influence. I search for and discern the heart of Jesus primarily through asking Him questions and studying His Word.

I ask questions like: *Jesus, do You agree? What do You think? Did You say anything about this? What do You want?* I cannot tell you how valuable these questions are to me.

Can we truly know what Jesus thinks or wants? We certainly can know if "it is written" (Matthew 4:4). We must diligently devour God's Word, allowing His Spirit to fold the Word into our hearts. The Holy Spirit also works through God's people (including reputable Christian books, tapes, etc.), circumstances, and in our hearts to increasingly give us the mind of Christ (1 Corinthians 2:10-16). Through these we can have our mind renewed in order to know the will of God (Romans 12:2).

### 3. Embrace the heart of Jesus, repenting of heart issues unlike Jesus

We examine our hearts. We consult with Jesus to discover His position. If His position is different than ours, who needs to adjust? Obviously, we do. Why do we adjust? Three kinds of authority! Jesus' love has captured our hearts and we want to please Him (relational authority). Jesus' wisdom leads us to confidence in His ways so that we know His ways are best for us (rational authority). We know the Jesus is the King of kings and Lord of lords. He, therefore, has positional authority in our lives and we bow before Him, submitting to Him and His will.

We change our minds and agree with our King (repentance, confession). Perpetual repentance (change of mind) and confession (agreement with) is how God's Word takes root in our heart. Confession and repentance include a very proactive, aggressive hatred of evil and agreement with God and right. This aggressive, proactive determination to unite with Jesus embraces Jesus' heart positions. As our thoughts and His Word become the same, His implanted Word will grow and bear fruit. Our mind fully agreeing with Jesus' Word will make our emotions and desires much more like His holy emotions and holy desires. This heart-likeness is the "two becoming One" of Jesus and His Bride (Ephesians 5:32). It is more than communion; it is union with Jesus. It is becoming one with Him as He is one with His Father (John

17:21-23). This is the Kingdom of heaven and the will of God on earth. It is the Word becoming flesh, again. It's almost unbelievable that King Jesus and I are being experientially united. His thoughts can be my thoughts; His emotions and passions, my emotions and passions. Any point at which my heart is united with His, I become a natural representative of Jesus wherever I am, starting at home.

Through bringing more and more of our thoughts captive in obedience to Christ (2 Corinthians 10:4-5), we can be united with Jesus (Philippians 2:1-2) and increasingly like Him (Ephesians 4:13).

Embracing the heart of Jesus through round table discussions can happen in public worship services, small groups studying the Bible, or as His people pray with each other. It happens most dramatically when you are alone with Jesus, free from all outside interferences. (You still have noise in your heart.) It sounds like bringing Jesus into conversations, asking what He thinks or wants. It looks like stopping to pray instead of worrying or arguing. It looks like finding a quiet place to meet with Jesus. For married couples, I pray it will happen as you meet with your spouse to help each other make disciples in your family. I pray it will happen as you meet with your children one-on-one, connecting hearts with Jesus. I pray it will happen as your family meets as a small group to look at Jesus, and listen, and respond to Him together.

We desperately need every one of these structures, but we can go through a worship service, small group, or prayer time and never connect with Jesus. I give my life to creating and leading these kinds of events. However, without repentance and confession regarding God's Word, we will not connect with Christ. The Word must not only be heard; it must be *received* into our hearts to take root and grow. There must be an actual embracing of the Word of Christ. Then we have a heart connection and not just an awareness of the Word. Without repentance and confession regarding every truth from Jesus, we remain hearers only, not united in heart and thus not doers of Jesus' Word and will. If we come from a focused round table gathering having exchanged something of darkness from our heart for something of Light from Jesus so that we are in agreement with Him in that area, we have a genuine heart union with Jesus. This is the crux of transformation (John 17:17; Romans 12:2).

"Above all else, guard you heart, for it is the wellspring of life." *Proverbs 4:23*

The treasures in the heart are of eternal value because each thought and emotion becomes the raw material from which motives, values, and attitudes are built. These heart conditions more than anything else govern the preferences, reactions, and conscious choices of your child. Your child's temporal and eternal destiny is determined more by the condition of his heart than by any other factor, including even the work of the Holy Spirit. The Holy Spirit knocks on every heart (John 16:7-13), but most do not respond because of the condition of their hearts.

Did the parable of the round table in a heart communicate the all-encompassing significance of our hearts? Did it make clear to you how our "hearts" work? It is our hearts that determine our interpretations of all that happens—our actions, our re-actions, our relationships, and our destinies. God works primarily in our hearts and evaluates us by our hearts. We absolutely must learn to guard our own hearts and the hearts of our children. How do we do that?

## How to conduct a meeting in your child's heart

To help your child connect with your heart and Jesus' heart, you must learn how to expose and eliminate lies from your child's heart. Then you must plant the truth *in his heart* not just "on his heart." To put truth "on a heart" means that the heart was not soft or open to receiving, and though the truth was said, it didn't go in. Truth can go *into* a heart that is warm, tender, and open to the source of truth. The truth in a receptive heart will bear good fruit.

Chapter 6 will demonstrate, and then Chapter 7 will describe strategies to conduct meetings in the heart of your child. More importantly, you will see how to help your child conduct his own heart meetings. (I often call this "pastoring your own heart.") To the degree that you learn how to conduct heart meetings successfully, you can be most optimistic regarding being empowered to lead your child to great maturity in Jesus.

# CHAPTER SIX

# From a Devastated Heart to a Discipled Heart

"His heart is steadfast, trusting in the Lord. His heart is secure, he will have no fear; in the end he will look in triumph on his foes." *Psalm 112:7b-8a*

"I am the good shepherd; I know my sheep and my sheep know Me—just as the Father knows Me and I know the Father ...." *John 10:14-15*

## Jesus would disciple His child's heart

Jesus, the Good Shepherd, said, "I know My sheep and My sheep know Me." (John 10:14). This knowing is more than just knowing external information, like knowing someone's grades on his report card, the number of points he scored in a game, or even his break-up with a girlfriend. The word "know" in John 10:14-15 refers to intimate knowledge—knowing the heart of a person—his thoughts about the game, attitudes toward his grades, emotions and desires concerning the break up, and motives in all these areas. The ultimate goal of this knowing is to be one in heart—the same—united. To know your child like Jesus knew His "sheep," you must study—be a student of—your child's heart.

The example and explanations that follow describes one of the very most important, most strategic—perhaps least practiced, even least known—keys to successful parenting.

## A devastated heart

One of our triplets, David, quit growing in the second grade. His classmates, including both his triplet sisters, increasingly dwarfed him. But his existing relationships minimized any negative ramifications—until we moved to Oklahoma City as he entered his seventh grade year. He left a small Christian school where he had been a popular leader. In Oklahoma City, he was enrolled in a 1,600 member junior high school, a literal foot or two shorter than all his peers and looking several years younger.

For years David and I had prepared for the teen years, agreeing that we would be friends no matter what. When he was nine, he and I were out on our weekly meeting. This weekly meeting was a time to listen, to ask, to get to know his heart, and to share my heart. It was a strategic "listening" event. We were talking about the future. I told him that many parents and their teenagers experience great conflict during the teen years. I shared my dream that he and I, and all of our family, could go through those years as very close friends. We could, I believed, be a house of friends. He agreed. (Incidentally, by God's gracious guidance and power, two parents and four teenagers went through the teen years without one major verbal or emotional blow up— that I know of. We had many quiet, long talks, but we stayed heart-friends then and remain so today.)

I began to notice a change in David just a few days into his seventh grade adventure. As I drove up to our home one September afternoon, I wondered if David would run to the door to meet me. Often he did. But for several days, he had not met me at the door. Instead, I had to go looking for him. I walked in the door and was greeted with silence.

"Dave?" I called out his name. "Dave, are you here?" Silence. I ran up the stairs to his room and knocked.

"Hey, Pal, are you in there?"

"Yeah," he answered in a quiet, slightly distressed tone.

"May I come in?" I asked.

"Okay."

I entered to find him crumpled up on his bed. This was uncharacteristic of my happy, outgoing junior high son. He stood up as I came in. The pain in his countenance told me he was not okay. I knelt on one knee, wanting to look into his eyes. But his eyes were riveted on anything but my eyes.

"What's up, Pal?"

"Nothin'."

"C'mon. You can tell me."

Silence.

"Did they jam you in a locker again? Steal your clothes? Did they call you names? What happened?" I wondered if he would open his heart to me today. It had become increasingly difficult this September.

"What happened today? Did they make fun of you again?"

Silence.

David and I had lots of good history, lots of open-hearted discussions where both of us shared deeply of our thoughts, emotions, and desires. But in one short month, it was rapidly changing. His new junior high career had been shocking and painful.

"Hey, kid," other students would taunt, "the kindergarten is down the street."

"Who let you in here? Go back to grade school!"

Relentless verbal mocking and rejection was just the beginning. The gym class guys thought it great fun to hide, even destroy, the underclothes of the "little kid." They would see if they could stash the "little kid" in a locker. Unbelievable! One boy on the football team, whom I'll call Joe, was nearly twice Dave's weight. He took great delight in consistently beating on Dave, punching on him just for fun.

It wasn't fun for Dave. Although the damage to his body was minimal, the damage to his heart was maximal. Right before our eyes, our happy, confident, fun, friendly son was becoming a sullen, angry, hostile loner. His behavior changed drastically and immediately. To be sure, the abuse was the catalyst of these changes, but the core problem and cause was in his heart.

## Heart damage

Try to imagine the invasive damage into Dave's heart when his peers verbally and physically abused him. How would your **thoughts** change if you went from being one of the most popular, cool kids on campus to being mocked and beaten daily? You might have different thoughts about yourself, the future, school, your peers, your parents, and even about the God whom you had come to believe was your Protector. You might respond with the **emotions** of fear, insecurity, resentment, anger, hostility, hatred, or guilt.

*Do your children know how to care for the wounds to their hearts?*

What about your **desires**? You might never want to go back to school. Or you might want revenge. Or you might want to find someone, anyone, to make you feel better. What about your **motives**? Would you be able to dig down to the core reasons for the way you feel or for the way you are acting at home? Would you be able to unpack the swirl in your heart and sort out the core reasons why you now are filled with fear and anger and hate? You might come to new **conclusions** (new, settled thoughts) about God, yourself, and your tormentors. Would your conclusions be accurate? Consider how your conclusions would affect every other area of your life now and in ten or more years. "As a man thinks in his heart, so is he." (Proverbs 23:7).

Would you be able to guard your heart from godless and immature conclusions? It is hard for Christian adults, but even harder for children or teens to guard their hearts.

Do you or your children have heart damage like David did? The answer is obvious. We can't go through life without being wounded. These wounds, if not cared for, will damage or disable us. Do your children know how to care for the wounds to their hearts? Do you know how to care for and facilitate the healing of the wounded hearts of your children? Of your own heart?

It was to this son with a severely wounded heart that I asked my questions about surviving the day at school. I looked at him and repeatedly asked, "Can you look at me?" It was usually too hard. Emotions that he did not know existed kept him from locking eyes with the one who had been his close confidant. Anger and newly experienced hatred, deeply rooted in the terror of going to school another day, hijacked our ability to connect.

It was not just David's heart that was hurting. My heart felt like a swirling, Oklahoma tornado. I felt anger at the perpetrators of pain to my son. I felt fear as I envisioned my son reacting in the crazy but typical method of gaining peer approval by doing anything to gain acceptance. I experienced heart-wrenching compassion for him in his pain. Several times in those days, when it was too hard to talk or even lock eyes, I would enfold my pal and partner in my arms. Sometimes both of us would weep.

## Appropriate touch connects with wounded hearts

At this time, hugs could do what words could not, and I knew it was okay to hug Dave. The "embrace" was more than acceptable. It often lasted for a long time. If you have years of talking and hugging in the good times, you can tell when it is okay to hug a junior high boy, and when it is not okay. A relationship is like a bridge; the stronger the bridge, the more freight it can carry.

If it were not for the years of relationship prior to this junior high terror, I would have been hard pressed to know what to do. Should I leave him alone because he doesn't want to talk, assuming the terrible silent years of teenagehood had begun? Should I pressure him to talk to me? Should I walk away, figuring that when he really needs to talk, he would? Should I just figure it is a season and let it go? Should I try to protect him by calling a principal? Should I insist on taking him out of school until we were promised help? Should I tell him to be tough and take it? Should I tell him to fight back?

Out of the shared tears and appropriate expressions of love, conversations occurred. "What happened today?" Depending on the day, I would hear different scenarios. Sometimes other students pulled his hair, other times it was the locker routine. Sometimes it was just being pushed or sworn at, or verbally mocked. We counted up to fifteen offenses one day. I listened patiently, hearing Dave out, and then responded by asking a heart opening question like, "Can you tell me how this made you feel?"

I was knocking at the door of his personal, secret, emotions. It is one of the rooms in his heart. At first, his response was guarded, but when he realized that I really wanted to know his true feelings without judgment, it was okay to share them. Out came statements like, "I'm afraid. Mad. I hate them." My response was, "I don't blame you."

Sometimes I asked David questions based on what I think I would have felt if it were happening to me. "Do you wish you could get even? Do you wish someone would deck them for you?"

—⁓—

*When he realized that I really wanted to know his true feelings without judgment, it was okay to share them.*

—⁓—

## Empathy opens and connects hearts

To unpack a heart, knock gently at the door by asking questions about a thought, or an emotion, or a desire. For David, "Do you wish you could get even?" was a question that knocked on the door of desire.

Simple empathy is a good way to come up with questions. By simple empathy, I mean putting yourself in another's place. Try to imagine what you might be thinking, or feeling, or desiring, if you were in the other person's situation. If the question probes too deeply, or feels too difficult, you're knocking too hard. Be gentle and humble like Jesus is. If you have a strong, positive relationship, you will better know what to ask and what not to ask. Be sure not to assume your child feels what you might feel. Guard against your child feeling pressure from you to say something he or she truly does not think or feel. Anything other than absolute truth will only confuse the issues. We are after truth in the innermost parts because the truth sets us free. (John 8:32)

## "Thank you for opening your heart"

Sometimes, after Dave shared his feelings with me, I would say something like, "I am so sorry. I know I can't feel what you feel. Thank you for telling me some of it." His response, as I remember, was often silence. Mine was often to hug him again. Although at times I felt angry and frustrated at what was happening to him, I believe that the Holy Spirit gave me ways to work the most important truths deeply into Dave's heart through careful questions.

When someone shares something from the heart—thoughts, feelings, desires, or motives—be extremely sensitive in your response. This person's heart is a secret, private, personal treasure. The tone, if not the very words, of your response should say, "Thank you for the gift of entrusting to me your hidden treasures."

My son-in-law (with whom I am well pleased), having just heard his wife pour out some less than pretty words from her heart, responded in this way: "It is not the substance of your heart that I call beautiful. It is the opening of your heart to me."

When someone shares his or her heart, it seems almost impossible not to pour out your heart. When we hear another's heart, the following easily spring out of our hearts: teaching, arguing, defending, correcting, disagreeing, and judging. Guard your heart. Let your will (the core of your heart) govern your emotions and thoughts. Try to respond empathetically to your child's heart before you pour out your heart. "I'm so sad to hear that. That must have really hurt."

When your child shares a thought or feeling, treat it with great tenderness and value. It is a treasure. Do not assume that you understand all that your child meant. Affirm the treasure and keep listening. Treat the heart secrets of your loved ones with the utmost tenderness.

## Opening my heart: Unconditional love for you

"Pal, do I really love you?" I asked Dave. Silence. "I'm serious, Pal. Are you important to me?"

"Yes." The weak, subdued answer finally came.

David and I had talked about thoughts and emotions for years, particularly about love between family members, friends, and Jesus. This is heart talk. To talk about being loved was not new. We had history in talking at these levels. To raise the issue of my personal valuing of David was my attempt to help him think about his situation from a greater perspective than he was capable of on his own. (In Chapter 8 we will see how God the Father gave God the Son a greater perspective.) The strategy is to get truth that makes the difference firmly planted in the mind, either by replacing a lie or establishing truth of greater significance than a secondary "fact."

"Is what I think about you as important to you as what the kids at school think about you?" This is a bad, pressure-creating question unless I had reason to believe that my son *did* greatly value our relationship and my love. The purpose continues to be to plant truth he can believe or bring truth into the open he already believes.

With a subdued tone, Dave's answer was, "Yes."

"Are you really sure?" I asked. I was digging deeper into the soil of his heart to make sure the seed was getting planted profoundly, not just superficially.

"Yes!" His affirmative reply was a little more emphatic this time.

"If you really believe that I love you, does that make any difference in how you think or feel about what the kids are doing to you at school?" By now, we are actually able to have a fairly reasonable conversation about a very difficult topic. I waited for his answer, which usually did not come. Then I would answer my own question. "Probably not much difference. But think with me."

## Planting Jesus' love and will into the heart

On paper the following conversation happened quickly. In real life, I asked these questions slowly, as I became confident that Dave was ready to consider each question.

"Is Jesus a real person?" I asked.

"Yes," David answered.

"Do you know that He loves you, David Perkins, right here, right now?"

"Yes."

I kept on. "Is Jesus the King of the universe?"

"Yes."

"Is He is always with us?"

"Yes."

"Does He know everything about everything?"

"Yes."

"Does He have all power to stop anything, or to do anything?"

"Yes."

"If He loves and values you, is that a big deal?"

"Yes."

"Do you know that Jesus really loves you?

"Yes."

"Are you important to Him?"

"Yes."

After each question I would wait for Dave to think and respond. Notice that each question was aimed at a most foundational, basic, doctrinal affirmation that almost every new Christian is willing to affirm. They did not require a theological Einstein to answer.

By that time in the process, David's answers were coming more quickly and with increasing certainty. I watched with my own eyes. Time after time, when somehow we got to the bottom line of Jesus' presence and love, I watched the power of the Holy Spirit working in a devastated seventh grader's mind. The mind is normally the key to heart health.

## From a devastated heart to a discipled heart

About this time, the truth started to set Dave free. His head would lift, we might lock eyes for the first time in the conversation, and he would answer, "Yeah ... yeah!"

The "minor" facts that he was small and that kids at school were making life very miserable for him were gradually being overshadowed by a major truth. The major but difficult truth was and is that the King of the universe is on his side. He is infinitely valuable to Jesus. This great King is always with him, loving him, and able to stop the storm or give Dave something better: the ability to overcome evil with good and reveal the very character of Jesus. The major truth was getting into his heart, creating not only hope, but faith. Don't be deceived: faith often requires diligent mental work.

"If Jesus really cares and is with you to give you what you need, can you go back to school tomorrow?" I was almost certain about the answer to this question before asking or I would not have asked. David needed to be strengthened by his own certainty.

---

*Don't be deceived: faith often requires diligent mental work.*

---

"Yes, I can!"

I watched Dave make a tough heart choice, day by day, to go back into his junior high pain because he believed that he was of infinite importance to Jesus and had a divine mission to accomplish. Imagine being set free by the truth to go back into that terror.

(Note: Many adults who are weary of hearing "Jesus loves me" continue to be ruled by the opinions of others, or the longing for approval, or the fear of loss of beauty, or change in the economy, etc. This is because they are not able to get the truth of their preciousness to Jesus worked deeply into the core of their heart so that they experience being valued by God. The result is that often they are not confident of being significant, secure, successful, etc. To help our children, we must "believe" our beliefs.)

## Guiding the heart: What do you think would be best?

A few days later, I began knocking at another door in David's heart—this time his thoughts. In emotionally painful situations, it is sometimes better to search out feelings before searching thoughts. When the time is right, ask what your child thinks about the situation and what he or she thinks is *best* to do, in the light of the situation. This type of questioning looks toward the future, toward action or resolution.

"Pal, what do you think would be the best way of coping with Joe?" (Remember Joe, the football player and ringleader of the abuse?) I was moving beyond binding up Dave's battered heart. I was preparing him for battle. I was getting him ready to respond to circumstances in a Christlike way. I was preparing him to love his enemies. I began by working into his heart the truth of his being loved, not only by his family, but most importantly, by the sovereign King of the universe, Jesus. Next, I worked on planting God's heart for David's enemies into David's heart. Not many Christian children will think about loving their enemies without help. Parents can plant God's Word into their children's hearts, but they must do so with great care. (See Chapter 7.)

When I asked Dave about what he thought would be the best thing to do about Joe, his eyes would usually drop and his countenance would be dark. It seemed to me that his pain resulted in an understandable attitude: "Do we have to talk about that?"

## Strategically opening my heart: "What do you think I think?"

Instead of telling David what I thought, I asked him, "What do you think I think?" Questioning is dramatically important. As parents, it is very hard for us to keep from telling our children what we think. At young ages, our children begin to hear our "telling" as "preaching at them." Therefore, we would be wise to ask, "What do you think I think?"

Suppose your child is able to quite accurately communicate his thoughts. You could say, "And what do you think about my perspective?" Now you can have a meaningful dialogue about whether your child buys your point of view. (As is always the case, the less mature the child, the less complex the questions. Remember that your child is probably more able to communicate on these levels than you realize. Give him a chance.)

If the child does not agree, it is okay. However, you have now earned the right, in essence, to ask, "What are the reasons why you don't agree with my perspective?" Your child once again has an opportunity in a safe place to sort out life-significant issues while under your guidance, instead of adopting values, attitudes, ideas, and behavior based on cultural influences, temporal desires, or reactions that leave God out.

Asking a question like, "What do you think I think?" is important because it ...

+ teaches the child to get outside his own perspective into yours.
+ keeps the child engaged in the process.
+ tests if the child has gotten your message or perspective. You'll be shocked at how early your child will be able to tell you what you think.
+ lessens the likelihood of frustrating him in hearing again from you what he already knows you think.
+ helps your child to be more open to the next step.

To tell your child what he has already heard you say will only build walls. A child normally hears the following message: "You think I'm stupid because you keep repeating this message."

## Knocking at a heart: Ask permission—"May I tell you what I think?"

Getting permission from your child to tell what you think (in the context described here) is like knocking on the door of his heart. It gives him the opportunity to open the door of his heart to you, if he desires. When we kick the door open by hurling our words and emotions at hearts (minds) without carefully knocking, they often feel invaded and are not nearly as willing to receive our thoughts. To plant good seed in the soil, we have to work the soil first.

If your child says "No" to your request to share your thoughts, you both know that he or she is closed to you. When you say, "Okay, I'll wait till you are ready to talk about it," you didn't get to plant the seed but you probably made points in the relationship and softened your child's heart for a future time. (There are emergency times when the child needs to hear your perspective, but not as often as most parents think.)

Usually children and teens will invite their parents to share thoughts if a history of caring has led them to practice the communication style described above.

## Connecting a heart to the heart of Jesus

Now let's return to my conversation with David. Once he answered about what he thought I was thinking, I was free to tell him my thoughts: "I try to think what Jesus thinks. We know that He knows what is best. Jesus loves you and He hates what is happening to you. However, He also loves every one of the kids who are hurting you, including Joe. He fully understands the reasons for what they are doing. The greatest reason for their terrible treatment of you is that they themselves do not feel enough love from anyone. They feel miserable, so they act miserably. The best way for Jesus to show them His love is for you to somehow be good to them, especially Joe. Can you pray for Joe and then go up to him and beat him to the punch by saying, 'Hi, Joe'? At the very least, you would be doing your part to overcome evil with good."

The Spirit of God enabled these words from Romans 12:21 to get into David's heart. He not only heard them, he received them. Little seventh grade David, with a giant of a God inside of him, headed into the dreaded halls of the junior high school, ready to return good for evil to his Goliath. David was empowered to overcome evil with good, to follow Jesus.

## A serving heart: More than conqueror

I have just shared with you the miracle of how God's Word and Spirit, working in a battered heart and body, can restore a child. The key is that someone needs to knock on the heart's door, receive entrance, expose the lies and distortions, and carefully plant good seed.

---

*Someone needs to knock on the heart's door, receive entrance, expose the lies and distortions, and carefully plant good seed.*

---

Dave, by God's truth and power in his heart, was not conquered by evil. First in his heart, then through his life, he conquered rejection and abuse. He was empowered to be more than a conqueror. He won the battle for his heart and then he went into battle for the hearts of his enemies.

I have heard Dave tell the story: "I went back to my school and would say to myself as I walked down the halls, 'Jesus loves me! Jesus loves me! Jesus loves them. Jesus loves Joe. Jesus wants me to love Joe.'" Dave was telling himself the truth—God's truth. The battle for the mind was being won!

The next semester Joe showed up in five of Dave's classes. Dave kept his commitment to be good and "do good" to Joe (Acts 10:38). Eventually, evil was overcome with good. Joe and Dave became friends. Joe was invited to our house to stay overnight. In the wee hours of the morning, he asked Dave, "What's up with you? I laughed at you and beat on you and you turned around and called me 'friend'?" When Dave told Joe why he "loved his enemies," Joe wanted to hear more. That night, Dave led his former enemy into an authentic relationship with King Jesus. Friends became best friends. They asked the question, *What can we do to change our school?* They heard this answer: *Start a prayer meeting every morning before school.* They found a teacher who would let them use his classroom. They started with five. Soon they were running 20, then 40, then 60. At this writing, 15 years later, 50-80 plus students still meet every morning to study the Bible and pray before school in that same teacher's classroom.

God's Word plus God's Spirit plus many family meetings allowed a young David to quickly grow into a man of God, defeating all sorts of giants. The Truth empowered him not to be a slave to the actions and opinions of others. With lies gone and Truth indwelling, he was free to follow Jesus and lead others.

Today, "Joe" is a missionary trainer in a missionary training center. Dave is the founder and director of a university prayer and disciple making ministry. His prayer and fasting conference this summer had over 7,000 students from 34 states in attendance. Many others from those morning meetings at the junior high became Christ-followers, including several who became pastors and missionaries. Good does overcome evil. The presence and power of God in a heart can turn despairing hearts into conquering hearts.

There is another benefit of learning how to teach and lead by asking questions. As our children learn to examine their thoughts, emotions, motives, etc., they become equipped to guard their own hearts. This is one of the most crucial skills to learn. When you help your child discover what is in his own heart and get his heart clean, united, and filled with Jesus, you are equipping a young saint for the ministry of pastoring themselves. Further, if he knows how to guard his own heart, he will be skilled in helping to guard the hearts of others. This is of greatest significance.

## The issue is the heart

Man looks on the outward appearance. God looks at the heart (*1 Samuel 16:7; Luke 16:15*). Our actions and reactions are based on our hearts. Remember: Our hearts are what we think, feel, value, and desire. It is what motivates us, what we know, what we assume, what we remember, what is buried in our mental and emotional subconscious that we don't remember. Our hearts shape how we receive every outside stimulus and how we respond to people, situations, and God. The reasons we do what we do is purely and simply because of the condition of the heart.

One person loses a job, turns to God, grows in faith, and learns a new career. A much less terrible thing happens to someone else—he gets temporarily laid off from his job—and he reacts with criticalness, resentment, fear, and depression. Why? The answer is the condition of the heart.

Wonderful things happen to two different people. One is delighted and responds with joy and thankfulness and desire to bless others. Another takes the good for granted, is not satisfied or delighted, and is even critical of the situation. Why? The answer is the condition of the heart.

Your children's hearts are like gardens. How can you help expose and remove the weeds of lies, distortion, ungodly attitudes and motives, confusion, error, negative emotions, and immature or errant values? How will you help plant the good seeds of God's truth, perspective, values, priorities, and wisdom in a way that your children can receive them? God has ways to empower your heart to influence the hearts of your children.

We have severe life problems because we try to control the outward appearance while not realizing that we need to allow God to deal with our hearts. Many people, including some very religious people, try hard to control the outward. However, God cares about and works on the heart. *Parents who work on the outward are working on the effect. Parents who work on the heart are working on the cause. If the heart is good, the outward will be good* (Matthew 23:26).

Let's look at a real life example. Suppose your nine-year-old does not want to do his homework. You want him to do it. The desires of your heart and his heart are different. Suppose you promise him a reward or threaten him with punishment, resulting in his "making up his mind" to do the homework. "Making up his mind" is setting his will to do his homework. At this point, his will and your will would be the same. But his desire and motive would still be different than yours. He desires the reward or to avoid punishment. You desire him to grow in knowledge, submission to the teacher's authority, self-discipline, etc. You also have different "minds" regarding homework. You see things he does not yet see. If through positive dialogue you can help your son to understand the values of doing his homework, he would think more like you think, have desires more like yours, and thus be more inclined to choose to do his homework for the same reasons you want him to do it. As it is, with rewards or punishments in place but lacking common perspective, you and your son's hearts are united in will, but separated or divided in understanding, desires, and motivation.

---

### *Law by the big and powerful is easier than relationship with the small and weak.*

---

Uniting our hearts does much more good than "getting homework done." It unites families relationally. God wants the family to be a house of friends. It is God's will to "turn the hearts of the parents to the children, and the hearts of the children to the parents." (Malachi 4:6). United hearts cause relationships to flourish. Divided hearts cause relationships to fester. Happy, holy families result from God influencing and uniting parents' hearts with His, and parents influencing and uniting the hearts of children with the parents' and God's heart. Houses of authentic prayer become houses of authentic friends.

It is easier to control behavior than influence hearts, but only for a while. Law by the big and powerful is easier than relationship with the small and weak. Although we start with some rules, we are made for relationship.

The fact is that our lives flow from our hearts. If our hearts are ugly, our lives get ugly. If our hearts are healthy, our lives will become healthy. Our hearts must be guarded with utmost care (Proverbs 4:23). Who guards the heart of your child? Who guards his thoughts, emotions, desires, and motives? And how in this world do you guard a heart?

## To open hearts, ask questions

Jesus was often with His disciples all day long. On those days, He didn't have to ask what happened. He saw what happened. But He did ask them questions about their heart, what they thought and wanted (Matthew 8:26; 14:31; 16:15; 17:25).

We cannot spend all day every day with our children, our disciples. However, we can know what happened in their days and weeks if somehow we can create an atmosphere where they are open to tell us their story.

"Lord, I ask You to ignite in the heart of every one of us the desire to know the heart of our loved ones, and to unite their hearts and our hearts with Your heart. Make us one with You and each other." (John 17:20-26).

The next chapter will detail practical steps for opening hearts, anesthetically removing weed seeds, and planting good seed which will grow and bear a crop, even up to one hundred times what was planted.

# CHAPTER SEVEN

# Parents: Heart Surgeons

"But the seed on the good soil stands for those with a noble and good heart, who hear the word, retain it, and by persevering produce a crop." *Luke 8:15*

"But the one who received the seed that fell on good soil is the man who hears the word and understands it. He produces a crop, yielding a hundred, sixty or thirty times what was sown." *Matthew 13:23*

I recently heard the following story: "Daddy, how much money do you earn in an hour?" Irritated by the question, the father brusquely told his son not to ask such personal questions.

"Please tell me," the boy pleaded.

The father relented and told his son that he earned $15 an hour.

The boy thought for awhile and then asked, "Daddy, can I borrow $7 for a little while?"

The father's response was not warm. "So that's why you wanted to know how much I make. Go to bed, and don't be begging for money."

The father could not sleep that night. His harshness toward his son troubled him. He lay awake wondering why his son wanted exactly $7. He wondered if his son truly needed something. Finally, he made his way to his son's bedroom. "Here's the $7 you asked for."

Suddenly alert, the boy blurted out, "Wow! Thanks, Daddy." Then the boy reached under his pillow. He pulled out a sock, filled with coins. "Daddy, I have $8 in here. With the $7 I borrowed from you, it makes $15. For this $15 could I have one hour of your time to be with you?"

It's in the heart of most children. Why not give them one hour of focused, undivided attention? What about one time per week? Or more?

This chapter is all about what you could do in one hour alone with your child. It will help you powerfully bond with your child. It will help you "open" your child's heart. It will help you locate and extract destructive deception (weed seeds). It will help you implant God's truth (good seed).

As described in earlier chapters, my dad was like Jesus in that he was very loving, gracious, and supportive. He took me with him on business trips. We went for rides and took walks together. He went to my ball games and band concerts. Whether he did it on purpose or not, he influenced and discipled me to think the way he did about life and about God. Unfortunately, his way of thinking was not always God's way.

I remember one time in particular when my dad discipled me—you decide if for better or worse. I was in junior high. Like my sons at that age, I was smaller than most of the other kids. Rusty, a chunky kid with red hair and lots of freckles, regularly began to push me around. I weighed about 80 pounds; he weighed about 140 pounds. If I reacted to him in any way, Rusty would respond with, "You want to make something of it?" This was his way of saying that he'd be more than happy to "clean my clock" right then and there for trying to stop him. I was terrorized.

I told my dad about the situation. I opened my heart beyond the facts of my situation. I poured out my fears and dread. Why not? Though I was in junior high, my dad was still my hero and best friend. His counsel to me was, "Stay away from Rusty as much as you can. But if you get into a situation where a fight seems inevitable, hit him first as hard as you can and don't let up." My dad's words were planted deeply into my open, trusting heart.

Guess what happened? One day soon I was in the Band Room. Rusty gave me the familiar shove. I probably could have avoided a fight that day. I could have once again been intimidated into taking it. But my friend, my dad, had planted a seed in my mind about how to handle Rusty. Without thinking,

I whirled around and smashed Rusty in the face. His nose started bleeding. We were both so stunned that we just looked at each other for a moment. Then Rusty turned and walked away.

---

*Sooner or later we behave according to what we actually believe.*

---

There are several points I could draw from the story, but the one I want to draw is this: one sentence by my well-intended dad influenced me to nearly get kicked out of school—maybe even beat to death. What he said went into my "heart." I believed him. What I believed I acted on. *Sooner or later we behave according to what we actually believe.* My dad was influential because he spent time with me and made me feel his love. I knew that I was important to him. In the process, he passed on his ways of thinking into my wide open mind. I was his little disciple. I opened my heart to him about what was happening in my life with Rusty and what I was feeling. He planted a seed into my open, vulnerable mind. The seed took root, grew, and bore fruit—I clobbered an unsuspecting, chunky, junior high red-head. The results could have been disastrous.

What seeds are in your child's heart? Who put them there? Are they good or bad seeds? Can anything be done about bad seeds? Can good seed be planted in the heart? How?

## Who will do heart surgery?

Jesus did heart surgery for His disciples. He purposefully selected twelve young men to disciple *by living with them* (Mark 3:14). He watched and listened to them. He asked them questions to expose and eradicate weed seeds from their hearts. He planted truth into their open, trusting hearts that grew into the explosion we call the church. By "heart surgery," I mean the elimination of error and the planting of truth into the mind.

The church, as it has evolved in structure and practice, is virtually incapable of extracting weed seed from your child's heart sufficiently to overcome the influence (discipling power) of his peers, the media, the dark forces of evil, and the natural conclusions of your child's immature, badly influenced, and unenlightened mind.

Some say, "But why is this such a big deal?" For starters, hearts get poisoned. The heart of the poisoned child is invaded and polluted with the weed seeds of confusion, fear, rejection, insecurity, futility, guilt, and shame. Words and acts impact a child's heart resulting in hurt, anger, resentment, hostility, rage, revenge, and bitterness. Often, these dreadful weed seeds take root and sprout into weeds that are visible, audible, and destructive. The child's countenance changes—a free spirit becomes a heavy spirit, a boy retreats to his room instead of running to the door to meet his dad, an open heart becomes a closed one, obedience decreases, candor is replaced by avoidance, and so on. Who will watch for these changes? Who will discern if the behavioral changes are normal childish behavior or the fruit of bad seeds planted in the soul of a loved one? Who will spend the time to find out what is going on in the heart of a wounded child? Who will be the human heart surgeon?

---

*My first disciple-making priority*
*was a small group called my family.*

---

## Consistent times to listen, to love, and to heal the heart

Do you remember how I influenced and discipled my son, David, through his traumatic junior high experiences? (See Chapter 6.) I would not have had the opportunity to help him if not for the many hours of strategic, consistent communication prior to the crisis.

When our triplets were born, Debbi and I already had a Spirit-led call and strategy to make disciples. Soon after their birth, it dawned on me that Jesus *chose* His disciples to live with Him (Mark 3:13-14). However, I did not need to stay up all night praying about with whom I would live. I had my disciples in David, Dana, Deborah, and later, Daniel. I may prayerfully choose to disciple some other persons, but my first disciple-making priority was a small group called my family.

Debbi and I prayerfully determined that the first priority for my time, after spending time alone with Jesus, would be one-on-one weekly meetings with each family member. On Monday, I would meet all day with Debbi. Tuesday afternoon I would meet with Dave, Wednesday with Dana, Thursday with Deborah, and Friday with Dan. These one-on-one focused times together—lasting about 30 minutes—started when each child was about four. The goal at this age was for each child to experience focused attention, feel valued, and become accustomed to the practice of dialogue, including answering questions about their experiences, thoughts, and desires. The activities were simple: go for walks in the park or mall, go for rides, get ice cream cones at McDonald's.

Out of need and desire, the length of our appointments gradually increased. By the time our children were in junior high school, I normally met with each for a couple hours, 4-6 p.m., leaving time for dinner as a family before I went out for evening meetings. The schedule was flexible. Sometimes we had to resort to early morning meetings. The commitment and priority were not flexible. If a conflict arose, we rescheduled for another time in the week. Parents, if you are not having regular, one-on-one times with your child of whatever age, I beg you to start. It's never too late.

By the time your child is ready to leave home, you will have had many opportunities to talk caringly and candidly about his immediate concerns and life's most significant questions, like:

+Can I have a new bike?

+Why do I need to study algebra?

+Is there a God? If so, why did He create us? How are we to respond to God?

+Why can't I "date" this person?

+What is real love? God's love? Our love?

+ What should I do after high school?
+ Is God's way the best way? Why?
+ What is the purpose of marriage?
+ What is most reasonable regarding the origin of the universe and of life?
+ Who is Jesus? What did He do? Why?
+ What does the Holy Spirit really do in our heart and lives?
+ Is there life after death? What will we do? How shall we prepare?

When Dave was about 10, we were out for our weekly appointment. We ended up talking about the power of God's truth—when known, believed, and obeyed—to save us. We talked about how we desperately need very close friends who will lovingly help us see the truth about ourselves. David said, "Dad, will you promise to always tell me the truth, even if I don't want to hear it, even when I am a teenager?"

---

*Disciples are made in the context of "doing life" together.*

---

Because of hundreds of conversations about life, love, relationships, and Jesus, a very strong bond was built between Dave and me. This bond could hold us together through the pain Dave was carrying. It dramatically strengthened our ability to connect with each other, which could finally turn into meaningful conversation about a very real Jesus. Your child's hardest times and greatest failures are your best opportunities to pour in grace, and then to work through to God's truth, starting with:

+ your child's perspective
+ moving through your perspective
+ ultimately discovering God's perspective together

## How to perform heart surgery

Disciples are made in the context of "doing life" together, unconsciously modeling and influencing. My experience is that something more is greatly needed: conscious, purposeful training.

Jesus consciously, purposefully withdrew to be alone with His Father for focused, reflective, direction-seeking times of communication in prayer. This is heart work. Jesus wanted His Father to coach Him. This happened in the many one-on-one meetings with His Father—we call this "prayer." Jesus also consciously and purposefully pulled His disciples away from everyday tasks in order to reflect on life and to work with their hearts. The best way for me to do the challenging work of making disciples requires—in addition to all the other ways of being together—conscious, purposeful *meeting alone* with the ones I am called to disciple.

Jesus makes it clear that a good shepherd *knows* his sheep (John 10:14). Parents are the human shepherds of their family. Parents are to help family members with the most important issues of life, starting with relationship with God. As the shepherd/parent of our families, we need to know each one, not just their grades, their activities, or even their friends. We need to know the heart of each child:

+what each one values … truly cares about

+what each one thinks about himself, others, and his circumstances

+what each one fears

+what each one wants immediately and dreams for long range

+what is frustrating to each one

+what pain exists in the heart of each one

Negative behavior is the effect, the weed. It is evidence of bad seed—heart "dis-ease." Bad seed (or no seed) in the heart is the cause, the root. If we deal only with behavior, we are temporarily or superficially controlling or manipulating external conditions. We are not creating real or lasting change. If we will work with the **cause** of the behavior (bad seed in the heart), God will work through us to create Christlike disciples for a lifetime and eternity.

Many of us can't be with our family members the way Jesus was with

His disciples. He was with them most days for a three-year period of time. We need to go to our jobs. Our children go to school and have activities. But we can consistently spend time alone with family members. We can establish and keep appointments with them. We can learn how to ask questions so that they honestly share with us, not only the outward experiences of their life, but their hearts. By listening to them talk about their lives and hearts, we can be "with them" through their story. We can know the most important part of their lives. Strategic one-on-one times together multiply the probabilities of positive heart exchanges.

When Deborah was filling out an application for Youth with a Mission (YWAM), she spoke about what happened on our times together. She wrote, "My dad would take me out, ask me questions, listen for the cracks in my heart, and then pour in love and truth."

Let's imagine you are out on an appointment with your son. It might be a ride to the next town. It might be a trip to a mall. It might be a hamburger at Burger King. Here are some specific activities for your appointment. Some may be obvious; others may not be.

### 1. Create casual conversation.

Tell a little of your story. Share some, but not too much, from your life that your son might be interested in or at least relate to. Examples include talking about food, clothes, people, games, disappointment, confusion, etc. See where it goes. Your goal is natural, easy dialogue.

Talk a little about his story. Comment on facts that you are aware of in his life, like shoes or clothing, successes, family, experiences, etc. It is like fishing. Put the bait out and wait to see if it is taken. Some children are very quiet. It takes great patience and skill to involve them in conversation. Others are constant talkers, so it takes great patience and skill to guide the conversation more productively. Please note that if from age three or four your child is accustomed to meeting and talking on one-on-one appointments, you and your child will be much more likely to communicate positively through the teen years.

Ask for some of his story of his week. You can casually ask, "What was one of the good things that happened today?" or "What did you get done yesterday?" It is a big deal to ask questions about the observable, material, tangible facts and experiences of your child's life. It is not hard for a child to talk about his life experiences. Communication occurs. The child gets used to talking to his parents. You are gathering information you need in order to better know your child.

Occasionally remind yourself and your child that your motive in asking is a sincere desire to know, understand, and as possible, be of help.

**2. Observe your child's body language; it reveals the heart.**

Observe your child's discomfort, excitement, boredom, facial expressions, tone of voice, etc. You may even want to ask a question about what you are observing. Observe silence. Ask the Holy Spirit to help you discern why silence is occurring. Be relaxed and comfortable with silence. Remember, you are trying to create an atmosphere where your child is free to share what is in his heart. Listen carefully to words for anything noteworthy to celebrate now or to investigate now or later.

Don't assume your interpretation of body language is accurate. Let body language give you a hint at what may be being thought, or felt, or desired. When appropriate, you can ask if your child is thinking or feeling tired, excited, bored, etc.

---

## Questions are the scalpel of the "heart" surgeon.

---

**3. Ask heart-opening questions about thoughts, emotions, desires, and motives.**

Remember the questions I asked Dave during his struggles in junior high? You can ask questions about what your son thought or even felt about a certain event. Look for a time when you sense it might be okay to go into his private world of thoughts, feelings, motives, or desires. This is the big moment of knocking on a door in his heart. Has the anesthesia of grace and patience and love been received into his sensitive heart? Questions are the scalpel of the "heart" surgeon. Is your scalpel sterilized from your own critical, careless, judgmental, or inappropriately curious heart? You are dealing with eternally significant issues, so be prepared. What types of heart-opening questions should you ask?

**Thoughts** Ask about your son's thoughts with a question like: "What did you think when he said that?" Or make a leading statement that serves to open the door: "I'll bet that you thought they were in trouble." Ask about ideas: "What do you think would be the best way of getting this done?" Ask about memories: "Did anything like this ever happen before to you?"

**Emotions** Ask about feelings and emotions: "How did it make you feel when you got up in front?""How do you feel about us leaving?" Note that some people experience their feelings far more profoundly than they remember their thoughts. Some are more willing to share thoughts than feelings. Both are massively important for you to know, value, and understand.

**Desires** Ask about desires: "What did that make you want to do?" "What do you wish she would do?"

**Motives** Ask about motives: "What is the reason you want to go?""Do you think you know why you don't like to be with him?" Be particularly careful when asking about motives. People often find it quite difficult to be introspective and honest about why they are behaving as they are. Be sensitive—your child may feel judged when you ask him why he behaved in a certain way, or why he wants to do a certain thing. Motives reveal very much about a person. Motives are often self-centered. Your son may not recognize his selfishness or want to admit it. On the upside, motives are often pure and noble, even though behavior did not appear good. One of the most important virtues for Christians to learn is ruthless honesty in the context of God's grace about their motives. Learning to talk about motives will help your child to recognize and evaluate his own motives. It will also help him to guard against thoughtlessly assigning negative motives to others. Equally important is that he will learn early to examine and honestly deal with his own motives. This is crucial in heart care. Many fail to learn this, to the disintegration, even demise, of their heart.

### 4. *Respond appropriately when your child opens his heart.*

Let's assume you have an appointment with your daughter. When she shares a thought, treat it with utmost care and honor. Be alert. You may fully disagree with the thought, but it is her thought, and it is reasonable and significant to her. If you respond in any negative way, especially with body language or tone of voice, it may hurt her. She exposed a part of her that is private and precious—the "pearls of her heart." Be more than gentle. Honor her thought because it represents who she truly is. If you handle one of her thoughts well, it will make it easier for her to tell you another one. If you do not respond well, she may not tell you another one. It is wise to learn to do what one of my friends does every time I tell him what I think. He says, "Thank you." Honor the treasure.

If you agree with her thought, affirm it: "Good idea." Verbally express agreement: "I agree." You are so important to your child—especially a younger child—that she feels good, smart, and close to you when you agree. After all, her very smart parent agrees with her.

To make disciples of Jesus, we want and desperately need to be sensitive to His perspective. We are not trying to make disciples of ourselves, but of Jesus. If what your daughter is saying seems to be in accord with Jesus' perspective and will, you can tell her how delighted you are that she is thinking like Jesus, which is wonderfully mature. We want to include Jesus in as much of our thinking and conversation as possible. We want to teach our children the same.

If what she says seems to be in conflict with Jesus, or dangerously ignoring Him, you have a challenge to face. You have just discovered a need for parental-pastoral care, a need to disciple (not discipline) her. You have simply discovered some weed seed. It may be deceit, or desire to get back at someone, or fear, or justifying and excusing selfish behavior. If your daughter is willing to open her thoughts to you, it won't be hard to recognize thoughts that are insensitive to God and His perspective. One of the greatest points of growth for Christ-followers is to include Jesus and His perspective in our thinking.

Now begins the challenge. A weed seed in the heart is any unChristlike perspective or value. The most common erroneous mind-set is simply ignoring Jesus—being insensitive or indifferent to Him. Jesus was unwilling to leave His Father out of His thoughts, conclusions, or actions.

Below are three practices parents must remember when a child reveals a weed seed:

- Do not immediately point out the error.
- Do not correct the error.
- Do not permanently ignore the error.

Think of the error as a delicate cancer attached to the heart or brain that must be cautiously and caringly extracted. Ask yourself questions like: Will this imperfect thought ever need to be removed? Is now the time for surgery? How much anesthesia (grace) is required? What preparation is necessary? Am I the surgeon or is a specialist required? What tools (questions) are needed to further open the heart? What will I find in the heart and how will I take it out if it needs to come out? What healing medication (truth) is needed and how can it be implanted in the diseased heart? Truth plus agreement (confession) plus commitment to walk in the truth (repentance) normally results in successful "heart surgery." Sometimes greater power is required. The Holy Spirit is always present, illuminating and inspiring, to make the "surgery" successful.

———

### *The key is getting the truth firmly planted in the heart.*

———

I paint this picture not to make it sound hard, but to illustrate the importance of replacing ungodly perspective—which gets in daily—with God's perspective. God's truth sets us free. The key is getting the truth firmly planted in the heart. This is the ultimate task of the Holy Spirit, but those who are undiscipled or disciples who are poorly developed almost always need great help from a more mature follower of Jesus to deal with weeds in the heart. When God's light is not known or recognized, our hearts are dangerously darkened and confused (Romans 1:18-32; Ephesians 4:17-18).

If you think it wise to not pursue a godless thought (or desire or emotion) at this time, you can choose to say something like:

• "That's interesting. Thanks for telling me what you think."

• "I want to think about what you are saying."

• "Maybe we can talk about it later."

If it seems good to pursue the idea or topic, you might say something like:

• "Are you thinking anything else about your teacher?"

• "I'm not sure I'm clear. Help me to understand what you are thinking when you say ...."

When your daughter has a history from an early age of telling you her thoughts about "her story," and of your listening and responding positively, it is not a hard thing to pursue a greater knowledge of her thoughts. Even if your child is older, start very gently and keep pursuing. It is worth the effort.

When you are quite sure you understand her thoughts on the topic or issue, it is very valuable to repeat back to her what you think she is thinking. You could say something like: "Let me make sure I understand. You think that ...." Simply repeat what you think she thinks.

---

## *"What do you think that I think?"*

---

If she says, "Yes, that's right," you may be surprised at how the Holy Spirit will use the conversation to reveal errors in her thinking. Often someone who reveals their ideas to a loving, spiritually sensitive person will find themselves saying something like: "That really isn't a very good attitude, is it?"

Suppose your daughter does not see the truth yet. You could ask a question that I have found to be very useful. You could ask, "What do you think that I think?" Memorize this question and choose to use it. Parents are tempted to tell their children what they think much too soon. You will be tempted to tell them what **you** think, but don't give in. You will be shocked to discover how even young children will be able to tell you quite clearly what you think. If they are correct, affirm them and ask the question, "What do you think about what I think?"

What we are doing is avoiding "preaching," lecturing, or correcting. Our children need to know for certain that we are sensitive to them, that we are for them, and that we are helping them discover truth instead of jamming it down their throats. Later we deal with how to *directly* speak the truth to our children when all other methods fail. A typical error of parents is to be the source of truth before seeking to be the facilitator of discovering truth. Children will generally enjoy dialogue with parents if, when sharing their ideas, they are not being told what to think. They enjoy searching for what is best when they are not being belittled or put down for not knowing the answer.

If your daughter doesn't know what you think, either through giving an incorrect answer or admitting she doesn't know, you can ask the question, "May I tell you what I think?" This must be an authentic request. You are truly seeking permission to speak into her heart. If she does not want to know, you would be wise to consider not telling her. If you respect her desires, the relationship will grow and you will be more likely to be invited into her heart on another day. But because the conversation has gone this far, and because you have established a very grace-based relationship, your child will almost always give you permission. You are being considerate of her and you are her friend. She will normally be happy to listen to what you think.

Jesus was full of grace and truth. You have been being gracious with your daughter. You now have an opportunity to hit what I call a "grace home run."

The first thing to tell your child about what you think could be something wonderful other than the issue at hand. You could tell your daughter what you think about one of your very favorite topics—her! "If you really want to know what I think, I think you are wonderful. I think you are my treasure. I think you deserve to have the best any person could have and I am going to try to get it for you."

Boom! You just put the greatest news a daughter can hear into a wide open heart. You have said that she is precious, regardless of her thoughts or feelings or desires. In telling her what you think about her, you have also told her what Jesus thinks and feels about her, even though you did not actually talk about Jesus. If she can believe it from you, she has been empowered to believe it from Jesus. This truth is the front door to the mansion that will empower her for a life of security, significance, and success in Jesus.

When she has clearly established this truth in her mind, she will feel safe to open her heart to your thoughts. After you tell her what you think, it is good to ask something like: "Do you know why I think this way?" This engages her, even at a young age, in wrestling with the reasons for your thoughts about her thoughts. It helps her understand your perspective. If you are giving your daughter the perspective of Jesus, and the reasons for this perspective, she will be strengthened in following Jesus and better equipped to lead others to follow Him. You are preparing her to think from God's point of view, to stand with the Truth and lead others into Truth.

---

## What really matters is what Jesus thinks.

---

One of my favorite moments in these types of discussions is when I can say, "It really doesn't matter too much what I think. I'm just a human being. What really matters is what Jesus thinks. He is the Genius of the universe Who created you and knows what makes you tick, along with everything else in the universe. What do you think He thinks about this issue?"

Notice the opportunity to accomplish two crucial objectives. First, Jesus can be sensitively brought into the discussion. With humility, I can say truthfully that my opinion really is not the issue, except that I know Whose opinion is crucial. Second, I can bring Jesus' mercy and grace to my child before I bring Jesus' call that requires an adjustment on her part.

After my daughter answers with what she thinks Jesus thinks about whatever topic we were discussing, I can say, "May I tell you what I think He thinks?"

If she says yes, I can tell her, "I think—in fact, I know—that He thinks you are precious. As precious as you are to me, it is nothing compared to how He feels about you." (When talking to a son, I'd use different language than "precious.") "He sees perfectly your heart to follow Him. He sees your will to trust Him and His heart is alive with delight as He thinks about you right now."

Once again, in a good moment, I have been able now to plant the greatest seed in the world in my daughter's heart: She is loved and cherished by the infinite Creator of the universe. The first great truth from God about God is that He loves us, including His grace and mercy that we all so desperately need to grasp. If there is other truth from God that we need to hear, like correction or direction, we and our children will be empowered to embrace it positively knowing that we are objects of His great affection and grace. When we are dwelling solidly in the foundation of grace, and we hear corrective or directive truth from God, we can run to Him and His open arms instead of giving in to the temptation to run away from a perceived glaring Father.

In the midst of talking about some area of confusion, neglect, or even unChristlikeness, your daughter has heard that both Jesus and her parent profoundly cherish and adore her, in spite of her confusion or weakness. What a moment! And it all came out of a commitment to having caringly guided conversations at McDonald's.

### 5. Plant God's Word into your child's heart.

As parent-pastors of our family, we want to keep expanding our child's knowledge of God's perspective. We want to equip them to take their own thoughts to Jesus (2 Corinthians 10:5). That way they can exchange their thoughts, feelings, desires, and motives for His. We want to equip them to pastor their own hearts. In the next chapter, we will talk about how to teach them to hear God's voice for themselves.

Right now, envision yourself at McDonald's with your son. An issue has come up that requires God's truth. Perhaps you clearly know God's truth about this issue. You will be tempted to tell your son God's truth. However, I strongly recommend *not* doing this. I recommend helping your son discover the truth by asking the kinds of questions we have already covered.

When an issue arises about relationships, attitudes, values, behavior, etc., another wonderful opportunity is presenting itself. Instead of asking your son what he thinks, what you think, or even what Jesus thinks, you could say, "Would you be willing for us to look in the Bible together to see if we can find out exactly what God says about this?" Note again that you are sincerely asking permission before proceeding. It reflects a constant sensitivity and honoring that oils the hinges of the heart's door.

Always carry a Bible in your car, purse, or PDA. Don't worry if you don't know how to find the answer in the Bible. Admit that you don't know, and show your son how you find answers when you don't know where to look. This is a great opportunity to train your child. Instead of giving him a fish, you are teaching him how to fish. Do you recall anything the Bible says about the issue at hand? If so, look it up together. If you can't, look up a key word or concept in your Bible's concordance (if it has one). If you can't find an answer, tell him that you will go home and dig out your study Bible, concordance, or Bible dictionary. If you still can't find the answer, tell your son you'll go to a friend or pastor and find the answer and then show him how you found it. (It is better to show than to tell.)

### 6. Secure heart commitment to God's Word.

Remember little King Will? We want to find out if our child (Will) decides to agree with, believe, and obey God's Word. Once we know God's Word and His will, we must secure a response. We want to lead our children to be doers of the Word, not just hearers. Remember, Jesus did not say to teach them everything He taught. He said to teach them to *obey* everything He taught. To do this, consider the following kinds of questions:

Do you believe what God has said? How will it affect you if you believe this?

Do you plan on obeying what Jesus is saying? How will you do it? How will you pray about it?

Can you hold as absolute truth what God says about you? How can you

119

establish His truth in your heart? What ways of thinking will need to change?

How will you do this at home, church, and school? Do you want or need help from me or anyone else?

Would you be willing to talk to me next week about any progress you see, or any problems that you are having?

I will be praying for you. Can we pray right now?

Do you realize how delighted Jesus and I are with you?

I pray that you will commit to this one-on-one discipling of your children. This is a lot of territory and I have just presented many optional questions. It is simply a guide, not a guarantee or a law. Your effectiveness will depend more on who you are becoming as you unite with and follow Jesus than your ability to develop all of the strategies outlined in this chapter. Further, your success will also be greatly determined by your sensitivity to both the Holy Spirit and to your child. It must not feel mechanical or programmatic, or it may feel manipulative to your child. Manipulation, in its negative understanding, is trying to control another person for one's own selfish reasons without the other person realizing they are being controlled. It is better to be totally responsive and real during this meeting and forget the plan than to push on toward the goal and turn off your child. Go at the speed your child is ready to go. Relax and trust the Lord.

## Personal appointments empower us to guard their hearts

Who will guard the hearts of our families? (Proverbs 4:23) Every day your child is bombarded with perspectives that leave God out (lies). What will prevent his heart from being seduced into temporal values, godless perspectives, fear, insecurity, and even hatred? How will it get done? Who will successfully open the heart, find out what is in it, and then have the grace and wisdom to pull out the weed seeds at the root, not just try to control the behavior? Who will plant good seeds in the place of the weed seeds? Weed seeds grow very quickly in the hearts of children and teenagers. It simply isn't enough to weed the garden of your child's heart once a year or once a month. Some parents hope for and depend on "natural, spontaneous, teachable" moments. I beg you not to depend only or primarily on these times. What is required is consistent, sensitive, intimate one-on-one listening to the heart.

Listen to what our daughter, Dana, wrote about one of our weekly meetings:

When a child, however old, has said yes in sincerity to Jesus, truly desiring to choose Him at all costs, one of the most needed things in her spiritual life is the continual call to whole-heartedness, given by one who knows of the rewards the heart experiences when this call is heeded. For me, one of the more significant of these calls came from my dad when I was in high school. At the time, I was in a dating relationship that was relatively serious. My heart was greatly intertwined and had there not been an intervention, the relationship would have more than likely headed into marriage. In and of itself this relationship seemed relatively good, having the approval of most everyone and leaving me somewhat convinced of why it was good. However, my father saw it differently, having a great vision for me to enter into the highest God had for me and on one of our weekly times together, he began to ask me some important questions based out of this vision. As we sat across the table, he asked me genuinely, "Do you feel that Jesus is calling you to this relationship?" Feeling the weight of this question, and the implications of its answer, my head went down as I felt the wrenching within—the tearing that comes between the tensions of either choosing my own comfort or reaching for the higher path that leads to life. In these times, the Holy Spirit loves to aid whatever flickering desire we have for godliness, and I remember this divine help as I knew, within a moment's time, that I must bring the relationship to a close in order to respond fully to the Lord. I lifted my head and said, "No. He hasn't called me to it," and the next day, with a heart scared to death, I broke off the relationship. My conversation with my dad changed my course that day, bringing me to a whole new plane in my walk with Jesus. And in response to my sincere reaching, the Lord answered me with a deeper intimacy with Himself—the most precious gift available to the human heart.

Why have regular, personal appointments with your child at as early an age as possible?

- ⁺To develop the positive habit of meeting and talking at heart levels so these meetings can continue throughout the challenging years ahead.

- ⁺To develop needed skills in talking at heart levels.

- ⁺To heal "heart disease." Hearts absorb poisonous debris. Second best is easily chosen. Weeds grow. Confusion, pain, and sin that will destroy lives temporally and eternally need to be exposed and eliminated.

- ⁺To prevent loneliness and provide heart knowing/sharing. Our children will look for someone—good or bad—with whom to share their thoughts, emotions, and desires. They are unconsciously looking for a way to not be alone in their hearts, and hoping to find acceptance, even value. If they do not have a follower of Jesus for a heart-friend, they will search for someone else, no matter what they have to do or where they have to go to find one. It is not good to be lonely, and loneliness is a heart issue (Genesis 2:18).

- ⁺To implant God's Word and will.

- ⁺To bond parents with their children. The family is in desperate need of help that connected hearts provide.

- ⁺To equip children to care for their own spiritual hearts.

- ⁺To equip children to connect with other hearts and connect those hearts to God.

♦ To overcome evil with good. The world is pouring into the heart of our families. The godlessness of peers, entertainment, and media infiltrate our hearts daily. Connected hearts provide the sensitivity and ability to overcome the evil with good.

♦ To do what the church cannot do. The church is critically important, a necessary help, and a reinforcement of the values being lived and taught at home. But one to four hours per week or month is a tiny fragment of influence. Further, church structures are primarily "telling structures," not "listening structures." Who in the church will consis tently listen and effectively minister to the confusion and pain in your child's or teenager's heart every day or every week?

♦ To do what Jesus did ( John 10:11-15) The caring and wise parent, like the good Shepherd, lays down his or her time for his "little flock" (family) instead of abandoning them. He or she knows his family intimately, by heart. The family knows the parent's heart.

---

### A Christlike parent does not see the problem as the child's problem, but as "their problem."

---

♦ To be like Jesus ( John 1:14) Jesus, full of grace and truth, left every thing to come all the way to us. Like Jesus, the Christlike parent does not ask a child to come to him, but the parent reaches all the way to the child (Romans 8:1-4; Matthew 5:17). A Christlike parent does not see the problem as the child's problem, but as "their problem." Like Jesus, a Christlike parent goes all the way to wherever his child is, in whatever condition of darkness, to demonstrate care and sensitivity, and to gently lead his child one step at a time to the Light, and thus to safety, security, significance, health, happiness, holiness, and heaven.

♦ To obey Jesus (Matthew 28:18-20) Christian parents are commis- sioned to disciple someone. Biblically and logically parents are to strategically disciple their children—immersing them in the character and activity of God, and teaching them to obey everything Jesus commanded. It is unacceptable for parents to assume that someone else will disciple their children while the parents disciple no one and/or give their time to other ministries while neglecting to disciple their own children.

Jesus said, "Let the children come to Me." Parents are to follow the living, incarnate Jesus, to walk as He walked, to be Christ-ian (little Christs). Parents need to be able to say, "If you have seen me, you have seen Jesus." (1 John 2:6; John 14.9) A parent connects with a child in order to connect the child with Jesus, one thought, one emotion, one desire, and one decision at a time. We cannot do it without God; God seldom does it without us.

—⁓—

## *A parent connects with a child in order to connect the child with Jesus.*

—⁓—

Do you remember the story I started the chapter with about the little boy who desired time with his daddy? Would you join me in praying for and working toward an army of parents who will consistently give their child "one hour"? Would you pray with me for an army of parents who will start to personally meet with and coach/disciple their sons and daughters? With God's help, parents can become sensitive, listening, spiritual leaders who turn their family into a house of friends and a small band of Jesus' disciples who will change their world.

Before we study how to spend "one hour" in intensively discipling your child, there is another issue. What you truly care about, when with your child formally or informally, will influence and shape your child as much or more than what you learn to do in formal discipling. Further, what you honestly care about is the solution for parents who believe that they do not have time to give "one hour." Finally, what you honestly care about is designed to model for your child the heart of a champion. The best hope for your child to have the heart of a champion will be for you to have the heart of a champion.

The next chapter discusses what you, the parent, care about most.

# CHAPTER EIGHT

—◈—

# The Heart of a Champion

"… the world must learn that I love the Father and that I do exactly what My Father has commanded me." *John 14:31*

" … My Father, if it is possible, may this cup be taken from Me. Yet not as I will but as You will." *Matthew 26:39*

Do you desire that your child be a winner—a champion? Many parents do. I wanted our children to be champions at only one thing—following Jesus. I told them time after time that if they were giving themselves wholeheartedly to Jesus that school, life partner, vocation, and everything else would work out just fine (Matthew 6:33; 2 Chronicles 16:9). Some parents are satisfied if their child does not get in trouble. Others, in their heart of hearts, dream of their child being much better than average. In fact, some dream of their child being a champion in God's army—serving with distinction and honor and passion. That dream is often realized. This chapter lays a necessary foundation.

## Full devotion

He told his story nostalgically, as one would relate a favorite Christmas memory. He was reflecting on a meaningful time in his life, a time when he was focused, single-minded, passionate. This is his story.

He got up early every morning because he had much to do. While he got ready, he mentally ran through his schedule for the day. He planned quiet time alone to meditate on his newfound faith, his dramatic purposes, and the new lessons he was learning. At breakfast, he read a newspaper to see what was going on the world. He needed to be able to relate to others in order to lead them from their point of view to his faith. After breakfast, he boarded a train for the commute to work. He took along several magazines that his new leaders had given him. He distributed them on the train seats where others might find them and—he hoped—read and begin to open up to his faith.

He arrived at work early. He wanted his employer and associates to respect him so that they would listen when the time came to share why he was such a good worker. He worked hard until break time. Then he would purposefully connect with other employees, asking about their concerns, needs, and frustrations. He empathized and helped when possible. Through this, he hoped to one day open the opportunity to share his good news about how their lives could be different. He did the same thing at lunch and all afternoon. Every moment of his work day was filled with meaning and purpose. He desired to lead others into the wonderful life of hope and purpose that he had discovered.

In the evening, he would race home to have dinner. He had important work to do after dinner. Some nights, he attended meetings taught or motivated by the leaders of his faith. Other nights he visited different neighborhoods to give practical help to needy people. As he grew in faith, he was asked to mentor new converts. Some nights he joined with others of his faith as they mingled at entertainment or eating locations downtown, seeking to connect with unbelievers in order to share their faith.

By the end of the day, he was exhausted. But he came home with a deep, profound sense of meaning and significance. He had lived every moment of his day on purpose, with purpose, to benefit his community and world. He fell into bed, thinking of what he could do better and how he could passionately, strategically, and purposefully give his life tomorrow to sharing his faith. There was fire in his heart. It was his passion.

This story was about a day in the life of a communist. The man's new faith was in communism. He had seen some communists doing good works.

He had talked with them and received, into his heart, their dream and strategy to make the world better. He bought it.

Ideas, good or bad, can enter our minds, set our hearts on fire, and then transform our lives. Jesus' mother, Mary, pondered things in her heart (Luke 2:19). Jesus said that evil thoughts come from our hearts (Mark 7:21). No one needs to tell us to live our beliefs. We live what we actually believe. We cannot help it. If we do not like the way we are behaving, we must change what we believe. Our behavior exposes our true beliefs. When we realize that our behavior reflects our beliefs, there is hope that we can improve. We can honestly look at our lives and use what we see to help us discover our true beliefs. We can change as we exchange the true beliefs of our heart to truth.

Our communist friend thought he was hearing truth, so he believed it. His new faith, which was authentic from the heart, determined his life. Day after day, he lived exactly as I described. He loved, and therefore lived every moment for, communism. He gave four of every seven dollars he made to the spread of his belief that communism was the answer for the world.

---

### *What actually fills a parent's heart consistently and inevitably spills out.*

---

The point I draw from the story of the communist is basic. What fills our heart inevitably spills out. What actually fills a parent's heart consistently and inevitably spills out. The communist was whole-hearted, single in purpose, passionate. He gave his life to an idea that entered his mind. His heart was ablaze with zeal. He lived out what was in his heart. What was in his heart made enough sense to him that he delightedly gave all he had to the cause. He turned to, trusted, served, praised, obeyed, and loved communism with all of his heart, soul, mind, and strength. He was wrong, but he was passionate. He had pure devotion. Incidentally, many years later, he had another heart change. He heard about Jesus and changed his mind. This change of mind—repentance—led to an authentic life of following Jesus.

## God created us to have full devotion

Our Father made us to be whole-hearted and passionate, not divided or ambivalent. He does not intend us to be half-hearted and bored, or confused and frustrated (2 Corinthians 11:2-3). He intends that we be whole-heartedly and passionately focused on Him and His purposes. Imagine millions of passionate Christ-followers like the former communist. Are there Christians struggling with divided hearts? Yes. Their hearts are divided. "Di-vision" comes from having more than one vision. A divided house or person cannot stand (Proverbs 29:18). We need to see Jesus clearly. The key to a passionate, fully devoted heart is seeing Jesus as He is.

Why do so many teens and young adults chase wildly after any extreme? They were created to be passionate. Consciously or unconsciously, they desire whole-heartedness. They refuse to live half-hearted lives without passion. How sad to be passionate about a deception, like the former communist was. Our children can encounter Him who is Truth. He can capture their hearts. He can satisfy their God-given longing for passion and pure devotion. Then they will truly be "alive with aliveness," as God intends. If we have this truth available, surely we would want to give whatever it takes for this truth to get into the hearts of our children to create the singleness of purpose that God intends. Without pure devotion, we are legitimately frustrated or bored.

Would it delight your heart to see your child living a totally devoted, single-minded, passionate, purposeful life with Jesus and for His purposes? Would it thrill your heart to discover your son sitting at a desk with his Bible open, writing letters to Jesus of thankfulness, trust, love, and promise in response to a personal Word from Jesus? How would you feel if your daughter's fourth grade teacher scheduled an appointment with you to tell you about how your daughter had started a Bible study during lunch that was influencing many students and even some teachers to follow Jesus?

Would it delight your heart for *you* to experience this kind of life? If somehow you could have this pure devotion for Jesus, you would benefit greatly because ...

+ You will be specially blessed by God (2 Chronicles 16:9)
+ You will experience the God-intended delight of single-minded devotion
+ Your child will probably be positively impressed and influenced
+ You will have the necessary motivation to prioritize your life for God's highest purposes, including discipling your family

Our Creator has repeatedly thought about and addressed these issues. A quick survey of the Bible reveals our God redundantly calling us to passionate, purity of heart—to pure devotion. He calls us to one unifying, integrating, singleness of focus of pure devotion. He calls us to:

+ Seek Him with all of our heart (Jeremiah 29:13; 2 Chronicles 15:12; 22:9; Psalm 119:2, 10, 58).
+ Return to Him with all of our heart (1 Samuel 7:3; 1 Kings 8:48; 2 Chronicles 6:38; Joel 2:12).
+ Trust Him will all of our heart (Proverbs 3:5).
+ Praise Him with all of our heart (Psalm 111:1; 138:1).
+ Serve Him with all our heart (Deuteronomy 10:12; 11:13; Joshua 22:5; 1 Samuel 12:20, 24).
+ Obey Him with all of our heart (2 Kings 23:3; 2 Chronicles 34:31; Psalm 119:34, 69)

Jesus said that these are all wrapped up in one great commandment. He calls us to love God with all of our heart, soul, mind, and strength (Matthew 22:37; Mark 12:30; Luke 10:27; Deuteronomy 6:5; 13:3; 30:6). To give ALL of our thought processes and strength to anything, be it another person, a career, security, reputation, or our perfect, worthy God, requires dramatic motivation and passion—pure devotion.

How does this pure devotion happen? Can our hearts be that pure, that passionate?

131

## Jesus had full devotion

Jesus had pure devotion for His Father, and for His Father's will. What the Father wanted Him to do He did with unspeakable love, purity, and passion (John 4:34; 14:31).

In the following story, watch what God the Father did to parent His Son and restore His Son's passion for saving the lost of the world.

One night Jesus needed purity in His heart. His vision was divided. He knew what He was called to do, but He did not have the inner resources to tackle it. In great pain, He went to the place where His heart would be renewed, re-kindled, impassioned to carry out His mission. He went to a garden to meet with His Father—to pray.

Jesus was suffering excruciating mental turmoil. His anticipation of the terror of the cross generated every painful emotion known to man. He knew it was the plan He and His Father had shared since before the foundation of the world. But now it looked different. Perhaps He had seen a Roman crucifixion. I think He sensed the terror that He would experience when He felt alone, forsaken by His Father. He knew that His Holy Father was furious against sin. He understood that somehow the sheer fury of His loving, righteous Father against every sin ever committed, past or future, would be unleashed. He knew that He would somehow be the One to absorb all the fury. He knew that He would identify with and be identified as the sin of the entire world, and thus absorb His holy, righteous, furious-against-sin Father's just penalty for the sin of the world.

Although we do not know what Jesus anticipated or experienced, we do know that it was enough to shake Him to the core. The One Who calmly reminded Pilate that no power on earth could hurt God's Son unless it was the will of the Father, now had sweat pouring from His body like great drops of blood. In anguish, He fell on His face, crying out to His Father to change the plan. "Father, if You are willing, take this cup from Me."

One night, while I was in college, I was thinking and meditating on what Jesus experienced in the garden. As I meditated, I became aware of the Father responding to Jesus. I didn't purposely conjure it up. I simply saw it happen in my mind. I do not claim that what I saw in my mind was from God, but I think it was. I do know that God has used this experience to create a life-long purifying passion in my heart that has dramatically shaped my entire life.

Jesus was desperate. "Father, do I have to do this?" Silence. Jesus repeated the question again...and again...and again. "Father, do I have to go to the cross?" Silence. "Isn't there some other way that we could get this done?"

Then I sensed God the Father speaking to Jesus. "Oh, My Son! With You I am infinitely pleased. You have fulfilled Your mission perfectly to this point. You were tempted in all ways, more than any person ever has been. You were even dramatically tempted to use Your relationship with Me to Your advantage. You would not. Not once did You ignore Me or leave Me out. You have been perfect. Oh, that You could feel the depths of My joy and delight in You!" Jesus' Father is pouring heart transforming truth from His heart into His Son's heart.

In my own thoughts that night in college, the Father continued. "I hate that men, especially religious leaders, are so evil as to be seduced into plotting against You even right now. Before You asked, a part of My heart was already yearning to pull You out of this mess and to simply let them all be destroyed as they deserve." Jesus' Father is further opening His heart to His Son. "But Son, You remember that as I love You, I love them (John 17:23). As I do not want You to suffer, I want them to not suffer. I want them to be with us forever. I am delighted with You; I love them. My heart is broken for them. How delighted I would be if somehow they would repent and relate to Me from their hearts in even a small way as You have." Jesus' Father is enlightening His Son's vision with the Father's vision. "Son, I hear Your cries and I passionately desire to deliver You. You have been free up to this point. I do not take Your freedom from You. It would be within My acceptable will to deliver You from bearing this heinous cross." Jesus' Father exposes an alternative. "However, I remind You:

You can be the Lamb of God that takes away the sin of the world. Through this dramatic act of selfless suffering and sacrifice, terrible as it will be for both of Us, Your shed blood can become the blood of a new covenant that will allow any person, regardless of the depths of his sin, to be fully and freely forgiven and given new life forever. I love You. I love the world of lost persons. The choice is Yours. You decide." Jesus' Father reveals a bigger, better—yet devastating—alternative.

It is one thing to make a request of a father and for the father to make the decision. It is another thing for a father, in love and wisdom, to give a hard choice back to a son.

---

## In preparation for the most difficult experience of His life, Jesus ran to a garden to meet with His Father.

---

In my mind, Jesus looked forward at the cross and shuddered. He looked upward at His Father and wept. He looked forward again at the cross and sweat like blood poured out of His body. He looked backward at Pilate, who had ordered His crucifixion. He looked at the Pharisees and soldiers making their way to arrest Him. He saw His disciples sleeping in spite of His plea for support. Compassion for every person's eternal well-being flowed through His merciful heart. He looked forward to the millions of redeemed who would sing around the throne, dancing in joy at the privilege of experiencing the goodness and glory of His Father throughout the endless ages.

In preparation for the most difficult experience of His life, Jesus ran to a garden to meet with His Father. He had had countless meetings alone with His Father. All of those meetings served to prepare Jesus for this most traumatic of meetings. The reason for His dying that had been securely planted in Jesus' mind was dimmed by the pressure and apprehension of the cross to come. He needed to be reminded of whom His Father was—why He, Jesus, had come—what the benefit of His suffering would be. It was this meeting with

His caring, wise Father that led to eternity being transformed. It began with a change in Jesus' heart. He poured out the pain and desires of his heart: "Let this cup pass from Me." His Father listened patiently for three hours. Then, the Father communicated with the Son. Eternity will proclaim and celebrate that the truth of the Father, planted in the mind of the Son, set the Son free in the most difficult moment in history. That implanted truth led to the possibility of freedom from judgment for every person on planet earth. It freed us to choose to walk away from our own government to follow the Lamb of God.

Jesus again riveted His attention on the cross. This time He was free. His perspective had been expanded by his Father. He could now see beyond the cross. He even had joy because of the vision given by his Father (Hebrews 12:2). No more shuddering or sweating drops of blood. He looked up to His Father and with Spirit-empowered resolve spoke the greatest words ever uttered, "Not My will, but Your will be done."

---

*But with great wisdom, born of good habit, He brought His heart to His Father. The perfectly wise Father influenced but did not control His Son in this crucial moment.*

---

Jesus' mind had been filled with thoughts about suffering and the cross. These terror-laden images affected His emotions. These thoughts and emotions caused Him to want to walk away from His purpose and mission. But with great wisdom, born of good habit, He brought His heart to His Father. The perfectly wise Father influenced but did not control His Son in this crucial moment. Jesus made the greatest choice of the eternal ages.

God sovereignly declared that we are free and must make choices. If Jesus had no choice, He would not have represented us. As our representative, He chose the cross. The victory was won in His heart where He made the ultimate good choice, aided by His good Father. In Jesus' hour of supreme weakness, He poured out His heart to His Father. In turn, His Father planted good seed in an open, pure heart. They'd had hundreds of meetings like this before on mountains, in early mornings, and all nights. All of those meetings had prepared Jesus for this one great meeting, the greatest moment in history. Aided by His Father, He won. His Father won. We won. Everyone wins when God's will is planted in a human heart that hears and responds, no matter the cost.

All it took for Jesus to quit running from the cross and to embrace the cross was a heart-to-heart talk with His Father. His Father could see better and further than Jesus could see in this, His hour of greatest temptation. How blessed we are that Jesus was in the habit of having personal, heart-to-heart meetings with His Father.

What God the Father did for God the Son is what parents in quiet one-on-one meetings can do for their child:

+ Examine alternatives

+ Expand vision

+ Empower noble choices

Do you feel the heart of the Father for Jesus? Do you feel the Father's heart for all of us? Can you imagine the tearing and ripping in His heart as He observed Jesus' pain? Do you feel Jesus' heart for His Father? Do you feel His heart for us? Do you feel the terrible tension of His heart, torn by the agonizing decision before Him? Torn by dread of the ultimate in suffering on one side, and profound love for His Father and us on the other? I feel it in both Father and Son, and it ignites passion in me for my heavenly Father, my Lord, my King, my Savior.

As His Father invited Jesus, so Jesus invites us to involvement in His eternally significant ventures. When we realize the cost and ask Him if we must sacrifice, even suffer, I believe He usually helps us to see the eternal benefits to everyone involved and says, "If anyone would come after Me, let Him deny himself, take up his cross, and follow Me." (Matthew 16:24)

## Full devotion empowers us to make disciples of Jesus

We will need full devotion to respond to Jesus' amazing invitation to make disciples of Him.

I was seriously committed to following Jesus. Logic, commitment, and some authentic love for Jesus helped me to be a sincere follower of Jesus. I had many times realized and experienced the wonder, grace, and genius of Jesus. Each encounter warmed my heart. Each led me to deeper resolve to know and follow Him. But something dramatic happened in my relationship with Jesus on the night I meditated on Him in the garden with His Father.

That night, I wept as I saw Jesus freely choose to suffer all He did for His Father and the world and for me. He became more wonderful and personal than He had been before. I remember that night as a high and holy moment in my relationship with Jesus. I believe the Holy Spirit somehow used this moment to powerfully purify my heart. By seeing Jesus as I did in the garden, my heart was captured, empowering a purity and passion that affected every part of my life. Did I love Jesus with all my heart before that night? I had thought so. Did I love Jesus with all my heart after that night? Only God truly knows the heart.

I do remember that after seeing Jesus in the garden, I wanted Him to have all of me—my time, money, energy and abilities. The issue was love for Jesus. The best way I knew to love Him was to give myself to Him and His purposes. I became a person so passionate for Jesus that I searched His Word for what He wanted. When I found what I believed He wanted, I gave myself zealously to Him and to His cause. His Word became my will. I made time with Him the first priority of my life. I experienced what Paul said, "Christ died for all that those who live should no longer live for themselves but for Him who died for them." (2 Corinthians 5:15)

I saw the heart of Jesus and the heart of the Father, and my heart became passionate and empowered. I learned that passionate hearts are the by-product of seeing Jesus' heart. I learned that for me to have and maintain passion for Jesus was to see and hear His thoughts, emotions, desires, and will. Hearts grow cold; they lose passion. By beholding the heart of Jesus, my passion and pure devotion for Him was renewed.

Soon after our triplets were born, I realized that Jesus wanted me to disciple them before anyone else. This pure devotion to Jesus of which I have been speaking made it an easy commitment. I do not think I would have been sufficiently motivated to make time to disciple my family had I not seen Jesus' heart that touched my heart. My job legitimately takes up far more time than most people give to their work. In retrospect, my personal encounter with Jesus in the garden had a most profound influence on my family. That encounter motivated me to sacrifice whatever I needed to be with my family.

Debbi explains her story about pure and passionate love for Jesus this way:

> I know that the Lord reveals His heart of extravagant love to us individually in unique, personal ways. For me, it wasn't in a moment, but over a season through circumstances, relationships, and scripture. In custom-designed ways, He satisfied the longings and desires of my heart that only He knew about. He convinced my heart that He truly has a Bridegroom's heart overflowing in joy, tenderness and passion for me (Isaiah 62:5).

> Little by little, I began to experience His rejoicing over me (Zephaniah 3:17.) It was not based on my performance, but on my heart that was seeking, thirsting, loving, obeying, and serving Him. It goes back to the very moment in Jesus' life that my husband just described. "For the joy set before Him, He endured the cross." (Hebrews 12:2) The joy before Him was those who had said yes to Him, including me. His heart was saying, "I'll do the cross thing. I want her with me eternally. Her affection-filled heart for Me has captured My heart." I then saw His provision, protection, and guidance throughout my life with enlightened eyes. I was staggered by His relentless pursuit to capture my little heart. This new paradigm, this depth of insight, experiencing His extravagant love for me,

tenderized my heart and invigorated me with passion to more fully consecrate all that I have and am to Him.

What Debbi and I have both found is that:

- The key to following Jesus when it costs and hurts is **loving** Him entirely.
- The key to establishing and keeping love passionate enough to make the difference is **seeing** Him.
- The key to seeing Him is **being with** Him.

Our problem is not with taking up our cross. A cross might be a hard relationship or situation. It is any invitation to serve or sacrifice or suffer for the benefit of Jesus. Running from our cross is always a symptom of something deeper. A deeper problem is insufficient love for Jesus, but this is still not the core issue. The core issue is that we have lost our revelation of the great heart of Jesus. This heart freely chose the cross—for the Father and for us. He chose the cross because He anticipated great delight in being with us eternally (Hebrews 12:2).

Being Jesus' disciple includes denying myself and taking up my cross to follow Him. Suppose that on the really tough challenges, Jesus gives me a choice to go the easier or the harder way. My spirit is willing. But without help, I'll probably go the easy way because my flesh is weak. I need help if I'm going to follow Jesus in sacrificial ways. It is through alone times in my garden of Gethsemane that my Father helps me.

To see the heart of Jesus is to see the heart of His Father. Even Jesus lost sight of His mission when He lost sight of his Father's heart. A vision of God's mission without a vision of God's heart will become legalism, institutionalism, dead orthodoxy, religion, or just plain death. On the other extreme, without a vision of God's heart, God's mission can become terrorizing, impossible, overwhelming, and too costly. When Jesus and you and I go to our Father once again to see His heart, life flows back into our hearts and we can all say, "Not my will, but Your will be done. I will take up my cross to follow You and Your will." (Matthew 16:24)

We can say yes and follow through on Jesus' call for us to disciple our children if we continue to be renewed in passion for Jesus. We'll be pulled dozens of legitimate directions that steal our time from our family. We'll get bored or frustrated in working with our family. But if we have passion for Jesus resulting in pure devotion, and we know Jesus wants us to disciple our family, we can keep going.

We may get discouraged about our own following of Jesus. We may feel like failures. We will face obstacles, even opposition. But if we have passion and pure devotion for Jesus, we can keep going. With passion for Jesus, we can deny ourselves, take up our cross, and keep on following Him. We can say, "Not my will, but Your will be done." Passion is primary. If we have passionate love for Jesus, we will have the heart resource to deny ourselves and take up our cross for Him, for eternity, for everyone. He announced that if we love Him, we will be empowered to obey Him (John 14:15, 21, 23; 15:10; 1 John 5:3; Revelation 14:12).

—⁓—

*If you will intensively, patiently meditate on Jesus' passionate love for His Father and all people—including you—the Holy Spirit will ignite your bored or divided or lukewarm heart with passion for Jesus.*

—⁓—

Jesus' passionate love for His Father and for us leads us to love Him. If you and I love Jesus passionately, we will give ourselves to Him. Relationship with Him will make us more and more like Him. Our children will see our passionate love for Him and for others. Seeing our pure devotion will influence our children to love us and want to follow us. They will like Jesus for what He does in us. We will have influence in their lives.

I pray you will never forget this promise: *If you will intensively, patiently*

*meditate on Jesus' passionate love for His Father and all people—including you—*
*the Holy Spirit will ignite your bored or divided or lukewarm heart with passion for*
*Jesus.* Your ignited heart will passionately desire to both cling to Jesus and serve
Him at any cost. Passion leads to radical, single, pure devotion. You will, once
again, devote yourself and everything you have to Jesus. If you have run ahead
of Jesus and been overzealous, you will be willing to back up. If you have been
too passive, you will be ready to become aggressive. If you have been wrong,
you will be ready to repent. If you have been right and effective, your ignited
heart will remember that every good thing in you was given by God, and you
will passionately desire that God be glorified. You will experience the heart of
a champion regarding the one contest worth winning.

Others, especially your family, will see your heart—the heart of a champion. Your champion's heart is passionate and devoted. You see Jesus more
clearly than most and give yourself to Him and His purposes without reserve.
You labor behind the scenes, but not for yourself. You labor for Jesus. Your
family will respect, honor, and support you, even in the midst of your human
frailty because seeing your sincere and passionate heart affects their hearts.
They are looking for a hero—someone noble, like you—to follow. From the
experience you have gained in serving wholeheartedly, you will be able to coach
and lead your son or daughter in this way of life. You are doing it so you can
coach it. It's all about the heart, starting with the great Father-heart of God.

I pray you are abundantly persuaded that it is God's will for you and
your family to live single-hearted, passionate, non-boring lives. No one or
no thing can adequately capture your heart in the long term other than Jesus
and His purposes. You are made first and foremost for Him. To find your
meaning and passion in anything less than Him is what He calls idolatry
and unfaithfulness (Jeremiah 3; Matthew 22:37). Wholehearted passion for
Jesus will empower you to courageously lead your family and others through
the pressures generated by fleshly passions. Jesus "died for all, that those who
live should no longer live for themselves, but *for Him* who died for them and
was raised again." (2 Corinthians 5:15)

A legend is told about a king. He was the most powerful king in the known world. The reason for his control over all other kingdoms was his superior army. The reason his army was superior was the superiority of the horses. His horse trainers had learned superior ways to train horses. In the midst of battle—with clashing of swords, screams of agony, even in pain—the horses were trained to remain sensitive to their riders' commands, or their nudges when the commands could not be heard. In the distraction, noise, and pain of battle, the well-trained horses could not be distracted; they must listen for and be obedient to their masters.

There was a test after all the training to see which horse would actually be suited and selected to be the horse the king himself would ride during battle. This horse had to be the best of the best. Many were equally strong. Many were equally fast. Many were equally trained. But the horse for the king had to have a loyal, passionate heart for the king.

The horse for the king had to learn to respond to many signals. One signal was a particular whistle. This whistle meant that, no matter what the obstacles, the horse was to come to the one giving the whistle—the whistle of the king.

The best horses were given a final test. A corral was built on the side of a ravine. The river that cut the ravine was splashing along, a few hundred feet downhill from the corral. The fastest, smartest, strongest, best trained horses were led into the corral. The gate was shut.

The horses were given no food or water for a day. They were hungry, but far worse was their thirst. They could see and smell the water in the river just down the hill from the corral. They scouted every section of fence, searching for a way of escape.

A second day came and went with no food or water. The horses were famished, but that was small compared to the scream of their bodies to quench the thirst. They could see and smell the river just down the hill. They pawed at the corral, attempting to beat down the sides to escape.

The third day was the same. No food, no water. Now, dehydrated, these best of the best horses were losing their fight. Hope of getting out was dying. They had spent all their energy seeking release from their captivity. They were broken.

During the third day, the gate was opened. The barrier was gone. Suddenly energy returned. Reaching the water in the river was no longer impossible. The gate was opened. It was downhill all the way to the water. The life-giving, life-saving water was within reach. Off these finest of horses bolted, through the gate, down the hill, gravity serving them in their mad dash to life. Then when they were at top speed, half way down the hill, THE whistle to return to the king was blown. It was the whistle that meant come to the king, no matter what the obstacle. The whistle to be blown in the most intense moments of the battle, when the king needed his horse at any cost, was blown. These horses were the best trained of all. Instinctively, upon hearing the whistle, they halted their mad dash to the river. For a bone-jarring moment, they responded—caught between their most legitimate, desperate need for water and the months of trained response to come to the whistle, regardless of any obstacle—but only for a moment. Almost all of these best trained, most suited for the king's service horses would give in to the scream of their flesh for water. They would ignore the whistle and satisfy their own needs. But every once in a while, every so often, a horse more noble, a horse more disciplined, would hear the whistle, and with whatever it took, stop the downward thrust of momentum and gravity, fueled by raging thirst. This horse would stop, go against the flow, painfully turn, and muster every available source of energy to get to the whistle, denying itself, being willing even to die, to serve the king. That horse was selected for special service—to be the special servant of the king.

Does anyone hear the whistle of the King? Our King? A thousand legitimate thirsts to be satisfied will scream at us to rush downhill. Most of our comrades, the best there are, will be heading full speed to the river. And it is understandable—if one loses sight of the big battle, and the King. Somewhere there is enough truth in taking care of our own temporal needs that it makes very good sense to ignore the whistle of the King and continue downhill. Our comrades will by their life and words call us to be reasonable and join them in satisfying our legitimate appetites and thirsts.

But every once in a while, every so often, someone hears the whistle of the King and denies himself and takes up whatever cross, gives up whatever is necessary, battles through every obstacle to follow the King—to respond to His whistle. That servant, that soldier, will be of special service to the King in the great war being waged to free every captive from eternal tyranny. Is your devotion to your King pure? Have you heard "the whistle"?

Flaming with passion, you can set your heart to the long, steady road of investing significant time to disciple each of your family members.

The next chapter will show you how to train your child to personally see, hear, and communicate with Jesus. This will empower him to be more and more a disciple of Jesus. This is the major step in transitioning your child from your leadership to Jesus' leadership in his life. The parent who inspires and empowers his child to effectively communicate and unite with Jesus has done the most important thing imaginable a parent can do. Enjoy.

CHAPTER NINE

# Coached by Jesus in Person

"Lord, teach us to pray ..." *Luke 11:1*

"Could you men not keep watch with Me for one hour?" *Matthew 26:40*

At age nine, our daughter Dana was diagnosed with Polyarteritis nodosa, a disease of the arteries that causes severe pain, fever, and fatigue. She had learned how to have meaningful, personal meetings with Jesus through family meetings with Jesus and personal training times. In her young lifestyle, Dana had already established consistent times to meet with Jesus. She knew how to ask questions of Jesus about her day, listen to Jesus speak to her through the Bible, and prepare through prayer for the upcoming day. She had learned to write to Jesus her thoughts, feelings, motives, and commitments. Read what Dana wrote to Jesus about her sickness:

> Dear Lord,
>
> Thank You, Lord, that I am alive and working for You. Thank You that the doctors found out what I had and Lord, whatever this thing may bring, by the power of Your love, I'm going to live through it. And even if it doesn't go away for my entire life, I get a new body in heaven. It doesn't matter at all what my body has, or doesn't have, for what matters is my heart, Lord, and my relationship with You. And if that's all that counts, I'm going to go a long way more, Lord.
>
> I love You,
>
> Dana

It's incredible for a nine-year-old to be communicating this way with Jesus regarding such a traumatic life issue. She is now a wife, mother, teacher, and speaker at the International House of Prayer, and author of a book on prayer, titled *Deep Unto Deep*. It all started very early.

Would you be thrilled to observe your child consistently sitting at a desk with Bible open, writing love letters back to Jesus in response to His personal love letter, His Word?

The goal of this chapter is for your child to be coached personally by Jesus. To reach this goal, this chapter will give a step-by-step process to train your child to literally meet with Jesus. You will learn ...

+how to lead your family, individually and as a group, to be coached by Jesus,

+how through genuine prayer—relating and responding to God—your child can meet personally with Jesus, resulting in his being coached and discipled by Him.

---

### *The key to passionate, purely devoted hearts for Jesus is to behold Jesus.*

---

This chapter will provide something else for you and your family. Do you remember the key to passion for Jesus? For pure devotion to Him? (See Chapter 8.) The key to passionate, purely devoted hearts for Jesus is to behold Jesus—Who is like His Father. Through meeting with and beholding Jesus, our hearts are continually renewed and transformed (Romans 12:1-2; 2 Corinthians 3:18).

## Can we really be coached by Jesus?

Many people do not realize that they can personally meet with and hear Jesus—literally. The Bible, the inspired Word of God, allows us to read and know the actual words of Jesus, including His passions, His purposes, and His plans. We can know His thoughts and desires as clearly as any soldier is aware of his wife's thoughts and desires as he reads her loving letters from home.

Not only do we have the Bible, a "love letter" from Jesus, but as believers we are indwelled by the Holy Spirit. Jesus said it was better for His disciples that He leave them than that He stay (John 16:7). Why? The Holy Spirit would not come to dwell in them unless Jesus was no longer *with* them. Jesus said that His indwelling presence by the Holy Spirit is better for His disciples than seeing and hearing Him in the flesh. His being in us is actually better than His being with us! If we are willing to slow down, look, and listen, we can experience Jesus now like the disciples did then, only better. The Spirit of Jesus actually speaks into our minds and empowers us to know the very thoughts of Jesus (John 14:26; 15:26; 16:13, 1 Corinthians 2:10-12).

---

*He will plant His perfect, heart-healing, heart-transforming Word into a heart.*

---

Therefore, if anyone is willing, he can be with Jesus. Jesus will help dig weed seeds out of the heart. We can have our wrong thinking exposed and replaced by the very thoughts of Jesus. He will plant His perfect, heart-healing, heart-transforming Word into a heart. Our hearts can thus be more like His heart, and our lives become more like His. The result: to the degree that we become like Jesus, there exists abundant life for us and blessing to those who live with us.

Jesus has called us to be with Him (Matthew 11:28). The ball is in our court. We can purposely be with Him to be discipled by Him any time we are willing to get alone with Him, take out our Bible, and dialogue with Him. As we behold Him, we will become more and more like Him (2 Corinthians 3:18). As we then follow Him, He will make us capable of leading our children to Him (Matthew 4:19).

147

## Training your child to be coached by Jesus

If Jesus were a parent, He would train His child to communicate with His Father—that is, to pray. Jesus' disciples actually asked Him to teach them to pray (Luke 11:1). It was His example of praying that motivated the request. Jesus' consistent example and even His expectation and directive (Matthew 6:5, 9) were to pray. He told Martha that Mary had chosen to do something better than serving Him. She had chosen to sit at His feet, communing with Him (Luke 10:42).

---

*This process can be so meaningful that Jesus replaces you as your child's primary Coach.*

---

A primary goal in discipling your child is to train him to pray. By "pray," I mean genuine communication with Jesus. It can and should result in agreement with Him. It is communion intended to result in union. This process can be so meaningful that Jesus replaces you as your child's primary Coach—the primary Influencer, Mentor, Discipler in your child's life. When you accomplish this, you have fulfilled one of the highest callings as a parent—probably the highest.

To train your child to meet with Jesus, the pattern is as follows:

- Explain what you are going to do.
- Demonstrate slowly, explaining why you are doing what you are doing.
- Ask your child if he understands or if he has any questions.
- When he says he understands, ask him to explain the concept to you. Celebrate everything possible.
- Ask him to try to do it, assuring him that any attempt is good. Celebrate whatever he attempts. The heart issue is that he

tried. If he really is not ready to try, relax and give it time.

Take turns going back and forth. You show him how, and then he tries it. You give him feedback. Then do it all again.

+When he can do it, he is partly trained. When he can explain why he is doing it, not only will he be better motivated to have these times with Jesus, but he will also be equipped to lead others. Followers know what; they are able to do. Leaders know why. They are able and more likely to do. They are far more able to motivate, train, and help others to do.

You can use the seven basic training steps listed above to teach and train your children in these three major concepts in meeting with Jesus:

+Worship

+Word

+Work

## How to meet with and be coached by Jesus personally

When our children were three, we began slowly going through each of the concepts described below—worship, Word, work. (At that time we called them accountability, discovery, and ministry.) Over and over, we trained them by explaining, demonstrating, discussing, and practicing. We gave them pennies for any contribution they made—the better the contribution, the more the pennies. We rewarded them when they met with Jesus on their own. Before they could read or write they experienced meaningful, personal communication with Jesus.

Obviously, we are meeting with God—Father, Son, and Holy Spirit. For ease of communication, I will talk about meeting with Jesus. In our time with Jesus, we seek answers to the following questions:

+Lord Jesus, what do I know about You? What have You done? (Worship)

+Lord Jesus, what are You saying to me through Scripture? What do You want me to do in response to Scripture? (Word)

+Lord Jesus, what do You want to do today? Through me? (Work)

The key to productive prayer is keeping the focus on Jesus' real *pres-*

*ence.* Keeping aware of Jesus' real, personal presence is the unique focus of what follows: Imagine you are meeting with your son. You can explain that Jesus, by His Spirit, is present. You talk to Jesus about His promised presence—including boldly giving thanks that Jesus, by His Spirit, is with you to communicate (Isaiah 40:31). Then speak to your son about Jesus' presence. Talk with him about the Holy Spirit who is present to speak, guide, and empower through bringing His thoughts to our mind. Ask if he understands. If not, ask what he does not understand. Remember not to tell your son anything that you can ask and help your son to discover for himself. When he understands, ask if he would like to talk to Jesus about the presence of the Holy Spirit. If he says no, it's okay. Don't press or push; be gentle and sensitive. If he says yes, then practice together thanking Jesus for the unspeakable privilege of actually being with Him. If he takes a stab at it, celebrate and give him any constructive, helpful feedback.

Next, explain and practice together each of the following steps: (If it helps, you may want to read with your child the things I have written below as the beginning way of explaining each concept.)

—⁓—

*Imagine yourself speaking
directly to Jesus. You are!*

—⁓—

### Worship

In this section we answer the questions: "Lord Jesus, what do I know about You? What have You done?"

**1. Meditate** Think about Jesus—or the Father, or the Spirit (Hebrews 12:2). Think about one or two of the most important things you know about Him. In your mind, picture Him, maybe in a scene from the gospels. Think about one of His names, like Lamb of God, or one of His activities, like walking on water. Or think about memories of Him and experiences you have had with Him. Read slowly and think about verses of Scripture about Him. Think carefully about the words of songs about Him, or listen to songs about Him. The beginning point is simply to fix your mind on Jesus. You are seeking to answer the question: "Lord Jesus, what do I know about You?"

**2. Praise** Imagine yourself speaking directly to Jesus. You are! Picturing Him, tell Him some of your thoughts about Him as you meditated on Him. Or you can write them to Him in a journal. This is praise. Praise is natural. If someone prepares a good meal, it is natural to say, "That was great." If you had seen the sunset I saw recently, you would have easily joined me in proclaiming, "Wow! How beautiful!" When you think about who Jesus is, or what He did or is doing, it is natural to tell Him of His wonder, His greatness, His goodness. Praise is proclaiming to Jesus the greatness of His personality and activity. It is seeing and celebrating who He is and what He does. The key is to keep looking at, thinking about, and talking to this real, living, present Person.

**3. Thanksgiving** Thank Jesus in all things, for all things (Colossians 1:16-17; 1 Thessalonians 5:18; Ephesians 5:20; Romans 1:18-32). Ask the question, "Jesus, what have You done?" Every genuinely good thing in our life is made possible by Jesus. Thank Him as profoundly as if you saw Him with your own eyes personally just hand it to you, gift wrapped from Him. He did—plus or minus the gift wrap. You can go beyond thanking Him to praising Him for being the kind of Person who would do this kind of good thing.

**4. Worship** Having meditated on some of the wonders of what you know about Jesus, it will be natural to go beyond praise and thanksgiving. It will be natural to express your faith, your love, and your commitments to Him. Declare to Jesus your intention to trust, love, and obey Him. It will be worship in spirit (the re-born you in agreement with the Holy Spirit) and truth (the revelation of Jesus through the Word and Spirit) that you express to Jesus what you truly want to do with and for Him. Formal worship is initiated by entering God's presence and beholding God. It is made real when, having been aware of God, we respond to Him.

Do you like to sing to Jesus? Do so, but be sure to be aware of Jesus as you sing to Him. Do you like to write letters? Write your praise, thanks, faith, love, intent to serve, etc., to Jesus.

When you are comfortable in focusing on Jesus, you will profit from following the same patterns in focusing on God the Father and God the Spirit. You may want to focus on one Person per meeting.

Genuine and perpetual thanksgiving is so important that it must be further explained in greater detail here. Jesus, our Sovereign King, has all power and all authority. Everything happening on planet earth is either caused or allowed by Him. He loves perfectly, has all wisdom, knows and accomplishes what is the best in the big picture, and has all power and perfect liberty to start or stop, to intervene or withdraw, from every circumstance. This includes your circumstances.

Jesus, in perfect love and infinite wisdom, consciously allows all that happens to us. Occasionally, love and wisdom require that He directly intervene, overrule human freedom, and cause things to happen. Normally, He rules by His Spirit's speaking into the heart of whoever will listen and respond. Either way, as directed by Paul in scripture, we can with integrity and faith give thanks, not only in all things, but for all things. By doing this, we can look behind what we call natural, and begin to better see the supernatural hand of God in our lives.

Paul says the only thing that counts is faith expressing itself in love (Galatians 5:6). If we will consistently and thoughtfully give God thanks for the hard things, we will be empowered to grow in faith in God and love for people like we grow in few other ways. Here is how and why: Select an important situation that is on your mind since your last meeting with Jesus. It may seem good, bad, or both, or neither. Sincerely thank King Jesus for either allowing or causing this situation to happen.

Suppose that what happened seems good. Every good and perfect gift is from God (James 1:17). In your heart, recognize and receive this situation for what it is: a gift from your loving Lord. Receive it from Him. Thank Him from your heart. Go slowly. Feel the love in His heart for you by giving you this good gift. It is the reigning King of the universe telling you about His heart for you by giving you this good gift. See the gift and the Giver. Meditating on His gifts allows us to experience His love and often sets our heart ablaze with love for our loving Lord.

Warning! Jesus constantly gives us good gifts and there are terrible consequences for failing to honor Him and give thanks for our good gifts (Romans 1:18-32). If we fail to recognize them as from Him, or fail to thank Him, or fail to see His heart of love as the reason for the gift, then we shut off His primary way of showing us His loving heart for us. When we shut off His love messages, we don't feel His love. When we don't feel His love, our hearts are not touched as they could and need to be to keep us bonded to Him. By looking at events in our lives and seeing the good in them, we recognize the fingerprint of Jesus in our experience. We are seeing Him at work.

---

*By looking at events in our lives and seeing the good in them, we recognize the fingerprint of Jesus in our experience.*

---

Consider another scenario. Suppose that your mind goes to a situation that seems bad. Jesus, through Paul, tells us to give thanks in this situation (1 Thessalonians 5:18). We can with full credibility and sincerity say, "Thank You, Lord. You could have stopped this, but You did not. You have promised to not allow more to come than I can bear (1 Corinthians 10:13). What is going on?"

Here is a small part of what is going on: Jesus wants to develop faith in you. Faith is one of the great qualities to be developed in this life (Galatians 5:6). Jesus wants to find faith when He returns (Luke 18:8). I do not learn much faith in Jesus for finances when I have a steady income that covers my expenses.

When something "bad" happens to my finances, I can view it as, among many other factors, my loving Lord knowing it is time for me to develop greater faith in Him to provide for me. I dare to rejoice in the promised provision of Jesus while I diligently do what I can to establish sufficient finances. I give thanks that Jesus is preparing provision, and that He is using this trial to strengthen my faith in Him which is more precious than gold. 1 Peter 1:7

If you are good to me, it is easy for me to love you. It takes minimal supernatural activity in my heart (Matthew 5:46-47). But when you are bad to me, my heart to love is being tested. Suppose you are breaking your promises to me, or you are hurting me with words or actions. When I think of you hurting me, I can sincerely thank Jesus for allowing it. He can see that I need to develop in love and forgiveness. By giving thanks in and for this situation, I *assume* Jesus' activity in my life in what He allows. He knew that through relating to Him I could handle your not loving me. He also knew that I could grow in love through this, and/or I could reveal His special love for you by forgiving and returning good for what felt like evil to me.

Warning! If we fail to expose the hurts, disappointments, fears, etc., of our hearts to Jesus for healing and restoration, our hearts get increasingly diseased with godless thoughts, emotions, desires, and motives. Then just when we can least afford it, our hearts are exposed, and long term damage is done to someone who is precious in our lives and precious to Jesus. This is why we must pastor our own hearts and equip our children to pastor their hearts.

As you train your child to meet with Jesus, take a few moments to look back at the most significant events in your life since your last meeting. Look at them from Jesus' perspective, giving thanks, and responding accordingly.

### Word

"Faith comes by hearing the message, and the message is heard through the Word of Christ." *Romans 10:17*

"Sanctify them by the truth. Your Word is truth." *John 17:17*

"Your Word is a lamp to my feet and a light for my path." *Psalm 119:105*

In this section, we answer two questions: "Jesus, what are you saying to me through Your Word? Jesus, what do You want me to do in response to Your Word?"

How often have you heard or thought, "If only I could hear God." Not only can you hear God, but you do. Jesus said, "My sheep listen to My voice..." (John 10:16, 27). Christians hear God, but they often fail to recognize His voice. They do not realize God is speaking to them. The key is paying attention to, recognizing, and responding to His voice.

When I open my Bible, I am opening God's love letter sent from His heart of love to me. It tells me about my Creator. He knows why I exist, my destiny, and how I am to live in order to have real life. I can hold the actual letter, a message from Jesus, in my hand. This letter is as personal, meaningful, and real as the letter that came in the mail yesterday from my doctor. In addition, the real presence of Jesus is with me and in me by His Holy Spirit (1 Corinthians 2:10-16). He empowers me to hear and recognize the words of Jesus in my heart. I have the most unimaginable opportunity: I can listen to Jesus talk with me by His Spirit through His Word.

---

## *I can listen to Jesus talk with me by His Spirit through His Word.*

---

The following relational, devotional Bible study—a method of listening to Jesus—has been helpful to many people. Select a book of the Bible to study during your appointments with Jesus. (At the start of your study, you may want to get an overview of the paragraph, chapter or book by reading it through or reading a summary in a study Bible or Bible handbook.) After reading the paragraph being studied, start your relational, devotional study as follows:

**1. Analyze the paragraph.** Read the paragraph very, very slowly—analytically. Think about each word, even the small, obvious ones, until you become accustomed to analyzing very carefully. Are there any words or ideas you do not understand? Look up unfamiliar words in a dictionary or Bible dictionary. Have a study Bible or commentary close by in case you need help with understanding what you are studying. If the paragraph is too complex, make note of your confusion and consider talking to a person who might help you at an appropriate time. For now, go with your best understanding, or go to the next paragraph. Normally, it is not best to let an academic question steal too much of your precious time with Jesus. Let's assume you understand the paragraph fairly well. Move to this next step.

**2. Categorize the paragraph.** It is very helpful in preparing to respond to Jesus' Word to go back through the paragraph, watching for several possible "categories" that may exist in the paragraph. Is there …

> ⁺a truth to believe? Put a *T* beside the verse.

> ⁺a promise to claim? Put a *Po* beside the verse.

> ⁺a prayer to pray? Put a *Pr* beside the verse.

> ⁺a command to obey? Put a *C* beside the verse.

> ⁺an example to follow? Put *Ex* beside the verse.

> ⁺an error to avoid? Put *Er* beside the verse.

> ⁺a warning to heed? Put a *W* beside the verse.

**3. Personalize the paragraph.** Simply take the exact understanding you have of the paragraph, and without changing the meaning, meditate on and picture Jesus saying the words directly to you. I like to picture Jesus writing the exact words and meaning of the scripture being studied. I record His words.

Assume I am studying Philippians 4:6: "Do not be anxious about anything, but in everything, by prayer and petition, with thanksgiving, present your requests to God." Having gone through this passage to be sure all the words and ideas are understood, I would look for any categories. I find the verse to be a command for me to obey. Because the Spirit of Jesus inspired these words, I am going to picture Jesus personally writing the very words of Philippians 4:6 to me. I record them as follows:

*Hal, be aware of your thoughts. Do not allow yourself to be uptight or to worry about anything at all. You sometimes do that regarding how you think the service went on Sunday; how the finances are going; how the small groups and disciple-making are progressing. Do not let it happen. Instead, I want you to bring your anxious thoughts to Me. Figure out if I am uptight about it. You will always know the answer. Ask Me to work in each area. Believe that I am listening and will in fact respond to you. Then give Me great thanks for what you are believing Me to do.*

This method of Bible study is like sitting at Jesus' feet—listening to, hearing, and recognizing the voice of God in the context of loving relationship. I have watched hundreds of people weep with amazement and joy as they listened to Jesus talk personally to them.

---

## *When Jesus talks to me, it is for a purpose. He intends for me to respond.*

---

What follows is a most important completion of this third step. If someone important to you sends you an e-mail, you respond. When Jesus talks to me, it is for a purpose. He intends for me to respond. In journaling, we say that Jesus wrote a letter to us so we will write back to Him. It is very helpful to write in a journal your paraphrase of the verse or paragraph being studied. The following is an example of a response to Him:

*Lord Jesus, I never want to let the problems govern my thinking. I know You want me to look at them, but to do it with You. Am I making any progress? (Pause and be still.) It seems that generally more and more I am thinking with You about challenges. Thank You for helping me to do this. Thank You for again reminding me that I must be confident in You to be at work in accomplishing through me what You have called me to do. I ask You*

*to strengthen my ability to be confident in You to do what I cannot
do. Thank You, in advance, for the victory that is ours. I believe
this all is according to Your will and in Your name. Amen.*

Since I am praying according to God's will when I pray the scripture, I
can pray not only for myself, but also for others, and it will be effective prayer.
For example, if Jesus tells me to forgive, I can pray that I will have spiritual
power to forgive, and that my child will have power to forgive, and that my
friend will have power to forgive. When we pray the Word like this, our prayers
will be according to God's will and will make an eternal difference, not only for
ourselves, but for our family, faith family, and friends.

Our children were raised doing this. They were shaped and discipled by
Jesus as they looked and listened to Him.

We can be with Jesus anytime we are willing to put other things aside
long enough to focus directly on Him. In our time with Him, He can unpack
and heal our hearts, and pour in His truth. As we look at Him and listen to
Him, He is influencing and discipling us just like He did Peter, James, and
John (John 14:16-21, 23-26; 15:26; 16:7-150).

### Work

In this section, we are asking Jesus two questions: Lord Jesus, what do
You want to do today? Through me?

My appointment with Jesus is more than worship and devotional Bible
study. It is to proactively prepare me to work with Jesus. It is to unite with Him
in doing His will and work in His world. His world for me includes my life, my
family's life, and the lives of those I work and live with in my church and community, and for the world mission areas He has called me to focus on.

Jesus seldom forces or coerces His will. However, He will increase His
work/activity as we with faith increase in our asking according to His will (1
John 5:14-15; Matthew 21:22).

The first work we are invited to is intercessory prayer. Effective intercessory prayer includes knowing, agreeing with, and believing Jesus, the One

who ever lives to make intercession (Hebrews 7:25). We work to a position of faith in Him for His Kingdom to come and His will to be done on earth as it is in heaven.

## "Lord, what do You want to do today?"

We start by seeking an answer to the question "Lord Jesus, what do You want to do today?" If I know of or sense something that I believe would be God's will in my life, I boldly and expectantly ask for His will to be done. I want to make sure I get to the point of faith so that I can ask with thanksgiving (Philippians 4:6). I try to focus with Jesus on the needs of my heart and the activities of the day or upcoming days.

Next, I apply the same question to my wife: "Lord, what is Your will for Debbi?" I meditate on Debbi's heart and life, waiting to see if I sense the Holy Spirit prompting me to pray anything for her. I try to repeat this process for my "standing prayer list"—the rest of my family, my small group in my church family, my pre-Christian friends I am praying for, etc.

## "Lord, what do You want to do through me?"

After discerning and believing for God's will, next I seek to find what God wants to do through me. I ask this question: "Lord, what do You want to do through me?" You may have heard the phrase "putting feet to our prayers." This is what I'm preparing to do according to God's guidance. This is preparation for obedience.

Staying alert to the presence and activity of the Holy Spirit, I meditate on the specific areas about which I have already been praying. I ask the Holy Spirit to help me recognize if there is something in God's will I am to do. If I sense something that seems right to do, I ask for God's power and commit to obey. If I sense no guidance or am uncertain, I try to make a wise decision, trusting God to guide me. This is not hard or mystical. It merely recognizes and honors the presence of the Holy Spirit, and makes a way for Him to whisper something to me if He desires.

During this process, it is good to simply think ahead about the main parts of your day and meditate on what you sense Jesus wants to do through you in each part. This becomes your marching orders or ministry description for the day.

I prefer to put the intercession and obedience questions, like: "What do You want to do?" and "What do You want to do through me?" together with each person or situation that Jesus and I are talking about. Look at the process in the following example. In this example, I am praying before meeting with friends.

*"Lord Jesus, do You have a specific will for this time with Joe and Sue tonight?"* I wait and think about Joe and Sue. If I don't sense anything specific, I go on.

*"Lord, I ask You to do Your will tonight in our time together. Is there anything You want to do through me?"* I wait a few moments. While waiting and anticipating being with Joe and Sue, I simply realize that they need to be encouraged and strengthened in the Lord.

*"Lord, I believe that You at least want me to help them remember what they mean to You, and that You are doing a good thing in them. I will plan on bringing this to their attention. I ask You to do anything in me while we are together that You want to do through me. Thank You. I am Your friend and servant."*

This briefly describes a process during your meeting with Jesus for intercession and obedience. It releases God's power and prepares you to "follow Jesus" in the coming day. It allows Jesus to coach you regarding living life with and for Him.

If you like praying the Lord's Prayer, but also like some of the components listed in this model, you can integrate anything from this model into the Lord's Prayer (Matthew 6:9-13).

### Journaling

It helps many to write or journal what Jesus says to them, and to then write their response to Jesus. Simply write your answers to the questions:

♦Lord Jesus, what do I know about You? Your names? Your nature? Your character? What good have You done?

♦Lord Jesus, what are You saying to me through Your Word?
What do You want me to do in response to Your Word?

♦Lord Jesus, what do You want me to pray for You to do today?
Lord Jesus, what do You want to do through me today?

If you journal your meeting with Jesus, you can also show your child exactly how you do it.

## Family prayer: A group meeting with Jesus

If you are meeting with Jesus with each of your children individually, it is a fairly easy step to gather your family together for a group meeting with Jesus. What your children have learned from being with you will prepare them to help you lead your family in meeting with Jesus as a family. Since your children understand Worship, Word, and Work, they will be able to help greatly in the group meeting. Also, because you are connecting with each of your children individually, they will be much more inclined to pull with you as you ask your family to join you in a group meeting with Jesus.

Why is it so important that we establish a family meeting with Jesus?

♦To communicate and unite with Jesus as a family (Jeremiah 29:11-13)

♦To unite with each other in agreeing with and following Jesus (Romans 15:5)

♦To do what Christians are expected to do with each other, including ...

1. Encouraging each other, especially through praising and thanking God and affirming the good in each other's life (Hebrews 3:13)

2. Studying and responding to God's Word (Colossians 3:16)

3. Praying for, loving, and serving each other, especially by helping each other know and follow Jesus (James 5:16; 1 John 4:7-8; Galatians 5:13), which includes sharing in one another's growth in the Lord, and prayerfully having faith for one another. It also

includes being kind to, compassionate with, and for giving one another, speaking the truth in love to one an other, and carrying the others' burdens (Ephesians 4:15, 23; Galatians 6:2)

+ To train and equip each family member for their personal meetings with Jesus (Luke 11:1-4)

+ To equip family members to start and lead prayer groups with peers (2 Timothy 2:2)

+ To experience the peace and joy of the Lord in the fam ily unit (John 15:5; Colossians 3:15-17; Romans 15:13; James 5:16; John 8:31-32; 16:13)

+ To welcome and include friends of the family of all ages into family meetings (John 1:46)

Here are some valuable steps to take in leading your family in a meeting with Jesus:

+ Cover your meeting in prayer. You will be opposed by evil and you will need divine power.

—⁓—

## Create a happy, positive environment.

—⁓—

+ Create a happy, positive environment. Some ideas: meet after family dinner just before a favorite dessert; meet at a fun place that is away from the television and telephones; pass around cartoons to start; announce a special upcoming family event; ask everyone to share one good thing; assign a different verse to each reader; sing a familiar song, etc.

+ Explain and practice worship, word, and work as you have learned

+ Be sensitive. If you only have the group's attention for 15 minutes, and all you can cover is one part of the meeting, it's okay. The goal is not to get through a process, but to connect with Jesus. Take your time.

Focus on Jesus. Do another section the next meeting.

⋆Consider making family meeting optional (with serious rewards for attending) for anyone over 13 who was not raised meeting with Jesus as a family

Below are additional ideas and questions for leading your family through the **Worship** section for your family meeting.

⋆"Let's think about Jesus (or God the Father or the Holy Spirit). What do you know about Him? Who would take what has been said about Jesus and say it directly to Him? Let's all take 30 seconds and write to Jesus, telling Him what you think or feel about Him."

⋆"Let's look at our lives for some good things. Who has one?"

Answers may include food, health, positive experiences, family, Jesus, church, successes, forgiveness, etc.

⋆"Where do good things come from?" God is the Giver of every good gift (James 1:17).

⋆"Who will tell God what you think and feel about His good gift to you?"

Let family members respond. Draw out or give examples as necessary.

⋆"Why does God give these good gifts?" The answer is more than because He loves us. The answer must include that He wants us to recognize His heart of love so that we are touched by His heart for us. This results in our heart being touched by His heart. We can consistently experience God's love in our situations by observing the good and recognizing it to be from God. The group leader does not want to push for the "right" an swers, but needs to see if the family understands the intent of God's good gifts and being touched by His love. If not, he or she can help connect the dots. The process is to: (a) see God's work; (b) see God's heart; (c) feel God's love; (d) feel love for God; and (e) express love for God.

⋆"Can anyone tell our Lord your thoughts or feelings about Him based on His good gifts to you?" Again, don't press for answers. Watch and wait. If answers don't come, you'll have some questions to ask on personal meetings with your child to find out what is in the heart. If outward behavior is positive, celebrate. But be discerning to be sure it is from the heart. If outward behavior is not positive, don't react. Instead, take note and determine whether to investigate hearts regarding the issue in private or whether to deal with the issue immediately.

Now look at some ideas and questions for leading your family through the **Word** section of your group meeting.

- "The next verses we are studying in 1 Peter are Chapter 1, verses 17-21. Dave, will you read these verses?"

- "Are there any words or ideas you don't understand or don't make sense to you?"

If someone has a question, ask the rest of family if anyone has an answer before you give an answer. If they raise questions for which you have no answer, good. This is an opportunity to let your family know that all of us have questions, and to show them how you get answers. Go to a dictionary, Bible dictionary, or study Bible to see if you can find an answer that helps. If you are unable to find an answer, tell your family that you will check with someone you think can help and bring back an answer for the next meeting.

- "Dana, would you be willing to turn this into words from Jesus to you?" Of course, you know Dana can do this because you have heard her do it during your personal meeting with her.

- "Thanks, Dana. Would you be willing to talk to Jesus about what He has just said to you?"

———

*I beg you to teach your family to take anything God says to them through the Word and turn it into prayer for themselves, each other, and others.*

———

You will watch the Holy Spirit touch your family as various ones share their communication from Jesus to them and their response back to Him. It is wonderful. I beg you to teach your family to take anything God says to them through the Word and turn it into prayer for themselves, each other, and others. It is also good to guide your family to do this in writing, followed by inviting anyone who wants to read what he or she has written to do so.

Finally, look at some ideas and questions for leading your family through the **Work** section of your group meeting.

+"Let's pray for God to do His will in any concerns we have for others or ourselves. I'll start." It is good to learn to meditate on the good God may desire to do in anyone's life, especially eternal good. It is also good to simply ask with faith that He will work to do His will in very particular situations. Guide your family in working through to faith for God's will. Study 1 John 5:14 together if you need help. When we ask God to do His will, we are working with Him according to His law of prayer: He will influence circumstances on earth if someone here will sincerely ask for and expect Him to do His will.

+"Does anyone have any ideas about what the Lord may want to do through us to help in what we have prayed?" Wait a few moments. If no one responds, but you think of something that could be done, ask what your family thinks about what you are thinking. If the Holy Spirit is guiding anyone, this becomes the obedience of faith (1 John 3:22). The work is Jesus working through our faith and obedience. This is also good to do in writing as a group, and then ask anyone who desires to share what has been written.

Conclude all meetings by proclaiming God's goodness, grace, greatness, and victory. You may want to ask family members to pray sentence prayers for each other. You can take hands and make a circle before a final prayer. See small group leadership books for many additional ideas.

Here are some general suggestions that may help you during your family meeting:

+Don't tell if you can ask.

+ Answer questions by asking if someone in your family has an idea about the answer.
+ When a need arises during a meeting, ask the group what can be done. Ask the group what they sense the Lord wants to happen.
+ Rejoice when others rejoice and weep when they weep.
+ Ask "why" after the group has figured out "what."
+ Share your vision of following Jesus and helping others to follow Him. Gently and humbly invite your family to honestly follow Jesus with you in the details of life.
+ Encourage your family by sharing what you see and believe will be by God's power.
+ Encourage each family member to go to their day or week as a missionary in Christ's cause.

*Worship* and *Word* without *Work* makes us hearers, not doers. *Work* without *Worship* and *Word* makes for dead works. Keep connecting *Worship* and *Word* with *Work*.


## What is your first priority?

Debbi and I packed up and moved to Kansas City for seminary when I was 24. Debbi taught sixth grade in a public school while I worked as a youth pastor.

During this time, I came to an important decision. I made the commitment that I would not substitute academic study required by the seminary for time alone with Jesus. I determined that my first priority each day was to meet alone with Jesus.

Within a few weeks, this commitment was severely tested. I had a philosophy test at 8:00 on Monday morning. I had been on a trip all weekend with the youth group, and I hadn't prepared well for the test. I needed about two more hours of study if I hoped to scrape by on the test. I would need to get up by 5:00 on Monday morning. But in order to have my time with the Lord,

I would need to get up at 4 a.m. At midnight, as I set my alarm, I was tempted to skip my time with the Lord. "No," I decided, "I'll get up in time to have my normal time with Jesus." God graciously intervened and gave me a better grade on the philosophy test than I would have had if I'd studied 20 more hours.

My point is I was convicted and committed to make Jesus, and meeting with Him, the first and most important part of every day. I pray that it will be the same for you. Through your consistent time with Jesus, He will make you a far better disciple and He will work through you to be a far better discipler of your family. You will be empowered to fulfill your high call as a parent.

Harry was a brand new Christian. He began meeting with his teenage son and daughter on Monday nights to help them meet with Jesus. They liked it and asked if their friends could come. In no time, between 15 and 30 kids were consistently showing up in Harry's home for a Bible study. Sound exciting?

## Who is the most important Person in your life?

A study was done of the most influential Christian leaders of all time. The study concluded that there was a single common spiritual discipline in every one of these leaders. Each was known to spend a minimum of one hour per day in prayer, alone with Jesus, meeting with and being discipled by Him.

What is your first priority? What will you get done each day if you get nothing else done? I pray you will determine or re-determine to establish a consistent time and place to meet with Jesus that is more important to you than any doctor appointment, work responsibility, or any other pressure or desire in your life. Who is the most important Person in your life? Do you need time with Him more than any other need in your life? Does He deserve first priority of your time to meet with Him? Even one hour (Mark 14:37)?

# CHAPTER TEN

# Coaching as Jesus Coached

"Follow Me ...." *Matthew 4:19*

What Jesus said to His disciples, parents inevitably say to their children: "Follow me!" As a parent, you are in a position to do for the spiritual maturity in the heart and life of your children what professional ministries—as well intended and equipped as they are—can seldom do. What can Christian parents do that the best pastors, the best children's and youth ministries, and the best churches cannot do for their children? The answer: live life 24/7 with their children, thus making disciples—of someone. In the process of living together, all parents inevitably—for better and for worse—do make disciples of their children. We need to realize the extent to which a child follows a parent.

Let me illustrate. What sophisticated skill do millions of Chinese preschool children possess that, with even years of university work, most Americans could not learn to do well? Can you guess it? The answer: speak Chinese!

From day one, a young Chinese child is immersed with words which, at first, are meaningless. But in the pervasive immersion and influence of Chinese being spoken, the child begins to associate events around him with symbols called words. By simply living in an environment where activities are associated with language that identifies, symbolizes, and communicates these activities, a child develops extremely complex language skills. Parents slowly enunciate words and then watch and listen to their children. In an American home, a bottle filled with white liquid is associated with a sound known as "milk." When a child points to his bottle and makes a sound something like "malk," though not perfect, it is so close that the parent goes ballistic with smiles and words of affirmation. The little guy thinks he just won an Olympic gold medal. For the next five years he calls it "malk" and no one can persuade him otherwise because he is sure he heard it from Mommy. When he said it, Mommy agreed and celebrated with him. He is unconsciously persuaded and knows he is right. As smart as his first grade teacher is in his eyes, when she tries to correct his pronunciation of "malk," he doesn't believe her. In his mind, the right word for the white liquid is "malk." And that's the way it is.

---

## *In the process of living together, all parents inevitably— for better and for worse—do make disciples of their children.*

---

Day by day, behavior and language are lived out in front of every child. Parents instinctively know how to train their children. Imagine a mother holding up a bottle filled with white liquid in front of her child. She then goes from the material reality (bottle, milk) to an abstract concept and sound. She slowly enunciates the word: M-I-L-K. The mother repeats the word over and over until she believes the child is ready for an exam. She holds up the bottle in front of the child's eyes and asks, "What is this?" or maybe just waits silently to see if the child will see the material reality, associate it with the sound, and mimic the sound. If the child doesn't understand yet, the mother is not derailed. She keeps working at it, naturally and persistently because it is *very, very important to her* that the child learns the language. When he says things incorrectly, she corrects him, in a good or bad way. But she does correct him because language development for her child is of utmost importance to her.

This mother probably coaches her child the same way her parents coached her. She probably does not realize she is coaching the way her parents coached her. She probably does not realize that the way she is coaching is good or bad. She simply learned—deeply, profoundly, permanently—from her parents, not only her language, but how to very permanently pass that language on to her child. The day he makes the sound "malk," she throws a party and reinforces his behavior. He is very seriously imprinted.

Our Chinese or English speaking mother is an effective coach. Her child is learning much more than a language from her. He is learning how to do life in every arena. He is learning behavior, reactions to circumstances, how to relate to others, how to make decisions. He is becoming like her, not just her language. This mother is unknowingly passing her values and conclusions on to her child. By watching her and listening to her, he receives into his open, teachable little heart her very heart—what she feels about the neighbors, how she values and spends money, acceptable ways of reacting to drivers who wrongly pull out in front of her in traffic. Every bit of input and feedback comes from her heart, good or bad.

The child drinks it all in, but not analytically or critically. Sometimes he interprets his mother accurately; sometimes inaccurately. But *he* is sure he is accurate. He absorbs what she is and does. He responds or reacts. Based on her heart—her thoughts, emotions, desires, motives—she responds or reacts to or ignores his response. And from her heart—her words, facial expressions, and tone—she coaches him further. She determines if and how to control certain behaviors based on what she is—her heart. She tolerates or ignores behaviors that are insignificant to her. The mother is consciously and unconsciously passing on to her child not only her language, but who and what she is—her heart. She is forming his heart. She is making him like her. He is becoming her little disciple.

A mother demonstrates the way to do life. Her child watches. She talks about life. He listens. She watches and supervises his life and words, and then gives him negative or positive feedback, depending on her heart: what she believes, feels, or wants—what she thinks about her husband, feels about being a mother, expects others to do. She coaches and shapes him from who she is: her concerns, desires, attitudes, etc. She sometimes controls his external behavior: "Go to your room"; "I'll spank you if you do that again"; "I'll give you a cookie after you put these dishes away."

Knowingly and unknowingly, the mother shapes her child's awareness or ignorance of God. She communicates and coaches what she cares about. To the extent that she cares about Jesus, she communicates something about Jesus. Every time the child sees or hears her, he is registering and interpreting (rightly or wrongly) an impression that influences his emotions and desires, which further influences his interpretations. All of this constantly solidifies and forms his trainable heart. If Jesus is included, he includes Jesus. If Jesus is ignored, he remains ignorant of Jesus.

Unconsciously, in a child's uncritical mind, everything he experiences is absolutely real and true. His conclusions are, to him, the way things truly are, yet he does not realize that he has come to dogmatic conclusions. He will live from these conclusions until they are confronted by life. Assume that his parents do not walk and talk with Jesus at the center of their lives. The child is also growing up in a culture with no absolutes to judge self or others by. It is a culture espousing pleasure at any cost. The culture is dominated by media and entertainment as major, often primary, influencers. This post modern culture in which he is growing up will only reinforce and support his unconscious assumptions: *God? Who is that?*

Conversely, if his mom and dad ...

+live from hearts radically dependent on and devoted to Jesus;

+talk naturally and consistently about Jesus;

+sensitively coach him about Jesus just as they did about their language, be it Chinese or English;

... then Jesus and His way of life will be seriously planted in the child's heart. He will be exposed to a world which replaces Jesus with selfishness, pride, peer approval, alcohol, drugs, pleasure, money, sex, success, etc. However, Jesus will have been in his experience so authentically lived out that when exposed to this new world, he will see and feel the contrast to his family experience. He will be in a position to not automatically nor easily buy into the world and its ways.

## Can the church adequately disciple your child?

Can anyone in the church be with your child day in and day out to coach him in the right direction? Who? Can anyone in the church watch and listen to the attitudes and motives of your child to see and graciously extract weed seeds and implant God's good seed? How?

Does it make sense that parents are absolutely crucial for making disciples of Jesus? The church and its ministries and institutions are dramatically important to your child. But it is not the church that children and youth see and hear in most real life situations. The best hope for seeing the acts of Jesus, and hearing the words of Jesus, and being coached to follow Jesus comes through parents in the home. Christ in you—living through you, the parent—is the best hope of glory for the young (Colossians 1:27). We must never discount the work of the Holy Spirit in every person's life, plus or minus any human influence. But God has directed parents to continuously and consistently live out faith, obedience, and communication with and about Him in front of their families (Deuteronomy 6:4-9; Ephesians 5:22-6:4; Matthew 28:19). If all that is necessary to assist children and youth to decide to follow Jesus is the convicting and convincing activity of the Holy Spirit, then every person could be expected to be Christian without help from family or church.

Parents are desperately dependent on an authentic disciple-making church. Children and youth are desperately dependent on an authentic disciple-making family—with serious support from a disciple-making church. The Word of God must become flesh in your family. It must be tangible, visible, and audible. The en-fleshment must occur in real life: dinner-eating, car-driving, vacation-taking settings. If not, Jesus is legitimately assumed to be the one-hour-per-week, in-church-only, Savior and Lord (Deuteronomy 6:7).

Do you want your son to speak excellent Chinese? As early as possible, put him in a family that speaks excellent Chinese. Speaking Chinese is difficult, but they will train him well. Do you want your daughter to get a good start in becoming a follower of Jesus? As early as possible, put her in a Christ-trusting, Christ-obeying, Christ-talking family. Debbi recently asked a nine-year-old girl why she wanted to follow Jesus. Her answer: "Because my daddy does."

The Christian family, whether consciously or not, is saying: "Watch and listen to us. We'll watch and listen to you. We will then give you feedback from our hearts—what we think and value—and in no time at all you will be living like us and talking our language."

The most serious Christian parents, living and speaking as followers of Jesus, have an important concern. We do not want our children to only mimic us, in that they learn the language and the behavior, but they fail to know, value, trust, and obey Jesus from their hearts. Every Christian parent runs the small but real risk of a child merely mimicking. Love and joy and peace and humility are attractive. Parents must persistently explain that the best thing in their lives is their relationship with Jesus. This will emphatically help their child to know, trust, and love the Lord Jesus Christ—not just mimic external behavior. Without the behavior and language of Jesus being seen and heard through the family, one or two hours per week with even a strong church are a terribly weak Christ-formation process.

---

### God does not intend the church to do for the family what only the family can do for the family.

---

Please consider this difficult point: God does not intend the church to do for the family what only the family can do for the family. I acknowledge the difficulty for the church to equip parents to be and make disciples of their families. I bless the church for stepping in to provide ministries for children and youth because parents were not adequately prepared to do it. Sending your child to Sunday school or your teen to youth group is usually a help. It is also almost always terribly insufficient to make him an authentic disciple of Jesus. We dare not ignore what Jesus did and told us to do: make disciples. Somehow we must obey Jesus in teaching our child (disciple) *to obey* everything Jesus taught (Matthew 28:18-20). Where and how? The family is where life is formed.

I hear reports of thousands coming to Jesus every day in parts of the world other than mine, and I rejoice. In North America, we are living in an increasingly darkened, fallen culture. Will the Holy Spirit, through the activities of the church, save and capture the hearts of your family? I pray so. However, I know statistics that cause me to warn you of the urgency to consciously disciple your family God's way. We biblically support and dramatically benefit from the church. I would be lost without it. But we dare not depend *primarily* on the church for the Christianizing of our precious child or teen.

Most Christian parents have sincere concern for their family's spiritual well being. They are not spiritually "dead beat" parents. Some have, in fact, fought very hard for their children's spiritual well-being. But instead of drawing their children to Jesus, many have alienated their children from themselves and Jesus. The most common reason: they focused on external behavior instead of heart. This is the very opposite of disciple-making principles and strategies. *Their method was to control behavior rather than know and influence the heart.*

---

### *We dare not depend primarily on the church for the Christianizing of our precious child or teen.*

---

I remember vividly a twenty-six-year-old pouring out his story to me, with tears. He was now an unmarried father, a graduate of "Drug University," financially challenged, and in a world of hurt. His story included the following:

- "I was required to behave according to my family's religious expectations without explanations."
- "When I asked questions about hard things that happened to me, I was told to 'get over it.'"
- "When I tried to get answers to my questions about God and the church, I was accused of being rebellious."

His parents failed to discover and solve the tension creating confusion in his heart. They expected him to behave in a fashion different than his true heart position—that which he actually believed and would choose if he had a choice. He was coerced into behaving in ways which he truly did not believe in. This resulted in serious inner turmoil and external disaster.

Without question, behavior must be governed in the very early years (see Chapters 1-3). Gradually and intentionally, effective dialogue—resulting in understanding and agreement—will eliminate the pressure to behave in ways other than that with which the heart believes (Chapters 5-7).

I feel only respect and compassion for these caring parents, for they were and are giving it their best effort, often based on how they themselves were parented (discipled). The fear that their children would become rebels, live a godless life now, and end up lost forever has driven many parents to only control behavior, which drove many children to the very thing the parents feared. There is a better way: make disciples the way Jesus made disciples.

—◇◇◇—

*Do not be disheartened. Children—even young adults— are still responsive and can unlearn and relearn through a gracious, honest, humble, gentle, patient parent.*

—◇◇◇—

Would you join me in the prayer to get the message out that well-intentioned parents do not have to be bound by the fear of losing their children to the world? You may be a parent reading this now, and you recognize that you passed on some "bad Chinese" to your child. Do not be disheartened. Children—even young adults—are still responsive and can unlearn and relearn through a gracious, honest, humble, gentle, patient parent. Note that these are the characteristics of Jesus. Weed seeds can be removed; good seeds can be planted. Much of this book is devoted to helping you do this very thing. Start now by honestly searching your own heart before God, including significant prayer for yourself and your child.

The unconscious ways a Chinese mother uses to train her child to speak Chinese have much in common with the conscious strategies Jesus used to disciple His men to change the world. These strategies are so natural that we fail to see them as strategies. Families are powerful influences. This is exactly why Jesus strategically adopted a "family" of 12 disciples to be with Him.

## How did Jesus make disciples?

*Jesus' first strategy: My disciples will watch My life*
"Jesus called to Him those He wanted ... that they might be with Him." *Mark 3:13-14*
"Jesus went out as usual to the Mount of Olives, and His disciples followed Him." *Luke 22:39*
"Come ... and you will see." *John 1:39*

Jesus chose to live with a family—His disciples. His strategy was to let them be with Him and watch Him. He was saying, "Come to Me. Follow Me. Watch Me." The thoughts, emotions, desires, and purposes of His great heart were visible. His way of living could be seen and absorbed into their minds and influence their values. A picture is worth more than a thousand words.

Jesus' disciples watched His daily routine—His decision-making process, His reactions away from the spotlight of ministry, His way of responding to criticism and conflict, His reactions to storms, His response to too little food or demands on His time. Through watching Him, they saw in detail how God empowers Spirit-led people to live, and they were permanently imprinted. By uniting with Jesus' "family," they watched Him and were powerfully influenced to be like Him.

God desires to help you effectively employ the strategy of Jesus. Think about the possibilities as your family watches your life.

**Your children can watch you ...**

#### ⁺work on your relationship with Jesus

Let them see your commitment to meet with and be coached by Jesus. They will come to see that you value your relationship with Jesus more than anything. You can make time with Jesus the most important activity or meeting of your day. Your family will then see that you work hard to keep this meeting, getting whatever help you need. They will not forget this. (Chapter 9 is to help you and your family with this.)

#### ⁺respond to life because of your relationship with Jesus

As issues come up around the table, at the computer, or in the car, your family could see that you are not seeking your way or your will, but what Jesus wants. They will be watching when conflicts come up, and they could see you as a peacemaker, or as one who forgives and loves even those who act like enemies. They will not forget. They can watch you demonstrate growth in the character of Christ, and will assume that this is the way Christians live. They will be right, and in most cases will buy in.

Your family can learn ways that Jesus did *not* live, not primarily from your verbal prohibitions, but from your lifestyle, which becomes a powerful example. When they see unChristlikeness in you, you could humbly tell them that what you did was not how Jesus lived or calls you to live. They could see how you hate coming short of God's will. They could see how you humbly face your errors and seek to make it right. If you do, they will respect you for being authentic, and decide again that they will follow Jesus. He calls them to Himself and His narrow way, and will be gracious and helpful when they wander from the truth or fall down on the journey. As you persist in following Jesus, they could increasingly see your gentleness, humility, dependability, goodness, love, service, return of good for evil, peace, self-discipline, patience, kindness, joy, etc. They will like what they see. They will respect, even like, the one they see growing in Christlikeness. They will like the One they are coming to realize makes it happen. They can watch you give yourself first to Jesus and then, in obedience to Him, give yourself to them on purpose and with purpose (2 Corinthians 8:5). (Understanding and practicing the preceding chapters of this book will help your family see Jesus in you.)

### ✦love, serve, and lead your family

I pray you will establish one-on-one appointments (Chapter 7), family devotional meetings (Chapter 9), and a whole array of family experiences (Chapter 11). If done well, this will forever positively impact each family member. When you talk about humility or gentleness or zeal, or when they hear of it at church or read it in the Bible, they will recognize and embrace it passionately for they have seen it in your life.

### ✦love, serve, and be loyal to your church family

I pray that your family will see in you faithfulness to your church family. They can learn by watching you give Sundays to working on your relationship with God, your family's relationship with God, and supporting and serving the church that Jesus loves and died for. They can watch you not give in to temporal desires that would compromise your Sabbath. They can watch you give time and money to God's work, and they will assume this is the way Christians live. They can watch you love and minister to other Christians: in your home, in groups, and spontaneously, all the while going about doing good like Jesus did (Acts 10:38).

### ✦love and serve non-followers of Jesus

They can watch how you perceive your neighbors and why you go to work. I pray that your family comes to realize that you understand Jesus has called you to go to work (or the mall), not just to work (or shop), but primarily to be good and do "good" so that you might influence others to consider Jesus (Acts 10:38; 1 Corinthians 9:19). They can watch your diligence and perseverance when things are hard or boring (James1:2-3). They can watch you incorporate non-Christian friends into meals, games, and parties, and understand that you have Jesus' purpose in all you do (Luke 19:5).

Your growing Christlikeness is one of the greatest weapons against Satan's purposes to steal, kill, and destroy your family. They will see your good deeds and praise your Father in heaven (Matthew 5:16). Dads, you can help restore the word "father" to an honored word. Moms and dads, through the character of Christ, you can restore the word "family" to our heavenly Father's high intent.

---

*Your growing Christlikeness is one of the greatest weapons against Satan's purposes to steal, kill, and destroy your family.*

---

Our children watch us. I am fascinated to hear our four adult children recount in detail what they experienced and absorbed from Debbi and me when we had no idea they were watching. Children absorb our daily routine. They often, unconsciously, mimic our words and tone perfectly which they experience in early childhood. If we have Kingdom priorities, it can be a powerful tool. They unconsciously watch what we decide to do. If they sense that we are seeking God's will, it will imprint deeply in the core of their heart. The power of our positive reactions to negative circumstances will influence them forever (Romans 12:21).

*Jesus' second strategy: My disciples will know My heart through My Words*
"But when He was alone with His own disciples, He explained everything." *Mark 4:34*

"Lord, are You telling this parable to us, or to everyone?" *Luke 12:41*

"After He was raised from the dead, his disciples recalled what He had said."
*John 2:22*

Jesus' family of disciples observed and absorbed His lifestyle. After the day of activity, they could sit around the campfire and talk about what happened and why. In these settings, Jesus could share His heart. The disciples could ask Jesus questions that would not have been asked apart from personal time with Jesus. With this deep, on-going relationship they could know what otherwise they could have only guessed. They could know Jesus' heart because they lived as a family and lived life together—and talked about it. If they did not ask Jesus about His reasons and power for doing what He did, He could ask them what they thought about the day, about what He did, how He did it, and why. One way or another, by personal relationship, they could see more than His behavior. They could hear His heart. They could understand. Then they could freely embrace his heart values, rationale, and motives, or question Him further.

—◊◊◊—

## *The "what" without the "why" leads to rules without relationships.*

—◊◊◊—

**Your children must know your heart by hearing your words.** Let your family hear why you do what you do. Children see, but do not automatically understand, their parents' actions. Parents must open their hearts by verbalizing their motives and reasons. The "what" without the "why" leads to rules without relationship. As you grow in being a disciple of Jesus, your family will learn a new language: Christian. The words will not be weird or foreign; your conversations will simply include Christian content. Bring Jesus into conversations, not flippantly, as if trying to sneak Him in on the sly, but openly (Matthew 12:34-36; Luke 9:26). He is your King, whether anyone else around has bowed the knee or not. Neither are you cavalier by flaunting your Christ-talk all over them. As naturally as talking about ordinary things like going to bed, it is important to talk about going to Jesus (Deuteronomy 6:7).

Trust Jesus. Storms come, and things seem impossible, but you know and affirm that Jesus is "in your boat." Follow Him. He said and did nothing independent of His Father, and has called you to learn from Him, to follow Him. (See Chapter 4.)

Your language includes much heart-felt praise of God, which is not in-your-face or a mindless and habitual "praise the Lord." When you see the good, you have learned to recognize God as the Author. You sincerely affirm your gratefulness for His good gifts. Often, in this context, you will communicate your honoring of, confidence in, and love for Him. This will flow from your times with Jesus (Chapter 9), where you purposely practice looking for the good to give Him thanks.

Our language can include Jesus in decision making, conflict management, and casual dialogue. We have formal meetings with Jesus (worship services, small groups, family small groups, one-on-one meetings) where the agenda is to talk with and listen to Jesus. Without these formal meetings it is much more difficult to naturally talk about Jesus in informal settings. Conversely, the formal meetings (Chapters 7 and 9) create common language and values to naturally speak of and with Jesus. It is desperately important that we talk with and about Jesus in the routine of our lives.

You may want to tell your family some ways Jesus would not talk (Ephesians 4:29; 2 Timothy 2:16). Tell them you do not want to talk in those ways. Tell them that if they ever hear you using these non-Jesus ways of talking, you would appreciate their kindly questioning you about it. Tell them you never want to speak words that slander God in any way. This includes language that communicates fear, doubt, unbelief, panic, complaint, grumbling, etc.

There are times when you may be led to purposely and honestly communicate a real fear or doubt. You would do this to be real and to show your family how you handle honest doubts and fears. It is helpful to purposely share your fears, but only if followed by articulating your commitment to trusting and believing Jesus to meet your need. Your family needs to learn that when you have doubts that you are learning how to face them. These words are intended, therefore, to help your family face and learn from you how to overcome their fears, doubts, etc.

You can tell your children that you will give an account on judgment day for every careless (insensitive, uncaring) word you have spoken about God or others (Matthew 12:36). Tell them that no unwholesome talk is to come out of your mouth, but only what is helpful for building others up according to their needs, that it may benefit those who listen (Ephesians 4:29). Words that tear down, find fault, reflect conclusions about others without knowing their hearts (judging), slander, or gossip, are unacceptable for you as a follower of Jesus. You even have a hard time with chatter among Christians that leaves God out, because it results in drifting from faith in God and leads to ungodliness (1 Timothy 6:20; 2 Timothy 2:16). That is one of the reasons you may experience Spirit-led tension with most of the entertainment that our culture indulges in. It simply leaves God out—which has always been the beginning of disaster (Romans 1:18-25). Our words, like arrows, go into the hearts of our children as good seeds or bad seeds. For better or for worse, they are powerful weapons. Take advantage of the power of Christlike words.

If the heart is what matters to God—and it is—and if the heart is what shapes lives and relationships—and it is—then we need to learn to talk heart talk. Christ-followers speak a different language, don't we? Imagine the power and influence all these faith-filled, positive, happy, encouraging words will have on your children. This language is no more difficult to learn than Chinese is to a child in a Chinese speaking family, especially if we start when they are very young.

If you are overwhelmed with this challenge of living and speaking with such sensitivity to Jesus, do not let yourself be discouraged. Accept yourself as Jesus does; not based on your attainment but on your trust in Him. Commit to God's will and to small steps of progress. Progress, not perfect performance, is what God calls you to. Remember to: 1) Commit to God's highest; 2) Be honest when you miss His highest; 3) confess freely to God and others involved; 4) receive grace and strength to help in weakness. (See Chapter 2.)

*Jesus' third strategy: I will listen to My disciples*
"Aware of their discussion, Jesus asked ..." *Matthew 16:8*
"Who do you say that I am?" *Matthew 16:15*
"What were you arguing about on the road?" *Mark 9:33*

There was something more difficult for Jesus to accomplish in a large group than sharing His heart. It was far more challenging to know their hearts.[1] Jesus wanted a group of men who would not only follow Him, but who would become like Him to carry on His mission. This requires dramatically more than training them in some theological understandings or in a few behavioral skills. It meant dramatically more than giving them an example. They had to have a heart like His heart. He must, therefore, know and work in their hearts.

Did they understand who He was? Did they passionately agree with His purposes? Were their hearts on fire with passion for Him, His Father whom He had revealed to them, and His mission to touch the whole world? Did they understand His motives, His source of energy and power? Were they committed to this as the only basis for success? Did they understand how He had discipled them? Were they resolved to do this with others as the means to go to all the nations and make all of them disciples? Jesus needed to know the heart of His disciples to prepare them for their high call.

---

1 This assumes my personal conviction that Jesus, while never abdicating or losing His full divinity, truly became flesh, was one of us and one with us, emptying Himself of the knowledge and use of His supernatural powers as God, becoming like us in every way, even being tempted in every way like we are. If He used any dimension of supernatural power that we don't have, He really was not tempted as we are. Thus, what He did of a supernatural nature He did by the presence and power of the Holy Spirit, through sensitivity, faith, and obedience to His Father (Philippians 2:5-9; Hebrews 2:17; 4:15; Luke 1:15; 2:52; 3:22; 4:1, 14, 18; 10:21; John 1:14; 5:19,30; 7:17; 8:29; Acts 2:22; 10:37-38).

## *Carefully listen to your child, especially in his unguarded moments.*

—⁘—

**Listen to your child.** God will help you learn to use listening as a major skill in discipling your child. Carefully listen to your child, especially in his unguarded moments. At those times, you will hear the contents of his heart without it being guarded and without having to do heart opening "surgery" (Luke 6:45). You will develop the skills of a surgeon in opening their hearts during formal listening (Chapters 5-7). Listening in informal settings is as necessary as listening in formal settings. In formal settings, children are inclined to say the "right" things; in informal settings, they are likely to reveal the unguarded contents of their heart. What is truly in their hearts can readily be known by what comes from their mouths (Matthew 12:33-34). Be alert. Don't ignore idle chatter. This is why you so carefully evaluate what you say in your unguarded moments; it tells you what is really in your heart that you don't realize (Jeremiah 17:9). Put a lock on your lips to prevent yourself from reacting to the speck in your child's eye until you have checked for a log in your own eye, especially the faithlessness that creates fear or carelessness that leads you to react ungraciously or even selfishly to your child's words.

Accurate heart diagnosis is necessary before a treatment or cure can be applied. By listening in the context of real life, parents can make out the contents of their child's heart in order to lovingly minister to a potentially life damaging heart disease in as painless but effective way as possible.

### *Jesus' fourth strategy: I will watch My disciples*
*"You of little faith ..." Matthew 14:31*

How could Jesus be sure the message was accurately planted in the hearts of His disciples? He knew they would live by the condition of their hearts. By watching their lives and listening to their conversation, Jesus could better tell what was in their hearts. Watching was better than just listening to what they said around the campfire. Life brings out and exposes our hearts—for better or worse.

Jesus could watch for ...

- ✦acts and words that reflected His values and He could rejoice with progress
- ✦reactions that revealed heart attitudes and motives like His own, and know progress was occurring
- ✦misunderstanding
- ✦clear understanding coupled with inability to implement the understanding
- ✦hypocrisy (claiming understanding and commitment for what ever reasons, but not being willing to follow through on promises).

---

*Parents must be sensitive to their child's behavior as a means to search out the child's heart.*

---

Watching His disciples' life was absolutely crucial for Jesus. He was on a mission to capture and redeem from an evil enemy the heart of every person. His disciples were the core of the army He enlisted to win the war. Their hearts had to be sufficiently informed and motivated to fight the good fight. He had to watch them in battle to see the progress and needs for improvement of their hearts.

**Watch your children.** Many parents who do "keep watch" over their children primarily watch and react to external behavior. Jesus, like His Father, watched the behavior in order to discern the motives, attitudes, and commitments of the heart. To follow Jesus, parents must look beyond the behavior to seek to know the heart. Debbi and I watched David struggle in pain as he was being attacked in junior high. He needed protection, not just from outward enemies, but from his heart reactions to those enemies. We watched Deborah as her heart was being captured as a sophomore. She needed greater perspective than she was able to see in that crucial moment in life. Parents need to look beyond the "what" to the "why." God wants to work in hearts and He will ultimately judge behavior by the condition of the heart. Parents must be sensitive to their child's behavior as a means to search out the child's heart. "Watch and pray" can be taken more literally than we sometimes do (Matthew 26:41). Guard carefully the inclination to watch and, without praying, speak or act. Seek to first go to your Coach for His perspective and power. He is the good Shepherd, the Good Parent. Parents must guard against looking at a child's behavior and making superficial judgments about the heart. The Holy Spirit will help you be slow to speak, slow to anger, and quick to listen (James 1:19). He will guide you into His wisdom and truth in your response to what you see.

### Jesus' fifth strategy: I will coach My disciples

Coaches watch their players practice and play games. After games, coaches watch game films. Coaches review what they see with their players either for encouragement or for supervised correction without rejection. They work with the perceptions, emotions, desires, and ultimately the wills of their players. Then they go back to the practice field to work outwardly (performance) on that which they have worked on inwardly (heart—understanding, motivation).

Jesus prepared to coach His disciples by watching and listening to them. Limited as He was in the flesh by time and availability, Jesus could not successfully coach one thousand or even one hundred men. He chose a family of twelve. The three we have record of Him spending the most time with—Peter, James, and John—are the ones we hear about most in the establishment and development of His army, the church.

Because Jesus lived with His disciples, He could observe godly behavior, discuss the inner heart causes, and celebrate. Based on what He saw and heard, He could in the right way also expose unbelief, fear, insecurity, confusion, discouragement, and selfishness (all "inner, heart issues"). He could then plant God's truth that, if received, could restore the heart to clarity, excitement, self-sacrifice, and confidence in God. In so doing, the disciples and Jesus would share the same heart. They would be united. Then they could return to the battleground for another day of on-the-job training to reach the world.

## Coach your child as Jesus coaches you

Remember: a Chinese mother coached her child in a most difficult skill—speaking Chinese. Jesus coached His disciples to prepare their hearts to lead a world-changing movement. He coached their conflicts, confusion, and choices (e.g., Luke 9:46; Matthew 14:26-27; John 6:67). He encouraged their progress and confronted their errors.

You can coach your family in the same ways a Chinese mother and Jesus coached. The perspective, character, and servant-heart of Jesus that you desire for your child requires you to be a "player-coach" demonstrating and coaching Christlike perspective, character, and serving. God chooses you to be your child's "player-coach." God, in and through you, can do it.

Now imagine yourself in the middle of a conflict, or terrible confusion, or a tough decision. You, the parent-coach, just watched and heard your child reacting in an unChristlike way. Others saw it, whether they recognized the error or not. It's a dynamic moment in your child's life. You have the call and opportunity to empower all involved to realize that Jesus is in the middle of this, and He has a gracious opinion that needs to be heard, believed, and obeyed.

What to do next is the topic of Chapter 11.

# CHAPTER ELEVEN

# Coaching Conflicts, Confusion, and Choices

"Hear, O Israel: The Lord our God, the Lord is one. Love the Lord your God with all your heart and with all your soul and with all your strength. These commandments that I give you today are to be upon your hearts. Impress them on your children. Talk about them when you sit at home and when you walk along the road, when you lie down and when you get up." *Deuteronomy 6:4-9*

My son loved to play basketball. He loved that I played with him. I had been a high school basketball coach. It was an easy, positive connection for us. We enjoyed watching basketball on TV, going to games, and talking about basketball.

*I'd like to coach you in life.*

One night, I was wondering how I might better coach him in a life condition that I knew needed help. I believe the Holy Spirit gave me an idea. I said to my son, "I love the way you like me to coach you when we play basketball. It's fun for me and fun that you want help. But I need to tell you that basketball isn't too important in the big picture."

"I want to ask you to give me a huge gift," I continued. "I'd like to be your coach, but not just in basketball. I'd like to have you on my team for life. I'd like to coach you in life. I've been living quite a while longer than you have, and I've learned some things about life that I believe will really help you. Would you be on my 'life' team? Spend time talking with me about life? Let me celebrate when you win? Let me blow the whistle when we need to talk about what's going on? If we are on the same team and you realize I am breaking my neck to help you and our team win, you won't mind when we call time out to talk about what is going on and how to improve. What do you think?"

To my delight, he thought it was a great idea. From that night on, he responded positively when I would say, "Time out! Can I coach you at this point?" He was honestly willing to respond openly to my questions and perspective. He grasped the significance of a "life coach" who wanted the whole team to win.

If you start early with formal appointments to love, listen, and coach in life issues, your child will assume that this process is normal and he will probably value it. He will love his coach and be coached well enough that through your time-outs together, you can avoid many of the terrible problems of the teen years, while preparing your child well for life and eternity.

Get ready for a great ride of coaching your child in knowing and following Jesus—not only in the classroom (one-on-one meetings) but on the playing field, in the middle of the action, where pressures build and promises are forgotten, where emotions flare and conflicts erupt and disagreements occur. Here is where families (and others) collide, even though their hearts are in many ways conformed to the image of Christ.

In this chapter we will work with insights in how to call constructive time-outs in the midst of great victories and turbulent tensions.

## Jesus would disciple His child spontaneously

"What were you arguing about on the road?" *Mark 9:33*

Jesus lived with His 12 guys. They watched, listened, and learned from Him just by being together. But Jesus also very purposefully coached them in conflict, confusion, and choices. He observed and responded to their acts, their words, and their motives.

Spending time together is not automatically positive. Sometimes conflict erupts on the perfectly planned family outing. However, a discerning and wise parent can be God's instrument to turn careless comments, confusing situations, and even times of conflict into something very good. These hard times are the best times to coach. Our response to life—good or bad—is dramatically significant in showing our children how to follow Jesus. Equally significant is showing our family the need to recognize their own responses to life, and respond well.

---

## These hard times are the best times to coach.

---

### Teachable Moment 1: Coaching communication and conflicts

A primary coaching time occurs whenever family members are in conflict with each other or with persons outside of the family.

Let's assume that there is a conflict between your two children. As the parent-coach, blow your whistle and stop the arguing, screaming, belittling etc. Next, silently run to Jesus in prayer: *Lord, we don't have peace or joy. This doesn't feel like love. You love us and are here to help us. I need Your help. We need Your help. We ask for it and thank You. Amen.* Depending on circumstances, this may be an audible or silent prayer. If it seems good to pray aloud, make it clear and short.

Now, ask the older or more mature child (let's call him Josh) to be quiet, not interrupt, and listen carefully as the other child (let's call him Mike) shares what happened, what he thinks, feels and desires to do. I repeat for emphasis: Be sure that Josh understands that he, along with you, are to be quiet and listen very carefully to Mike. When you understand Mike, ask Josh not to defend, explain, or excuse his behavior, but to explain what Mike thinks and how he feels. This must continue until Mike can say, "Yes, Josh understands me."

Then reverse the process, having Mike listen (without interrupting) to Josh until Mike can explain exactly what Josh thinks and feels to Josh's satisfaction. You have now helped both sons be able to explain the other's perspective, to understand, and maybe even to agree.

An ideal next step is to ask the boys, "What do I think about each of you?" At this point, I remind you again, you have a golden opportunity to introduce the infinite value of each person in the conflict, and your love, valuing, and willingness to suffer in order to serve each one. You can be the example of God's grace to your children and His willingness to suffer in order to serve and save them. Sooner or later, God talks to us about our ungodly behavior and also the cause of this behavior in the context of His grace.

Wait for one of the boys (let's say Josh) to be able to meaningfully look you in the eye and say, "You love me."

You then ask, "And what about Mike?"

"You love him, too." This should not be rote. Do your best to help each one realize the value of each other because of the value you the parent place on each one. The key is to put the conflict into perspective by establishing the bigger issue of the significant value of each person.

Now, ask something like, "What does Jesus think about each of you?" Again, go slowly enough for the truth to sink in and for each to respond meaningfully to Jesus' love. You'll have to say it differently at different times. If you prayed aloud earlier, and have been humble and gentle, you led your sons to Jesus by your example. Now you will lead them to Jesus with your words. Your family will be helped if they feel Jesus' love and grace through your expressions and tone. You capitalize on the conflict by expanding their thinking to include the reality of their value to their Creator, the Living God.

We are ready to move into problem solving and conflict resolution. Start by asking, "Mike, what do you think should be done?" Don't let Josh answer your question. "Josh, what do you think?" Now Mike needs to listen. If you agree, tell them.

Say something like: "My task is to help us to discover and do what Jesus wants done. Mike, what do you think Jesus wants?" Josh listens carefully. "Josh, what do you think?" Mike listens carefully. "What about forgiving as we have been forgiven? Do we need to do that? How?" Listen to their perspectives and respond. "Good. How do you think we should handle this the next time? Good. Josh, do you see anything else? Good. Mike, do you agree? Okay. Now, how do we pull this off?"

Pre-school mothers, you are with your children 24/7. You could be overwhelmed if you try to dialogue every issue throughout the day. Instead, control the external conflicts as necessary. Show your children that you are writing a reminder of the conflict on a list on the refrigerator. At an appropriate time, the appropriate issues will be talked about in an appropriate way.

Conflict resolution processes create a great opportunity to involve Jesus' perspective and desires! The parent must be very sensitive and wise. A few talk about Jesus too much, usually because of the way they do it. Most Christian parents talk about Jesus too little. It is often good to ask permission to talk about what Jesus thinks or wants.

If a family member is uncommitted to Jesus, or not quite ready to have Jesus brought into the middle of the issue, it is wise to help all involved search for what each one thinks is best, or for what Mom or Dad think is best. If what is truly best can be determined, you will have found what Jesus thinks and desires regarding resolving the conflict, whether you mention Him or not. Don't leave Jesus out unless you believe—this time—it to be His will for wisdom's sake.

---

## *Conflicts are poignant, powerful opportunities.*

---

Don't waste the conflicts! They expose the need in the hearts of your children. They give you a chance to relate in love. They also let you disciple your family in how to communicate, how to handle conflict, and how to find and follow Jesus in the details of life. They are also helpful for the future to be a successful spouse, parent, and Christian leader at school, or work, or church, or play. Conflicts are poignant, powerful opportunities. You can, by God's power, turn conflict in family struggles into an encounter with God's grace and wisdom. Problem situations are often the best opportunity to reveal your faith in God and your love for God and your family. The problem, if handled wisely, can be your great ally in helping your children in dealing with life and with Jesus. This is the greatest benefit. Lead by watching for conflict and wisely bringing Jesus into the middle of the conflict to be the Peacemaker.

As a parent, you need to be aware of what is happening in your home. Take responsibility for the atmosphere in your home. Refuse to let sin and bad behavior reign in your family. However, do not respond to bad behavior by merely slapping on a law with penalties. You may need to put a short-term law in place until you can establish grace and truth. "Both of you sit at the table and be absolutely quiet until I come back." Sometimes a child will not receive grace and truth, and at those times, the parent must impartially put a law in place. The law is a means to control behavior because attempts to influence the heart (their perspective, their emotions, and their desires) did not affect the core of the heart—the will.

Law is power, but it is not leadership. If I threaten you with pain, I am not leading you; I am dominating you. If I bribe you, I am buying you. In either case, I am not leading you. Positive and negative rewards are not intrinsically wrong. In fact, God uses them. Sometimes they are our only alternative. Nonetheless, parents can and must learn to go beyond power and to use influence. Those who can't lead have to control or just let go. The law alone is external and often leads to either thoughtless dependency or rebellion. Grace and truth are essential in establishing internal motivation.

### Teachable Moment 2: Coaching choices and decision-making

Our daughter, Dana, recorded her experience following the discovery of a serious childhood disease.

I remember sitting in the specialist's office at nine years of age when I was diagnosed with an autoimmune disease called Polyarteritis nodosa. It was one of the scariest moments in my little life. Immediately the flood of accusations came against me—that I would never be normal, that I would always be different because I was "sick." Later on that day as my triplet brother and sister asked me about the doctor's appointment, I suddenly felt so different than them, so separate and alone. Overwhelmed, I burst into tears and ran inside. There to meet me was my father, embracing me in my tears and taking me upstairs to talk about what I was feeling. Little did I know then all that he must have been feeling as a father, aching over the pain of the difficult diagnosis given to his daughter, asking the Lord his own questions and experiencing his own inward wrestling. Yet he did not treat this more challenging time any differently than all the ordinary times, but rather began to ask me the familiar questions that I knew so well, leading my heart back into truth. He began to tell me that Jesus was giving me an invitation right now—He wanted to invite me to know Him more deeply through this circumstantial difficulty. Dad asked, "How do you want to respond to Jesus in this?" Even at age nine, I remember my heart arising to the invitation in front of me as my emotions aligned and my focus moved out of feelings of "woe is me" into the truth of God's desire to bring me nearer in relationship to Himself. I responded with a "yes" to Jesus' invitation, and the Lord answered this response, by moving my little heart out of darkness and into light—just as He is always faithful to do.

Major decisions, like who to marry, come up rarely. Minor decisions, that usually determine major decisions, are made every day. When you or your family needs to make a decision, it is a perfect time to align the nuts and bolts of life with the thoughts and perspectives of Jesus. "Jesus, You are present. You are the Head of our family. Do You have an opinion or desire regarding this decision?" I hardly ever consider an evening's activity apart from consulting my wife about her perspective and/or preference. Why? I love her and want to be sensitive to what she thinks or desires. How much more the One whom I love with all my heart, who gave His life for me, to whom I have voluntarily given my entire life, AND whom I call Lord! We are not our own, we have been bought with a price (1 Corinthians 6:19-20).

## Discernment for decisions

Of first importance in Christlike decision making is simply being sensitive to Jesus. We are made for real relationship with Him. If by seeking Him and His will we secure His guidance for a decision, it is a win-win for all involved. With the Holy Spirit guiding us, we can grow in discerning God's will through ...

   *knowing the scriptures

   *securing godly counsel

   *thinking clearly

   *prioritizing eternal values over temporal values

   *prioritizing relationships over things

   *prioritizing needs over desires.

———

*How can our children learn to give Jesus input into their decisions if ... we don't demonstrate that we are seeking Jesus to coach the details of our lives?*

———

How can our children learn to give Jesus input into their decisions if in most of our day by day living we don't demonstrate that we are seeking Jesus to coach the details of our lives? How can they learn to seek to find out what Jesus wants if parents don't bring Jesus into the decision making process with them? Many, if not most, of these decisions are not between good or evil, but between temporal versus eternal, things versus people, desires versus needs. We don't want to demonstrate to them the habit of doing what we think or what we want independent of consulting Jesus. If we do, Jesus is ignored and we are acting as if we are the "lord." Dare we assume we are doing His will until He screams so loudly we stop? Being Christian is more than not committing a few sins and doing a few religious exercises each week, with the rest of life left for us to live according to our perspectives and preferences. When and how will Christians learn to slow down and follow Jesus, Who did nothing apart from what He saw His Father doing and said nothing apart from what His Father taught Him (John 5:19; 8:28)? The best chance is to learn it while young through weak but sincere parents.

Remember in all this discussion of seeking and finding what Jesus wants, I am talking about the heart—the intent—the commitment. I am not talking about perfectly seeking and finding and doing what Jesus wants. I am begging for sincere commitment to seek, to find, and to do what Jesus wants.

## Decisions about details

One of the things we felt confident that God wanted was for us as a family to play together. The family that prays—*and plays*—together, stays together. On our family day, which will be described later, we incorporated time for play. Usually this went smoothly. The story that follows illustrates one of the most difficult but best "play" days in our family.

One summer, our vacation was legitimately filled with many days in the car, driving across the country visiting extended family and preparing for college. We had had very little time to simply "play." On Sunday, we were in Bakersfield, California. As a family, we decided to attend a church in Los Angeles, three hours away. To make the service, we had to get up at 5 a.m. After the service, we had time for a quick stop at McDonald's. Debbi thought we should eat out on the tiny grassy area in the parking lot to make the meal more like a picnic. Next, we went to visit the children's great-grandmother in the nursing home.

Finally, we headed to the beach. After jumping the waves and playing in the sand for a couple of hours, someone asked, "Can we go to Disneyland?" The park would be open for six more hours and Debbi was all for it. Night rates would be in effect, she assumed. She further assumed, based on her perception of Jesus, that it would absolutely be His delight and highest will for us to finish this special vacation day at Disneyland. We lived in Oklahoma, far from Disneyland. It was unquestionably obvious to her that going to Disneyland would be perfect.

Everyone was ecstatic, except me. I joined the discussion after the decision had pretty much been made. To the best of my memory, I read the situation and was aware which way we were going—toward Disneyland. Hearing the idea jarred my heart. My first thoughts were not about having a great family day, or about what Jesus wanted. My first thoughts were about the money—would the cost of going be worth it? I quickly calculated my guess at the cost for what I assumed would be a couple hours, at most, in the park. It did not seem at all worth it to me. Debbi was thinking, "With night rates, and only one real day to play on vacation, why not?"

After a few moments, one of my highest passions came into play. I remembered Jesus, and silently asked, "Jesus, what do You want to do?" Maybe He did not care if we went to Disneyland. Maybe He even wanted our family to have one final fling, but it didn't feel that way to me.

As we headed away from the beach, the atmosphere was not as ecstatic as it would have been if everyone knew that I was excited about going to Disneyland. In spite of my feelings, I do know that I did not care as much about going or not going as I hated for us to make decisions independent of Jesus. I vividly remember thinking: "The cost of getting in is a small price to pay for the value of practicing bringing every thought and act into obedience to Jesus."

At that point, I opened a conversation: "Gang, let's try to figure out if

Jesus wants us to go." In my mind, we were going, but I wanted to have a good discussion while we drove. In their minds, the decision was now officially up for grabs. Some of the family, maybe all, assumed that I thought Jesus did not want us to go so maybe discussing the issue was a losing battle. The silence was deafening. I was aware of what appeared to be anger on more than one face. Then I heard a muffled cry.

"I am not saying it is right or wrong," I said, "or that we should or should not go. I'd just like for us to see if we can figure out what Jesus wants." The discussion began. It became lively, even animated. One thought Jesus did not care and it was up to us. One thought He wanted us to go. Both had their reasons. One did not care as long as we did not have tension over it. It was a painful but valuable discussion. I hoped, maybe even prayed, that God was using it to help us learn how to discern His will in decision making and perhaps to strengthen our commitment to be sensitive to the Lord in the decisions and details of life.

After a while, I announced that the excellence of the discussion was worth far more than the cost of entrance into Disneyland, so I felt very good about us going. We pulled into the huge parking lot and paid to park. We discovered that there were no night rates, and easily agreed that the cost was not worth it. We went out to dinner and had a hilarious, happy time. We afterward agreed that it was one of the best times we'd had together as a family.

---

*I announced that the excellence of the discussion was worth far more than the cost of entrance into Disneyland.*

---

When Scripture is clear, we need not ask God's will. We simply need to honestly seek to apply it to specific situations. But the Bible does not tell us if to go or not to go to Disneyland, or most day-to-day, detail decisions of life. Time and money are limited. To know how to invest both requires sensitive wisdom. To grow as Jesus' followers, we must learn to prioritize eternal values over temporal pleasures, even those we sometimes call needs. Will children learn to follow Jesus—Who did nothing apart from His Father—on their own without help from parents?

I would rather be too sensitive to Jesus than not sensitive enough. I want to bring every thought captive into obedience to Jesus. I want to walk by His Spirit, not by my flesh. I love Jesus and want Him to have His way through the life that I have freely given to Him. Further, I know His will is by far the best for God, for my family, for the people of God, and for the lost people of the world.

How seriously do we desire to follow Jesus? He did nothing apart from His Father (John 5:19, 30; 8:28-29; 12:49-50). His food was to do the will of His Father (John 4:34). The Holy Spirit inspired Paul to share with us this way to live: "We are destroying speculations and every lofty thing raised up against the knowledge of God and we are taking every thought captive to the obedience of Christ." (2 Corinthians 10:5) Could we commit to this height of communion with Christ and include our family members in our decision-making process as we discover what Jesus wants? Could our passion for Jesus be so great that we cry out with Him, "Not my will, but Yours"?

—⁓—

### When do we learn to bring our thoughts and desires to Jesus to give Him an opportunity to be Lord of the decision?

—⁓—

We can invite our families to join us in finding Jesus' desire in the everyday decisions of life. To follow Jesus authentically is to increasingly seek His perspective and will in the details of our thoughts, attitudes, words, and activities. To the degree that Jesus is given a voice (the Voice) in decision-making, He is given the opportunity to actualize who His is—King of kings and Lord of lords. He is King and Lord, which means that nothing happens apart from His awareness and permission. However, when we help our family to slow down and seek God's will in the details of life, Jesus' lordship is taken from potential to actual, from theoretical to practical.

As we enter the arena of our family, those we are called to disciple, issues are constantly raised:

- "Why can't we watch that?"
- "Dad, why aren't you excited about me dating Jim?"
- "Do we have to go to church today?"
- "Can I stay over at Jamie's house?"

In and of themselves, most of the questions are not make-or-break issues. The real issue is *when* do we learn to bring our thoughts and desires to Jesus to give Him an opportunity to be Lord of the decision? Will children and teenagers learn to follow Jesus in the details of life without a Christian coach to graciously help them consider giving Jesus a voice in the decision? How will our children learn to walk by the Spirit and Word and not by the flesh, to think from God's perspective and value system? Like conflicts, decision times are wonderful training and testing times for the parent-coach.

## Danger

For the parent who desires to help his or her family walk by the Word and the Spirit as Jesus did, a great danger looms. No matter how graciously, tenderly, and caringly parents bring Jesus into the specifics of life, we run the risk of being interpreted as critical, condemning, or controlling. All three must be avoided.

The parent-coach must always go to Jesus to discern when and how to help a child consider Jesus' point of view. In decision-making times, some of the following types of questions are helpful for opening hearts:

- What do you think? Feel? Want?
- What do you think is best? Why?
- Do you know what I think? About you? (Some examples of answers: I care, I am for you, I want what is best, etc.)

- Do you know what I think would be best? (If you don't know, be candid.)
- Could we try to figure out what Jesus wants? Tell me how He feels about you.
- Do you trust Jesus?
- Does the Bible give us guidance? (If not, move on.)
- What do you think Jesus wants?

These questions do not make up a formula that will crank out a solution. They are ideas to use as tools. By the presence of the Holy Spirit, you can know if and when to slow down decision-making moments to seek what Jesus wants. Your children will know and feel your love, grace, and desire for their best through your lifelong friendship. They must know you desire God's best for them and are not trying to manipulate or pressure them into your will. There were many times when we chose not to bring Jesus into the decision-making process because we thought it not wise at that moment.

The Holy Spirit is absolutely faithful to work in the lives of our children. However, if He were all that is needed, children who receive Jesus would automatically become like Jesus. We know this not to be the case. Further, there would be no need for Jesus to have commanded us to make disciples if the Holy Spirit would take full responsibility to nurture and mature believers. Young Christians (and more mature Christians) are greatly locked into personal perceptions and habits. Even with the Holy Spirit's speaking, we routinely drift into non-eternal, selfish, proud decisions. Our children need other Christ-followers around them to raise the issue of God's will in the details of life. We live most of life in the details. If Jesus is not invited into the details, He isn't invited into much. I pray that you will consider leading your family to Jesus in the decisions of life.

Sometimes the Holy Spirit guides us into very difficult decisions. It happened for us several times. The following event was very challenging: We had just finished building a new sanctuary when the triplets were 10 and Dan was 5. During the four years of building, we had sacrificed quite significantly in order to contribute to the building fund. Some of the sacrifice included several breakdowns with our old family car. Now that the building was finished, I found a nearly new "nice" car with which our family immediately fell in love. Debbi felt like it was her "friend" because it had so many conveniences to help her. She nicknamed the car "Love Compartment." We enjoyed the car for six months before I had a thought that seemed might have come from the Lord. I went home and announced it to the family. "There is still quite a debt on the building and I would like for all of us to spend this next week praying about if the Lord wants us to sell the car and give the money to the church." After each one had spent a serious time seeking God's guidance, they came back with what they believed the Lord was saying.

"I think it is a test to see if we will put a car ahead of Jesus."

"I think it is our opportunity to deny ourselves and take up our cross."

"We have to obey what we think God wants."

"It's God's car. If He wants it back, it's His anyway."

We all agreed it to be God's best for us to sell the car and give the money to the church. Debbi has never pushed for material things, but this time she was being asked to give up what had become very dear to her. She, too, denied herself, took up this cross, and followed Jesus. Children watch and learn big lessons from their parents. (God may not always do this, but several years later He asked someone to give Debbi a far nicer car, which they did.)

### Teachable Moment 3: Coaching good behavior

In business, the phrase "Catch them doing something right" has become popularized as a key to successful leadership. Jesus, the greatest leader of all time, tells us through His Word (a manual on success), to encourage one another daily (Hebrews 10:25).

Debbi is the queen of encouragement. The massive doses of encouragement that she gives have been a big factor in making our family a house of friends and a visionary can-do group. Debbi encourages anytime she caught any of us doing anything even close to being good. She can find good in almost anything or anyone. In so doing, she sees and points out the activity of God, for He is the Author of every good thing. To ignore the good around us is to ignore God's special, personal gifts, and it takes us down a dangerous road (Romans 1:18-32). To see the good, give God thanks, and recognize His love to us touches our hearts and strengthens our bond with Him.

When we see something good in a family member, it is crucial to recognize the good in that person as a gift from God. Further, it builds a positive fire in the heart of one who hears encouraging words from a parent. Look for good in your child—both behavior (outward) and especially character (inward).

+ "That was a very kind thing you just did. It was just like Jesus!"

+ "It was so thoughtful and generous of you to give your brother the biggest piece."

+ "I am so excited about how patient you are being. I know that Jesus is more excited than I am."

These kinds of statements do several things. They encourage the person who did the good. They reinforce the good behavior. They build relationship between the encourager and the one who is encouraged. They are a model for encouraging others. Encouragement multiplies healthy encouragement in the family unit. Most importantly, encouragement affirms that God is at work in and through the person. It brings God into life, and brings glory and praise to Him. If done well, encouragement communicates the wonder that we, as God's people, are empowered by Him to co-operate with Him in bringing good to our world. What a volume of good is done through watching for and celebrating good!

Many have been deceived into not celebrating the good, not giving thanks for the good, or simply taking the good for granted. I admonish you to talk about this issue with your family. Tell them you want to encourage them. Ask them to practice encouraging each other. Talk about how to do it and explain why it so important.

Find something good in your family members to encourage daily (Hebrews 3:13). When your young child obeys instantly by taking his plate to the sink, celebrate. When your teenage daughter makes a good but tough choice to pass up a popular but questionable activity, rejoice in her response to the Holy Spirit and celebrate her integrity. Watch for and celebrate the good. Another spin on encouraging is that family members can encourage one another daily to obey God's Word. As your family's coach, you can lead your family to Jesus through encouraging them.

### Teachable Moment 4: Coaching inappropriate behavior

When a child behaves inappropriately, don't waste this golden moment to demonstrate grace, then truth, and to then apply the appropriate discipline! Instead of immediately reacting with judgment and penalty, or ignoring the issue and abandoning the child at a point of need, it is important to have a caring and honest talk. The child needs to be able to see the bigger picture—the way this behavior is affecting others and especially what this behavior says about his relationship with God. If a child will not respond to grace and truth, a law governing this and future behavior may have to be established, but as the last alternative, not the first.

—⁓—

## *Find something good in your family members to encourage daily.*

—⁓—

One night my son was staying overnight at a friend's home. The curfew was 11 p.m. At 2 a.m., he and two friends decided to toilet paper someone's house. Since the toilet paper was at our house, they snuck in to get it, forgetting that I'm a light sleeper.

At this point, most reasonable, "logical" parents would have punished the children or lectured them or promised to talk to them in the morning. But I responded differently. Upon discovering the three "thieves," one of them belonging to me, I made them sit on our sofa while I sat on the fire place. Now, I have to confess that I'm not pretty at any time. But at 2 a.m., dressed for sleeping and with my hair going all directions, I was scary.

I said nothing because I could not think of anything of any value to say. When they tried to make excuses for themselves, I told them to be quiet and think. We sat there a very long time. Finally, I went to my normal tactic. I sent a barrage of questions their way. They responded to each question.

"Are we having fun yet?"

"What do you think about sneaking out at 2 a.m.?"

"Is your fun worth violating your agreements and trust with your parents?"

"How do you feel about sneaking out and breaking curfew?"

"What do you really want?"

"What do you think we should do now?"

"What would you do if you were the parent?"

By this time, we were having a moderately valuable discussion. We got to evaluate our behavior based on *our* hearts. (Please note: The behavior of my son is the fruit of his heart. My son's heart is connected to my heart, so it is our heart that we are working with.) I asked my son more questions. "What do you think about this? Have I left you with the impression that violating our agreements is okay?" I think it was 4 a.m. when the marathon discussion was over. It ended up going where we always want to go—to Jesus.

---

### *The attitude is not, "You've got a problem."*
### *It is, "We've got a problem."*

---

When God's family messed up, His ultimate response was to suffer for their sin, and call them to repent in order to restore the relationship. Giving up a couple hours of sleep in the night is not a big deal, but in a little sense, when my son messed up by ignoring his parents and breaking their law, I was willing to enter into his arena and suffer a tiny bit with him. The attitude is not, "You've got a problem." It is, "We've got a problem."

Recommendations and ideas for coaching inappropriate behavior:

+Be poised, deliberate, and gentle, not harsh or loud

+Silently (or aloud, if it seems best) pray for grace for all involved, wisdom, and other kinds of help

+Express your commitment to what is best and your desire to be of authentic help

+Ask questions that establish exactly what happened, what the reasons were, what the anticipated or hoped for outcome was to be, what the outcome actually was (or would have been), etc. (Listen before you come to conclusions.)

+Ask those involved to evaluate their answers: What do you think about what happened? What do you think about your reasons?

+Ask what seems best to do now and why

+Ask the child if he knows what you think and why

+If appropriate, ask what the child or children think Jesus thinks about the whole situation. Ask what Jesus wants.

Don't waste these "teachable moments"!

There are times when you cannot and should not bring up Jesus because the timing is simply not right. In those times, asking "what is best" works well. The discussion of what is best often leads into a discussion of what God says is best. This often results in discussions about Christlike relationships and eternal values.

In the situation with my son, the boys' behavior would not have done much damage: a little wasted toilet paper, a few hours lost sleep, someone having to clean up a mess. But the bigger issues of disobedience and violated trust were at stake. Parents can capitalize on these moments dramatically. There are times when it is best to talk later, or force behavior alteration, or instantly punish. However, in general, a parent can decide that the inappropriate behavior is a wonderful opportunity to coach about life. It is an opportunity to sensitively open the heart and wisely ask questions about what happened, how and why it happened, what we should do now, and if we agree that this is what Jesus wants.

When a child's behavior is inappropriate or simply not as good as it needs to be, parents have two simplistic options at this point: 1) ignore the "bad" behavior, assuming that "it's just a phase"—which might be true, or 2) attempt to modify the behavior, either by sudden and severe punishment, verbal chastisement, bribes, or threats of punishment. These and other similar tactics are fairly easy to use, but they are fundamentally unsound because they deal only with the behavior (the fruit), not the cause of the behavior, the heart (the root).

A far better response to inappropriate behavior occurs when the parent can use the issue at hand to search out the child's heart. This is more than dealing with abstract ideas and ideals. The child has been caught red-handed. He knows that he is wrong or has a need. The parent must not react in rage or even anger, but sensitively and thoughtfully.

To help you recognize inappropriate behavior for Christ-followers or Christian-led families, carefully study passages of scripture like Matthew 5-7, Romans 12, I Corinthians 13, Colossians 3, etc. These passages illustrate God's will for His people. God, Who made us, knows how we work best. We need to coach our family in living these ways so our lives and relationships work. In Matthew 18:15-17, Jesus tells that when we see someone else's faults or sins, we should go to him in private to talk about it. Note: be as aware and open as possible about your own inappropriate behavior to minimize perceptions of hypocrisy. You don't want to confront the splinter in your child's eye while being oblivious to the log in yours (Matthew 7:1-4). Nor do you cop out on skillful parenting because you know you are not perfect. Deal with your own need honestly, and then lovingly serve your child.

## Jesus would "do life" with His child

A major thesis of this book is that Jesus did what it took to be with His disciples. He took them with Him on ministry trips. He took them with Him on prayer retreats. He strategically called His disciples to be "with Him."

### *Do life together: Make time and redeem the time*

We need time together as families. Why? Among other things, to help each other grow as followers of Jesus. This includes seeing and celebrating the good. It also includes seeing and coaching inappropriate acts, confusion, conflicts, and choices.

A place to start is to organize family life so that we do life together. It is imperative for families to spend positive time together. Because family life is fading, our culture is disintegrating. With the disintegration of our culture, family life is fading. Who will stop the cycle for your family? There are disintegrating forces that rip our families apart, both outside and inside the home.

Remember that Jesus invited His disciples to live with Him. Establish family events that you will do together routinely. Decide which activities you will do without interruption. Great family activities include mealtimes, family meetings, family church, family day, family ministry, family celebrations, family revival, and the necessary routine of life.

**Mealtimes**—Will you eat breakfast, lunch, or dinner together as a family? If not, why not? This powerful time of mingling two of our greatest needs—food and caring relationships—has been met for centuries by families eating together and relating positively during the meal. Mealtime is one of the best times for mutual knowing and encouraging, watching and listening, as well as positive coaching. The following are a few ideas of how to incorporate meaningful, Kingdom-valuable elements into conversations. During meals and most times you are together, find positive words to say about every person in your family, including Jesus. Be genuine. Purposefully use supportive language that blesses those present. If you don't know something good to share, you have work to do in knowing the life and heart of your family members. Find the good and affirm it. Give your family an opportunity to share something good about others, including each other. "Let's all tell something we appreciate about Mom."

Give your family an opportunity to share good things about their lives. "Dana, what was one of the best parts of your day today?" In the right dosages, ask if anyone can see how or why Jesus was working in the situation, since He is the Author of every good gift.

Young children love to ask the question, "Why?" Occasionally, it is great to ask, "What do you think the answer to your question is?" The purpose is to engage them and help them to think. This is a powerful opportunity. They are willing to find out what is in your heart. They need to know why you do what you do. They need to know what you think about what is happening. Sensitively respond when they ask questions about what you desire, think, and value. They are being trained very easily to value this mutually meaningful conversation.

If conversation is negative, stop it. Don't automatically impose a gag rule, although occasionally that may be the only appropriate action for the family coach. Consider asking permission to investigate the negative conversation. "Do we need to think about what we are saying here?" or "Is everyone okay with going on with this conversation?"

Before responding, consider what seems to be the best of the following options:

- Ignore what has just been said?
- Bring it up at a private or less dynamic moment?
- Respond right now because it is a dynamic, teachable moment when issues are obvious to everyone present?

Meals together are the cornerstone of your family life. They must not be seen as a necessary nuisance. Make them good in every way possible.

**Family meetings with Jesus**—Every Christian family can become a little church that has regular church meetings. The parent or parents are the lay pastors. The family is the church. They meet together to ...

+encourage one another

+give thanks and praise to the Lord

+listen and respond to God speak through His Word

+bear one another's burdens

+love one another

+pray for one another

+prepare to serve each other and those outside the family unit.

(Chapter 9 explained in detail how to do this.)

I believe with all my heart that the core organizational structure, the most basic universal set of small groups in the church, is the family unit. Here is part of my dream:

+Every family is a small group with one or both parents serving as lay pastor.

+The leaders of all the family small groups (parents) meet in groups to help each other and to be trained in leading their family groups

+All the additional training given to small group leaders is available to the parents of the families, to equip them to be lay pastors for their families.

Until our triplets were about 15, our family normally met together with Jesus five times per week during and after the evening meal. We relaxed the schedule as their lives got more complex, but kept working at gathering consistently to be with Jesus as a family.

**Weekly family meeting**—Weekly family meetings were the "business" meetings of our family. They included more of the day-to-day issues. They occurred on family day. They included ...

+asking if there are any questions, ideas, or difficulties that anyone is having personally or with each other

+talking about difficulties

+learning to communicate and resolve conflicts

+praying for and with each other

+planning what we are going to do this week

+determining what activities need to be communicated for the family calendar. (Examples: Who needs a ride and when? Do we need to plan anything for next month's family days?)

+thinking together about what the Lord may want the family to do for Thanksgiving

The family unit is big business and needs consistent "business meetings." Some of our children's leadership positions can be partially attributed to them participating in and learning leadership skills in family meetings.

---

*The family unit is big business and needs consistent "business meetings."*

---

**Family day**—One of Debbi's wonderful ideas was to make every Monday our family day. As our family got older, what we did changed. Summer family days were all day long. When school was on, family day began at 3 p.m. But our kids grew up knowing that every Monday the Perkins family would have a party. We did it all: cook outs, camping, hiking, fast food, games, camp fires, friends, swimming, inner tubing in the snow, building snowmen and forts, wiffle ball, basketball and football, kick the can, and so on. We had no idea how important it was to the kids. It helped to bond us as a family into a group with a common identity. Since we were all following Jesus, we became a little church, growing in common values, vision, mission, and strategies. Debbi and I poured our hearts into our little group during these fun times. Family days were strategic glue that helped bond us together. They generated further relationship the rest of the week. These days gave us an opportunity to slow down and work on our hearts. As an adult, Deborah said this about family day:

Every Monday as I sat in school, I would be excited. I knew that both my Mom and Dad were coming after school to pick us up for a fun family time together. Part of the strength of family day was that Mom and Dad had been on a date while we were in school. That modeled much to us. They came up with fun, meaningful things for our family to do and that went in very deeply. Their marriage and union provided a security for us we didn't even realize then. Every week they had an all day date. That was powerful to us. If my dad had only dated us, but not Mom, it would not have worked like it did. There is power in partnership. Mom was a full-time mom, yet she gave every bit she could to help dad, understanding and believing in who he was before God, counseling and serving together with him. They felt like a unit, a team. That was a powerful force.

**Family ministry**—We helped our family join us in serving others. They watched us invite people to our home. The children were coached in serving our guests and in caring for the children of our guests. They understood the significance of practicing hospitality, and learned to serve in Jesus' name. They went with us to meet and pray with people. They worked on the church building. They served and gave leadership in the children's and youth ministries of our church. As ten-year-olds, they were challenged and responsive to serving as lay pastors for their peers in our church's lay pastor ministry.

**Family celebrations and identity**—Debbi, with an intuitive genius about family cohesiveness, used every birthday, holiday, or community event to pull together our family for a party. She gently and persistently suggested we do things together like going to events, having events, taking pictures, singing songs, or doing just about anything as long as it got us together. She created a song for each child that we sang to the child every family day. The songs became so much a part of us that we sang "their song" at their wedding rehearsal dinners and a newly written song for their spouses. Every holiday, birthday, and community event became its own unique tradition. Do it once, and if it's worth anything, do it again, thus making a tradition out of it. The traditions were good moments that we looked forward to during the next month or year. The value of the relationship building and restoration during these times strengthened the bridges between us to carry the heavy freight of everyday life. Another comment from Deborah:

> I think one of the great things we did together was sing in the car. It was like glue that made our family work. And Mom and Dad praying together was powerful. Whatever humps you have to get over to sing and pray together are powerful in making a family work.

**Family revivals**—Our family took vacations. We called them "family revivals." This was a two-week period, usually in July or August, when we would jump into our station wagon or a graciously loaned vehicle from someone who recognized we needed it. Sometimes we drove to a camping site or halfway across the country to be with family. Other times we drove to conferences. Sometimes we just drove to one spot until we were ready to drive to another. The key in all this is that we *drove*. In the car, there were few distractions, and we had hours and hours to read, pray, talk, sing, play games, ask questions, connect, and bond. It was like a huge family meeting. Its purpose was to work on relationship with the Lord and with each other. God led and used these times.

**Annual family meetings**—Your family is big business. There needs to be time once a year for evaluating and dreaming together about your family. We planned this during our family revival (vacation).

You can ask some of the following questions very early in family life. In fact, it is best for spouses to work on these family issues even before they have children.

+ What are the five most important things for our family?

+ If we could do those things for five years, what would our family look like?

+ How are we doing in those five most important areas? Can we do them better?

•What do we need to change to move in this direction together?

In essence, you can ask your family to think and talk about the values your family holds, the dream or vision for your family, the ways to accomplish the dream, the cost and resolve to realize the dream, how to measure progress in the dream. All responses to these questions become opportunities for listening, affirming, considering other's perceptions, asking what children think parents think, asking if anyone has an idea about what Jesus thinks, etc. A side benefit: You are modeling leadership methods and skills for your children. This will help equip them to be leaders.

**Routine**—The routine events of each day and week are just as or even more important than consistent structures and special days and events. What do we see and hear from each other when we get up? Brush our teeth? Get ready for the day? Driving to school each day was a time to discuss the following question: Today will you be a missionary or a mission field? We decided to greet each other after a day of being separated with delight and celebration instead of a casual or cool greeting. We determined to sing our praise to the Lord part of the time when we did dishes together. Guide and guard these routine moments.

"Hear, O Israel: The Lord our God, the Lord is one. Love the Lord your God with all your heart and with all your soul and with all your strength. These commandments that I give you today are to be upon your hearts. Impress them on your children. Talk about them when you sit at home and when you walk along the road, when you lie down and when you get up." *Deuteronomy 6:4-9*

Thank you for choosing *If Jesus Were a Parent*.  We pray that God will empower you to take the principles in this book and mold them to fit your life and ministry.

If you find it has helped you in being and making disciples and disciplemakers, I'd love to hear your story!  Please feel free to e-mail me: hp@gvnaz.org

*Hal Perkins*

# CHAPTER TWELVE

---

# Impacting the Next Generation

"... make disciples ... teaching them to obey everything I have taught you ..."
*Matthew 28:19-20*

You have read much about coaching and discipling your child to follow and become like Jesus. Now, let's dream. Can you see your child as a disciple-maker? Even a maker of disciple-makers?

Two major steps are required:

+parenting your child *to make disciples.* This means helping others to know and follow Jesus.

+parenting your child *to make disciple-makers.* This means helping their disciples to help others to know and follow Jesus.

This chapter will help you see how to do this.

When our family moved to Seattle, Dan was a junior in high school. Having spent most of his education in public schools, he chose to enroll in a Christian high school in Seattle. The first week of school it was announced to the students that the chapel speaker had cancelled. Dan immediately raised his hand and said, "I'll speak." In that chapel he called the students to whole-heartedness in following Jesus. We saw this as very bold—and very delightful.

Nearing Dan's graduation, a lady from our church went to one of the school's events to evaluate the prospects of enrolling her daughter in the school.

She approached a math teacher and opened the conversation by saying she knew Dan Perkins. The teacher replied, "The level of spirituality in this school has significantly increased because Dan Perkins chose to go to school here."

According to the teacher's perspective, Dan had significant positive influence in his school. He was a leader during his two years there. Was it just his personality that would give him the confidence to volunteer to speak the first week of school? Maybe. Maybe it was also some concrete steps that had already been taken to disciple him and equip him to be a leader.

—⌇⌇—

## Making disciples is God's way to lead the most people possible to Jesus and eternal life.

—⌇⌇—

You may recall my story from the introduction of this book. In it I explained how the Holy Spirit led me through the gospels to realize and be convicted of Jesus' ministry strategy to reach the world. Jesus' mission was then, and remains today, to seek and save every person. His primary strategy is through multiplying Word-knowing, Spirit-empowered disciple-makers. Remember that the Communists captured the hearts of one-third of the world in a few years by using the disciple-multiplying methods of Jesus. Seeing the power of disciple-making in the Communists was the picture God used to confirm what I knew He said to me through Jesus life: Making disciples is God's way to lead the most people possible to Jesus and eternal life.

Imagine that your child hears, by the Holy Spirit through you, the call of Jesus to make disciples. Imagine he "gets" why making disciples must be embraced. Imagine that he sees through you what disciple-making looks like. He now has the seeds of disciple-making in his heart! You simply need to water, weed, and feed his heart. God will provide supernatural power to see that making disciples and making disciple-makers takes root and grows.

You can plant the seeds into the heart of your child to be a conscious, purposeful disciple-maker for the rest of his life. Teach him to obey one last thing Jesus taught all His disciples to obey and to teach others to obey—to make disciples.

Do *you* see that by making disciples who make disciples, you are employing strategic divine wisdom to reach the masses? If so, the disciple-making vision is in your heart. Do you believe that Jesus has called you to raise Christian children who leave home heart-equipped with passion, purpose, and a plan to unite with Jesus in His world reaching mission? If this disciple-making mission and ministry are in your heart, it can come through your words and life to be securely planted in the hearts of your children. Is it your dream for your child that he not only be an authentic disciple of Jesus, but that he be a mature disciple—one who makes disciples? If so you are already well on your way to seeing the dream fulfilled.

Look at what has already occurred, assuming you have are following the steps outlined in this book so far:

+Your child is obedient from the heart, not only to you, but to Jesus (Chapters 1-3)

+Your child has a picture through your life of honest faith and pure devotion (Chapters 4 and 8)

+Your child is learning to "pastor" his heart (Chapters 5-7)

+Your child is able to meet with Jesus and to be coached and discipled by Jesus (Chapter 9)

+Your child is learning to live the Christ-life through your life coaching (Chapters 10-11)

In short, your child is an authentic follower of Jesus who is becoming more and more Christlike. What he is becoming qualifies him as an example, thus a disciple-maker. What he has learned to do from you greatly qualifies him to do with others.

You now need only to work on the following six steps to lead your budding disciple into being a full blown disciple-maker and maker of disciple-makers.

### 1. Pray

Long before you approach the topic of making disciples, be faithful in prayer for your child to begin and continue on a disciple-making mission. Through prayer, your child will be helped to stand firm in all the will of God with maturity (Colossians 4:12). If we ask anything according to the will of God, we know that God hears and answers (1 John 5:14-15). It is unquestionably God's will for your child to make disciples of Jesus, especially all of his own children that he may sometime have (Matthew 28:18-19).

For your child to become a disciple-maker, he will need to be consistently empowered to believe that making disciples is God's will for him. Our Living God will powerfully speak when you plant the Great Commission in the heart of your child. But there may still be mountains in your child's heart or life called diversion, fear, insecurity, confusion, disappointment, etc., that will require mountain-moving prayer to release more of the Spirit's power. Therefore, pray without ceasing.

### 2. Secure commitment

Communicate the reasons for your child to become a disciple-maker.

* *You can bring to your child this reason to make disciples and disciple-makers: Jesus clearly commands it.*

Our sons and daughters need to understand clearly that Jesus intends that someone disciple them—including discipling them to make disciples. They need to have this clear revelation: "Jesus directed my mother or father to make disciples. I was chosen to be discipled by one or both of my parents. Part of my parents' mandate is to disciple me to obey everything Jesus taught. Jesus, through the scripture and my parents, is teaching me that I am to obey His call to make disciples. I will respond to that mandate." (Matthew 28:18-20)

The disciple-making mandate has been greatly lost. It must be revived. Our children are to be taught to obey all of Jesus' commands. He commands that His followers make disciples—be purposeful disciple-makers. For Christians the issue really is not if to make disciples; it is who and how.

There are potentially as many divergent God-given visions and ministries as there are Christian groups. Every snowflake is unique. Each of us is uniquely created to do specific good works for specific purposes. However, I believe that regardless of our unique purpose and work, as we are going wherever we have been led to go, we are to purposely make disciples of Jesus. We are to inundate others with the character and activity of the Holy Spirit through us, teaching them to obey everything He commanded—including making disciples. *Every Christian is to mature and be discipled into becoming a conscious disciple-maker.* How that is done will be unique. *That* it is to be done is universal for Christians. My disciples are to be committed to knowing and obeying everything Jesus taught, including teaching their disciples to make disciples.

I encourage you to very carefully study Matthew 28:16-20. Personalize it. Do you clearly see that Jesus is calling you to make disciple-makers? If so, wonderful. If not, ask Him to open your heart to whatever it is He wants for you.

I ask you to consider something else. Study Matthew 28:16-20 with your child. Personalize it. Give him a chance to hear and reflect upon the Great Commission personally. The Holy Spirit may do a special miracle. You might consider prefacing the study by asking your child if he has given much thought to what God has called him to for his life. Has he thought with the Lord what his life might or could look like 20 years from now? Does he have a sense of destiny (destination)? In this context, he needs to know that no matter what God may call him to regarding marriage and vocation, God is calling him to making disciples of family members, church family, and friends.

+ *You can bring to your child a second reason to make disciples and disciple-makers: Jesus clearly did it.*

221

Our sons and daughters need to understand that Jesus, guided by the perfect genius of the Living God, invested a great deal of His time on earth in a very small group of men. He was on a mission to see that every person possible repent and receive eternal life. He had only three years to accomplish His mission. His time was limited. The way He used His time is of extreme interest. How did Jesus invest His time? He made disciples. He was strategic. His great strategy was to invest His life, first in prayer with His Father, and next in a few men He would invite to live with Him in a family-like arrangement. He would direct them to invest their lives in a few who would continue the process. It was His leadership development process. Jesus said, "Follow Me." Because we are committed to following Jesus, we must be committed to making disciples.

• *You can bring to your child a third reason to make disciples: the power of multiplication through making disciple-makers.*

It may help your child to understand the potential power of a disciple-making ministry. Organizations, businesses, para-church ministries, even enemies of our Lord have used disciple-making as a strategic and powerful tool to advance their cause. The Lord worked dramatically in my life to confirm the power of disciple-making. I shared the stories of the Communists with you for only one reason: I desired to help you see the blatant potential of working with individuals and small groups (as they—and Jesus—did) so you can see that the greatest movement in the history of mankind (Christianity) and a relatively short-lived but dramatically powerful and pervasive movement (Communism) used the same strategies to motivate and multiply converts: disciple-making.

Would knowing Jesus' mission and strategy motivate your child to adopt a disciple-making lifestyle? If you were sitting at a McDonald's right now with your child, you might lean forward and look him in the eye and say, "We are called to make disciples of Jesus, and we must." He might say, "I can't do that." You could say, "If I show you how, will you pray about following me as I follow Christ?" He might respond with, "If that is what Jesus wants, I will." You would say, "Good. Here's how..."

**3. Learn to lead**

Have your child take over leadership of the meeting the two of you experience. Role play (pretend) that you are a brand new Christian. Have him first lead you in talking about needs in your life in following Jesus (Chapter 7). Raise every problem and obstacle you need to help your child get practice in responding to the life and spiritual needs of a young Christian. Do this until your child is gaining confidence in facilitating a meeting talking about following Jesus in life (still Chapter 7). Then, after he is getting the basics of working with you in your life, have him lead you in the content of Chapter 9. (We trained and equipped our children to lead others by letting them take turns in leading our family meetings of worship, Word, and work as discussed in Chapter 9.)

**4. Select a disciple**

Shortly after your child starts leading the meeting with you, prayerfully select and invite an appropriate person to pray about being your child's first "discipleship partner." Be sure his friend understands that your child is leading the meeting and you are simply there to help in case you are needed. In your selection, you are looking for a friend of your child that we call **F.A.S.T.**

- **Faithful**: a friend who will make and keep promises to God and your child
- **Available**: a friend who will make the time to meet together and learn to work on relationship with God, his family, his friends, and his church family
- **Submitted**: a friend who understands that faith in Jesus includes seeking to obey whatever King Jesus says through His Word
- **Teachable**: a friend who is hungry for God's truth and committed to change when truth is known

It would be ideal if your child's "F.A.S.T." friend would commit to and be accountable for the four sets of essential relationships:

+Loving Jesus, and being His disciple

+Loving family members, and helping each be Jesus' disciples

+Loving church family, and helping some be Jesus' disciples

+Loving lost friends, and helping them become Jesus' disciples

At the very least, your child's first discipleship partner should understand what you and your child are going to do, and agree that he wants to:

+Consistently meet and pray to help each other live as followers of Jesus

+Learn how to meet alone with Jesus and "do life" with Jesus

+Be accountable for relationships and ministries with Jesus, family, lost friends, and church family

What about feeling inadequate? Strategic disciple-making requires knowledge and skills that can be learned. These skills are most efficiently learned under skilled coaching. Your God-empowered wisdom and experience, coupled with what you can pick up from resources like this book, can keep you growing and effectively coaching knowledge and skills into your disciple-making child. Give him the best resources you can find. Encourage or send him to the best conferences or mission experiences possible. Help him develop for a life time. Never forget: The Great Disciple-maker lives in us. We all have His "Love Letter" on our table or desk—be it King James Version or New International. We have some of His great disciples (our mature, fully dependent and fully devoted Christian friends) to help us.

### 5. Meet with disciple

With mutual agreement, include your child's first discipleship partner in the meeting with your child. The *life situations* of your child and his discipleship partner are the "curriculum" (Chapter 7 meetings). Soon your child will introduce Bible study (the Word section of Chapter 9) into the meeting. Then add intercession and ministry (the Work section of Chapter 9). Pray for and develop ministry plans for family members. Gradually introduce prayer for and ministry plans for lost friends. Then add prayer for and ministry plans for church family. Finally, begin the meeting with all present giving a brief account to God of praise and thanksgiving for all He has done, especially in the areas of ministry to family, friends, and church.

You coach as your child disciples his friend. If you are really needed, you speak—usually only by asking questions that bring issues out into the open. You give feedback to your child in private after the meeting. For things done well, make positive observations; for issues you think needed help, ask your child what he thinks. Give much encouragement, either in private or in front of your child's friend.

The goals:

◆your child and his discipleship partner helping each other know and follow Jesus in the specific details of life

◆your child discipling a friend to meet with Jesus on his own

If your child still wants to meet alone with you (in addition to meeting with his discipleship partner and you), make time for it. You'll be glad you did. Your child's *ability* will be strengthened through continuing *accountability*:

*Accountability*—Few have the character to persevere in the high calling of making disciples without great support and shared commitment. Working with people and their hearts is challenging. The positive results of planting good seeds in hearts often take years to be revealed. Your son or daughter will need to have you available to be a life-time partner in making disciples, if they desire. As they have their own sons and daughters, they will need and want accountability for this new role of discipling their sons and daughters. They are now adults. You were very wise in how you advised them when they were younger and under your authority. You will maintain this wisdom, giving input only by request or with permission. They may well want to establish the same values and vision that you have. They may ask you to help them live out the commitments you helped to work in. They could become your lifelong partner in being and making disciples. If they are to persevere, they will need someone. Help them to understand this. You know it is true. You still need someone to help you to keep on.

## 6. Multiply

Finally, disciple your child to make disciple-makers.

"...teaching them to obey everything ..." *Matthew 28:20*

One final strategy is yet to be established. It is Jesus' strategy and commandment to us. It is the *least practiced but absolutely necessary* strategy for world evangelism. The strategy: not just making disciples, but making disciple-makers

Jesus taught His disciples to teach their disciples to obey all He taught His disciples: "... teaching them to obey *everything* I have commanded you."(Matthew 28:20) *Everything* includes obedience to Jesus' farewell commandment to make disciples (Matthew 28:19). The disciples of Jesus have not completed their disciple-making mandate until they have discipled their disciples to be disciple-makers. To teach them to obey everything includes teaching them to make disciples who make disciples. For Jesus' disciples to have not made disciples would have been disobedience, and for them to fail to teach their disciples to make disciples would have been disobedience.

**Disciple (teach and train) your child to lead his disciple to make disciples.**

The following illustration is not of a child or teenager. It is a story of a 24-year-old who just became a Christian. It illustrates the dream and the steps you can use to train and equip your child to make disciple-makers. I have watched children and teens progress and do what this 24-year-old did.

I was standing in an outdoor, above ground swimming pool in Jim and Carol's backyard in Mount Laurel, New Jersey. We were baptizing new Christians. These new Christians had mostly come out of a small group (house church) in Bill and Kathy's house. Attendance had jumped from four to forty in a few weeks. Barbara, who lived in Philadelphia, was one of the new attendees. She converted from being deeply lost in darkness to becoming a follower of Jesus. She had done a 180 degree turn. It is called repentance—a sincere confidence and commitment to Jesus resulting in every part of her life gradually being renewed. She was one of those being baptized. She had asked me to pray for Danny, her husband. He thought she had totally dropped off the extreme edge of sanity in her new "religion." Danny himself was very much lost and in extreme darkness.

I was delighted but very surprised when Barb came running (literally) up to me before her baptism and said, "Pastor, Danny came to see my baptism! Come meet him." I had only heard about Danny, and wasn't at all sure what to expect. We had a pleasant introduction, and got on with the baptismal service.

About ten people were baptized that night. Most of them were in their twenties. Each told his/her own story of life before Jesus, of coming to trust and follow Jesus, and the difference He had made in each life. Most told about bad history with drugs, alcohol, and relationships. It was a happy, high, holy moment. We finished and I was standing behind the pool, drying off, when I heard a voice. "Pastor!" I looked up. It was Danny. "Can we talk?" Of course I said yes and Danny rapidly told me his story and what was happening as he watched the baptisms. He finished by saying, "I thought Barb was crazy in her new religion. But she has changed so much, and now I think I understand what happened to her. Can I be baptized?" He had just heard ten people talk about Jesus, the cross, their sin, repentance and faith in Jesus. He needed no more information. I heard clearly in his words that he had genuinely repented and determined to trust and follow Jesus. I called for a re-assembly. Danny told his story and was baptized. This made for a happier, higher, holier evening than any of us could have dreamed. But you must hear the rest of the story.

Danny started attending the Tuesday night house church. His zeal was so great that in a few weeks I asked him if he would ever be interested in meeting with me personally to be discipled (Chapter 7, then 9). I strategically watch for followers of Jesus to disciple …

> ◆who keep their promises even when it is inconvenient
>
> ◆who love Jesus enough to use their time for Jesus and His purposes instead of their own pleasures or pressures
>
> ◆who are hungry and humble enough to think honestly and openly about Jesus' Word and ways
>
> ◆who relentlessly embrace the Word and will of Jesus when they know it.

Danny qualified. He was obviously F.A.S.T.

On Tuesday nights Danny watched and learned from me in a small group setting about how to connect with Jesus (the worship, Word, and work described in Chapter 9). What he learned to do in the group setting he practiced on his own. He was now leading himself to Jesus for Jesus to disciple him. He was learning how to "pastor" a group by watching me; he was learning not only methods but biblical truth and theological perspectives because he literally sat at my feet absorbing everything I said and did. We started meeting together at his house in Philadelphia on Thursday nights. He had a long list of questions. He would often come with his eyes a bit drooped. I came to realize the drooped eyes meant he had somehow lost focus that day or week and we needed to work back through grace, repentance, and faith. Every bump and fall that we talked about became wonderful opportunities to understand how to walk as a Christian. We covered many important theological issues by simply talking about Danny's life and walk with Jesus. We were, simultaneously, studying through a basic core curriculum of theological essentials.

Soon I quit answering his questions. He would ask, and my response was, "What do you know about that?" He had learned quickly—and well. Everything about Christian theology was totally new to him. In many ways, his newness made things much easier for him to get a solid grip on many of the issues covered in this book:

+ Heart issues when contrasted with performance issues
+ Grace issues when contrasted with law issues
+ Communing with Jesus issues when contrasted with normal concepts of prayers
+ Christlikeness issues when contrasted with cheap grace and legalism.

He studied the assignments I gave him. I grilled him, often playing the devil's advocate to make sure he was getting his foundation clear.

Then it was time. We made a list of his Philadelphia friends. He and Barb started inviting them to the "church that meets in their house" (Philemon 2) on Thursday nights at 7:30. I had gradually turned parts of the Tuesday night house church in New Jersey over to Danny to lead under my close supervision. When we started the new church in his house on Thursday nights, Danny left the Tuesday night meeting. Danny and I met at 6:00 before the meetings to continue to work on his life and questions. Soon, Danny was pastoring his own church—at 7:30 on Thursday nights. I sat there and watched him. If he started to get in a mess, I would ask a question that would guide us back in the right direction. If he didn't know what to do, he might look at me. Often I would simply smile, which meant, "You can do this. Go ahead. Give it a try. I'll bail you out if necessary." I was simply doing what coaches and mentors and parents are called to do.

It was not long until Danny was transferred to another part of the country. One day I received a long distance call. It was from a pastor. He asked if I knew Danny. I told him I did. He then told me how impressed he was with Danny, but there were some questions he (the pastor) wanted to ask me. I was wondering where this was going. To get to the bottom line, Danny had come to his new pastor, suggesting that they start a house-church planting, disciple-making, leadership-multiplying ministry. Of course, I was excited about that. The pastor continued to explain. To get this new ministry going, Danny had invited the pastor to meet with Danny—to be discipled by Danny. I was on the verge of embarrassment. But the pastor continued. He so loved what he saw and heard in Danny that he was ready to do it, even though he was a seminary graduate. He had called me to get the clear purpose and plan regarding house-churches, disciple-making, and leadership multiplication before he jumped in. He also wanted to make sure I had no reservations about his being "discipled" by Danny.

---

*I have not taught my disciple to obey everything Jesus taught until I have taught him to make disciples.*

---

My point is this: Because Danny had been willing to be discipled, he (still a very young convert) was qualified in the eyes of his new pastor to make disciples of Jesus. How exciting! It should be more normal! Danny knew that he must do more than make disciples. He must make disciples who make disciples. He must not only start "little churches" (small groups). He must help others to start little churches—who would help others to start little churches. *Everyone must learn to make disciples, and everyone must learn to make disciple-makers.* New converts being taught to obey everything Jesus taught—including making disciple-makers—is God's will. It is to be normal.

Jesus unambiguously said, "Teach them to obey everything I have commanded you." Within the great commission is a great commandment to "make disciple-makers"! I have not taught my disciple to obey everything Jesus taught until I have taught him to make disciples. Our disciples are called to pray, love, serve, disciple others, and *disciple those they disciple to disciple others.* This is your goal for your child.

Your disciple-making goal for your child is for you to coach him in helping his disciple to make disciples. It is one disciple making one, with both then making one, the two becoming four who become eight who become sixteen, etc. The Christian movement grows exponentially when Christian disciple-makers not only help their flocks (be it a church of 5000 or a family of 5) to know and follow Jesus, but also disciple each one to not only help others to know and follow Jesus, but to also become disciple-makers. In short, everyone possible must be discipled to be disciple-makers. "And the things you have heard me say in the presence of many witnesses, entrust to reliable men who will also be qualified to teach others." *2 Timothy 2:2*

Parents: Jesus calls us to disciple (teach, train, and coach) our children to obey everything He taught—including making disciple-makers. In order to help your child commit to a "making disciple-makers" mission you need a Spirit-guided vision and strategy. You can then paint the "making disciple-makers" picture for your child. If his heart is open, the Holy Spirit will begin to profoundly work God's will into his heart.

I share a very general, brief, and simple plan for this last step. It is the critically important step. This step, if left undone, leaves us failing to finish the disciple-making mandate.

In general, repeat the first four steps of this chapter, but this time see that your child, instead of you, is doing the steps. Completing these steps sets the stage for the final stage, which is making disciple-makers. This means you, the parent, are observing your child help his disciple become a disciple-maker.

Here is another way of saying the final step in the cycle: *Coach your child to take his disciple through the six steps of this chapter, just as you took your child through the same steps.*

You will need to prepare your child to explain why his disciple needs to prepare for making disciples by leading meetings. You must not do the explaining to your child's disciple. It is your child's task to explain why and how his friend is to become a disciple-maker. It is your task to be sure that your child is equipped to call his friend to become a disciple-maker. Unless it is impossible or unreasonable, watch your child as he role plays and coaches his disciple in leading meetings. Persuade your child that what you have done in *coaching him to coach* he must always be doing in every serious discipling relationship. You can make no higher investment in lives than in the lives of the young. They respond to ideals and visions. They are ready to give themselves to a worthy cause.

---

## *Your child will best understand and see disciple-making by experiencing the process through you*

---

Your child will best understand and see disciple-making by experiencing the process through you. If he grows up with an authentic, growing, disciple-making parent who purposefully discipled him, he will have much of what he needs to pass it on. He will likely assume this is normal Christianity, which it is. Someday he will disciple his own child, probably in much the same way as he was discipled.

The various emphases of this book need to be built into the lives of disciples and disciple-makers in order for reproduction of the heart and life of Jesus to occur.

+Heart obedience—faith that obediently follows (Chapters 1-3)

+Growing toward pure dependence on Jesus (Chapter 4)

+Guarding one's heart—removing weed seeds and receiving good seeds (Chapters 5-7)

+Establishing and maintaining passion and pure devotion for Jesus (Chapter 8)

+Establishing and maintaining meaningful communication with Jesus (Chapter 9)

+Turning heart intent and commitment into actual faith and obedience in life (Chapters 10-11)

Along the way, your child will need help from a personal discipler who is passionate about and has experience with Jesus' call to make disciples. It *could* be you. There could be natural and perpetual conversation about making disciples.

I pray that you will be in a position to coach and partner with your child as he learns how to disciple your grandchildren. If you are willing to meet with and disciple your child somewhat as described in this book, there is a good possibility that through these disciple-making practices you will start an explosion of making disciples of Jesus.

One of the statements you may want to make to your child goes something like this: "For Christians the issue really is not *if* to make disciples, it is *how* to make disciples. Your ultimate opportunity and challenge of discipling will come if you get married and have a family. You must meet your family where they are so that you can lead them to Jesus and then coach them through life's tensions, fears, pressures, passions, conflicts, and decisions. Your family members can become discipleship partners with you. You coach them into maturity so they are radical disciples of Jesus, with or without you—who mature to be disciples, make disciples, and make disciple-makers."

The whole concept of every leader making leaders must be profoundly built into the DNA (heart) and methods of those you disciple. Talk about it urgently. Model it. Coach it. Hold your disciples accountable for making disciples and making disciple-makers.

A simple overview of the whole process looks like this:

+Be Jesus' disciple by...
  +meeting with Him
  +ministering with Him
  +maturing toward being like Him
  +making disciples by helping others do what you are growing in: meeting with Jesus, ministeing with Jesus, and maturing toward being like Jesus
  +making disciple-makers by helping your disciples do with others what you are doing with them: hling some of their family and /or friends to meet with Jesus, minister with Jesus, and mature toward being like Jesus

Don't do anything for your disciple they could possibly do for themselves. Teach and train them to do everything Jesus commands, and teach them in the process to teach the ones they work with to do the same thing. Demonstrate. Delegate. Supervise. Coach. This may come "down the road," but put it in your vision now.

Imagine how open our sons and daughters are or could be to us. Imagine the value and impact of sending them out from our homes as passionate, mature, disciple-making, leader-multiplying servants of Jesus.

Is your heart saying "yes" to discipling your sons and daughters? "Yes" to Jesus? To His mission? To your mission with Him—your co-mission? If it is in your heart, God will empower you to get it into your life—and then into their hearts—and once in their hearts, with a minimum of your help, into their lives.

**A reminder: This is more about Jesus than about you.**

You can be a disciple of Jesus. You can make disciples of Jesus. Why? Because the One who called you lives in you to equip, enable, and empower you to lead your child—even in his uniqueness. As you trust Jesus—and obey Him—He will actually interact, intervene, and empower your heart and your activity. If God be for you, who can be against you (Romans 8:31)? The One who calls you is faithful to do it (1 Thessalonians 5:23-24). You can do all things through Christ who strengthens you (Philippians 4:13). Above all, all authority in heaven and earth has been given to Jesus. He has authorized you to go and make disciples, baptizing and engulfing them in the character and activity of the Father, Son, and Holy Spirit by your life and words, and teaching them to obey everything He taught you. Here comes the clincher: In making disciples, Jesus will be you with you, always (Matthew 28:18-20)! Jesus is with you in this venture! God is on your side. Your faith is not in your knowledge, your zeal, and your ability. This is not nearly so much about you as it is about God. Don't quench God's Spirit in and through you by believing it is impossible, thus not going for it. With God, all things are possible.

Debbi and I never dreamed of our fourth grader initiating and leading a Bible study for peers over the lunch hour. We never dreamed of dozens of junior and senior high students meeting every morning of the week before school for Bible study and prayer. We never dreamed of a high school junior, having just begun attending a Christian school, volunteering to speak for the student body chapel and a faculty member saying it created a whole new level of spiritual life at the school. We never dreamed of a college freshman being asked to lead a full time discipleship school for a national youth ministry. We never dreamed of our twenty-four-year-old discipling forty-six interns from around the world 24/7 in prayer and fasting—or her sister discipling and training sixteen leadership teams in an international house of prayer. Who would dream that in their twenties they would regularly and individually be speaking to thousands? Who would dream where the thousands of appointments to disciple—the hundreds of family meetings—the challenging times of coaching choices and relationships—would lead? Those times of purposeful discipling opened doors that opened doors that opened doors. Our children have now been discipled better and more by great men and women of God far more advanced than we are. But wholeheartedness and some foundational discipling opened amazing doors to our now young adults. Little is much when God is in it. One date at a time-one weed seed at a time pulled out—one good seed at a time, planted deeply in an open heart. With God, all things are possible.

**Some serious advice: Seek and secure help from other disciples.**

Do you have a family member or Christian friend who is willing to help you follow Jesus more closely? To help you help each family member know and follow Jesus? If so, ask for help. Read this book together. Establish a weekly meeting to be accountable for and to supportively pray regarding these four basic life commitments:

+to consistently meet with Jesus

+to meet with and disciple your family members

+to serve and connect with your church family.

+to consistently connect with pre-Christian friends

At this weekly meeting, do four basic activities:

✦Start with praise to God

✦Reflect on the four commitments that you and your discipleship partner are committed to, and give God thanks and praise for any progress or good you see.

✦Talk candidly about difficulties you are having. Ask your partner to ask you questions to help you honestly know your thoughts, desires, and motives about what you are doing in the four commitment areas. Try to discover what God has said through scripture. Try to settle on what the Spirit is guiding you to do this week. If issues too complex to deal with arise, call a lay or professional pastor for help. They should be ab solutely delighted to help you with biblical, theological, or practical questions too complex for you or your partner. Consistently review the reasons for your commitments and practices.

Pray for God to empower what you together sense you need help with, and the things you sense Him calling you to do.

It would be wise to secure the agreement of a pastor who knows the person you are asking to meet with you. Some pastors themselves would be delighted to meet with you in this kind of arrangement, but most would feel incapable due to time pressures.

I also encourage you to secure some persons who care about your spiritual development and ask them to pray for you. You might prepare a monthly written record of your progress and prayer needs to distribute to them.

God, plus your best, plus a spouse or Christian friend, plus some prayer support, are far more than enough to get you on the road of growth as an authentic disciple of Jesus who is discipling family members, loving some neighbors, and serving as led in your local church. As you are practicing and growing in these areas, you are being equipped by the living God and your practical experience to disciple others in your local church to meet with Jesus, to disciple their families, and to love their neighbors. Every chapter in this book is strategic. If I can be one who helps you in any way, e-mail me at hp@gvnaz.org.

Do you remember the story of the horses from Chapter 8? If you don't, consider reading it again, right now. I ask again the question at the end of the story. Can you hear the whistle of the King? Our King? A thousand legitimate thirsts to be satisfied will scream at us to rush downhill. Most of our comrades, the best there are, will be heading full speed to the river. And it is understand-able— if one loses sight of the big battle, and the King. Somewhere there is enough truth in taking care of our own temporal needs that it makes very good sense to ignore the whistle of the King and continue downhill. Our comrades will by their life and words call us to be reasonable and join them in satisfying our legitimate appetites and thirsts.

But every once in a while, every so often, someone hears the whistle of the King and denies himself or herself and takes up whatever cross, gives up whatever is necessary, battles through every obstacle to follow the King—to re-spond to his whistle. That servant, that soldier, will be of special service to the King in the great war being waged to free every captive from eternal tyranny. Do you hear "the whistle"?

# Particularly for Pastors—
# A Church that Equips Parents
# for Ministry

"... Pastors ... prepare God's people for ministry ..." *Ephesians 4:11-12*

To my pastor friends in Jesus' mission, thank you for reading this afterword. You may remember reading my dream that there would exist at least one leader per church who understood and was committed to living out a disciple-making, leadership-multiplication ministry. The dream has changed markedly. I now dream and pray for there to be one Jesus-following, disciple-making, leadership-multiplying minister in *every household* in the church. I see it! It can be! It should be! I think it must be.

I dare not guess what God thinks about the condition of the church and the family unit in America. This morning I read in *USA Today* that 40% of Americans attend church at least once a week. With 17% more who attend at least one or two times per month, 57% of Americans are fairly "churched."

I have doubted the polls affirming that church attendees have almost as much struggle with various lists of godless behavior as the unchurched. However, I recognize that an unacceptable portion of the thoughts, emotions, desires, and motives of our congregations have been discipled far more by the godless influence of the world than the clear Truth of God's Word and the power of the Holy Spirit, especially through His body, the two or more who gather to help each other honestly follow Jesus. The result is a disappointingly low level of Christian character, service, influence, and power. God alone knows our condition and the reasons for it. Do you desire with me far better disciples of Jesus, resulting in far more disciples?

I believe that good preaching and teaching are necessary but not sufficient ministries for the church to be in the world but not of it. Can we come anywhere close to replicating Jesus' ministry of prayer and discipling to His twelve disciples? Could that create a level of heart-confidence in and heart-affection for Jesus that would translate far better into our moment by moment living than we now see? Could there ever become a multiplying wave of Christlike influence that would generate an authentic revival in our post-modern culture?

I think so, and I think it will happen when Christ is aggressively included in our conversations, in our family rooms, our kitchen, our bedrooms, our cars, our time and financial priorities, our relationships, our decision making—in short, when the church meets in relational ways to model for and coach each other in being doers of the Word, not just hearers. I think it will happen when somehow an army of us do the heart work with God necessary in ourselves and others we live with to recognize His presence and give honest consideration to the voice and will of our King.

---

*God will most help others through what*
*you learn through your heart work.*

---

How will this happen? Someone must respond better and more to God's grace. This will provide godly leadership. Someone must have the sensitivity and wisdom to lead themselves to Jesus, and then to lead the ones with whom they live, work, and attend church to Him, also—without driving them away in the process.

How will this happen? Prayer? Of course, and much more of it. Worship and teaching ministries? Certainly. Small groups? Yes. And there are many other good services to which we give ourselves. Children and youth ministries. Conferences. Compassionate ministries. Missions ministries.

But somehow, someway, it seems we must more strategically reconsider disciple-making. Could we possibly give what Jesus *practiced* and *commanded* another shot? Make disciples! How?

## 1. Be discipled by Jesus

To make disciples, we must be disciples. Pastor-friend, as always it starts with us. Let's do the old self-examination for authenticity—again. Do we need to let Jesus disciple our own hearts a little better? Do we—from our hearts—trust Him with our family? With the future? With His church—having faith for *His* vision and being obedient to *His* priorities? Do we need to invest time alone with Him as the first priority of our lives—letting Him pastor our hearts—connecting with Him regarding the good, the bad, and the ugly? Have we been strong enough in seeking Him to retain our first love? Have we been whole-hearted? Loving Him, not just with part, but with all of our hearts, so that we, like Jesus, seek to do absolutely nothing but our Father's Word and work? Does the sweet aroma of love, peace, joy, kindness, etc., flow through us, or is there a lot of relational shrapnel in the air? Of course, I have to raise the last issue. Are we purposely living with a few potential and emerging leaders to carefully work into their hearts what Jesus has worked into ours? The temptation is to think that if our hearts are too messy in any of the first four areas we might simply be making a bigger mess by getting too close to our sons, or staff, or deacons. Don't buy that. Simply be honest with God and go to work with Him on and in your heart. God will most help others through what you learn through your heart work (2 Corinthians 1:4). You know a major reason that lay people fear to take up "ministerial" work is that they perceive themselves to be too ungodly. Interesting that some of us "of the cloth" folks don't really feel comfortable in saying, "Follow me as I follow Jesus!" So, all of this is simply an invitation to more authentic discipleship. It is an invitation to walk in intimate communion and union with Jesus—uniting with Him to let Him make us like Him so that our lives will increasingly be instruments for His glory. This empowers us to purposefully select and effectively make disciples.

All of this is simply an invitation to very intentionally ...

⁺meet with Jesus personally

⁺minister with Jesus at home, in the church, and in the community

⁺mature to being more like Jesus, which includes ...

> ⁺make disciples of Jesus by helping them to meet with Jesus, minister with Jesus, and mature to being more like Jesus

> ⁺make disciple-makers by helping them to make disciples as stated above

## 2. Disciple your family

> ⁺If you are married, you have already chosen your first disciple. Ask your spouse to be a discipleship partner with you. This includes setting aside specific times to ...

>> ⁺*meet with Jesus* together, including sharing each other's heart and life battles, helping each other to ultimately bring each issue to Jesus, securing confidence in and commitment to His grace, His truth and His power in every arena, and being mutually accountable to each other for your...

>>> ⁺*ministry with Jesus* together with family, in church, and in the community

>>> ⁺*maturing to be more like Jesus*, including *making disciples* together, especially of your family, and *making disciple-makers* together (helping her lead women in the church to be disciples and disciple-makers)

> ⁺If you have children—certainly if they are still at home—you don't have to pray all night whether or not to disciple them; just how to do it

(Chapter 1-12). I am challenging you to help every parent in your church become a conscious disciple-maker of their at-home children. They will need to see you leading what you call them to do. You may want to ...

+Meet with Jesus together by establishing a weekly "appointment" with each of your family members (Chapters 5-7, 9). Reflect on the story of the night I was with David when I had a board meeting but we were not finished.

+Meet with Jesus as a family by starting a small group meeting for your family at least once a week (Chapter 9).

+Minister with Jesus together by occasionally or systematically leading your family in hosting a "friend event" (i.e., barbecue) for neighbors and friends, etc.

This will be a wonderful start for many. Others already do more than this.

### 3. Disciple an "open to anyone" group from your church

If you presently lead a small group, consider employing some of the principles and practices described in Chapter 9 of this book to help group attendees grow in being disciples of Jesus. If you do not have a small group you lead, you can start one. You can decide if you want it to be by invitation only or if anyone is welcome. I recommend making an open invitation. If you are concerned that too many would come, you can make it based on some criteria so everyone understands who is invited—like elders, or staff, or worship team. For example, if I had a concern that too many might come through an open invitation, I might invite all the men of the church to meet me at 6:30 a.m. on Wednesdays. My experience is that inviting all the men of the church to a group to meet with Jesus is a good way to start to determine who will be your "disciples." I strongly recommend that the meeting be a time to "look at" Jesus (worship), "listen to" Jesus (Word), and unite in prayer and ministry (work) with Jesus as described in Chapter 9. Here's why:

⁺You are facilitating each attendee in connecting with Jesus. You are helping them be disciples of Jesus through the meeting.

⁺You are training them for their own time with Jesus by explaining what to do, doing it, having them explain what is being done and why, practicing it under your coaching over and over until they've got it. They can then meet meaningfully with Jesus on their own. If you desire a copy of my booklet, "Meeting with Jesus," e-mail me at hp@gvnaz.org (handling charges may become necessary).

⁺What they have learned with you and are now doing on their own becomes the knowledge and skill development they need to meet with and disciple their family members individually.

⁺As they help their families to develop relationship with Jesus individually, they are preparing each family member to participate meaningfully in a beneficial family group, using the same skills learned while meeting in your group to benefit them in hosting the family groups.

⁺These family group leaders are now adequately skilled and comfortable in leading groups (they started with their own family), thus they can invite others into a group at their home, just like you are doing with them.

⁺You cannot personally disciple every person in your "open" group. Encourage prayer/accountability partners among the attendees, helping them to "grow up" in ministering to others as all Christian—not just the "pastors"—are called to do.

⁺You greatly enhance Christians experiencing authentic fellowship, building relationships around Jesus and His purposes and plans for life (1 John 1:3-4).

## 4. Disciple a group for disciple-makers

Gradually transition your group of disciples to a group for disciple-makers (only those you have prayerfully and carefully selected to be your long-term disciples invited).

I suggest some guidelines, not laws, for transitioning:

‣**Call to discipleship**—Consistently explain Jesus' call and invitation to your group for us to be His disciples. Call and send out all who come to your group for disciples to the lifestyle of discipleship, including …

> ‣meeting with Jesus, which you are showing them how to do in your open meeting. Ask all to be accountable to your group for progress.
>
> ‣ministering with Jesus—praying for, listening to, and blessing/serving their families, church family, and lost neighbors. Ask all to be accountable to your group for progress.
>
> ‣maturing to be like Jesus through loving and seeking His truth, honestly repenting of unChristlike motive, attitudes, words, and acts, being committed to being Christlike to all. Ask who will be accountable to your group for progress.
>
> ‣making disciples.
>
>> ‣strategically and formally meeting with individuals (family members, church family members, friends) to help each know and follow Jesus.
>>
>> ‣inviting those meeting with individually to meet together in order to meet with Jesus, thus forming their own meeting for disciples.
>>
>> ‣ask all in your group to be accountable for their progress in making disciples individually and in their group.

‣**Observe their discipleship**—Listen and watch carefully to find out who is actually working on his relationship with Jesus (meeting with Jesus, ministering with Jesus, and maturing to be more like Jesus), and helping his family, church family, and friends come to know and follow Jesus. Through inviting persons who meet with you to join you in Jesus' mission to disciple everyone possible, you can carefully watch for the ones to give yourself to on a long-term basis to help each other in making disciples of Jesus. You "date" them in the group for *disciples* to see whether or not to invite them into a "lifelong commitment" as one of your disciple-makers.

♦**Invest privately in disciple-makers**—Give primary attention—and as much as possible—to those who are following you in making disciples. They are responding to your challenge to make disciples. Invest in them outside of your formal meeting to help them mature not only as disciples of Jesus but as disciple-makers.

♦**Transition the focus of your group from being disciples to making disciples**—Give increasing time in your group for disciples to report progress in *making* disciples of Jesus (helping others know and follow Jesus) as compared to reporting progress in *being* disciples of Jesus (personally knowing and following Jesus). Those interested only in their own relationship with Jesus (or fearful of trying to help others) may be unhappy, even drop out of the group. Pray for them, seek to help them to plug in to a group that is dealing with their maturity level, or even invite them to stay and give God a chance to help them develop as disciple-makers. They can be invited to attend one of the new groups for disciples being started by those in your/their present group (because your group is transitioning into being a group for disciple-makers.)

> ♦Note: For many years I have maintained both kinds of groups, but this requires more time and fails to model for "my disciples" the transition if they are only able, for the long haul, to lead one group per week.

> ♦It is possible for your disciple-makers to lead two groups for a short period of time while transitioning the original group from a group for disciples (knowing and following Jesus) into a group for disciple-makers (helping each other to help others know and follow Jesus).

> > ♦While leading your group for disciples, start another group for

those from your group who have started their own group for disciples, agreeing with them (due to time constraints) that they would attend your group for disciple-makers and quit attending your group for disciples.

◆Those who stay in your group for disciples would gradually be led to either plant their own group and thus become eligible for your group for disciple-makers, or they could be guided to attend one of the new groups for disciples, led by one of the former members of your group.

◆Soon, your original group for disciples would either all be disciple-makers or be in another group for disciples, allowing you to lead only one group—your group of disciple-makers.

### ◆Who to select for long term disciple-making relationships

◆Select through serious prayer those you believe God has called you to. Jesus stayed up all night over this issue (Mark 3:14).

◆Select only those who have responded to your challenge and are committed to being and making disciples.

  ◆They meet with Jesus.

  ◆They minister with Jesus—at home, in the church, and in the world.

  ◆They are maturing in Christlikeness through awareness of Jesus and His truth, and demonstrated humility, repentance, and increased faith and obedience.

  ◆They make disciples—not just informally, but formally by gathering family members and others together to help each other know and follow Jesus.

  ◆Their goal is to have 10-12 lifelong disciples, and that each of their disciples will also have 10-12 lifelong disciples, thus multiplying the disciple-making process.

◆Select those who want to be with you, who value your walk with

Jesus, and who value your vision and strategy to make disciples. They are "loyal comrades." By giving yourself to them for as long as they continue to make disciple-makers, you maximize your (and their) potential for Kingdom impact.

♦**What to do in the meeting with disciple-makers** (contrasted with your meeting for disciples as discussed in Chapter 9)

  ♦Praise and honor God, invoking His presence and guidance.

  ♦Give God thanks and praise for *progress* through His empowerment in the following four goals all of the disciple-makers are mutually committed to and practicing (one of the pre-requisites for being invited to this meeting):

    ♦Loving Jesus and being personally discipled by Him.

    ♦Loving family members and discipling each personally and/or in a family group (see above and throughout this book what I suggest you do with your family).

    ♦Loving lost friends and informally and formally discipling them—praying for, connecting with, serving, and seeking to develop influence—especially with new or fringe church attendees. (Don't forget accountability for the lost around the world: praying, giving, and going as guided.)

    ♦Loving and formally discipling faith family members in a group or one-on-one.

  ♦Openly and mutually report *challenges* and *difficulties* in these goal areas. These become the areas for prayer, heart searching, faith, and growth. Ask questions as described in Chapter 6 and 7. Observe each other's thoughts, emotions, desires, and motives. Learn to exchange the darkness in hearts for the light of Jesus' truth. The truth seen, believed, and obeyed will empower these willing leaders to become excellent leaders. It will also model how they can help to "do heart surgery" with their disciples.

✦Make commitments based on God's guidance—including the commitment to be accountable at the next meeting—and pray for God's empowerment for success in commitment areas.

✦Watch for, and privately respond to, special needs of your group of disciple-makers.

If time limits prohibit the covering of all of the above each week, start the following week where you left off in the preceding week. The next week, start where you left off the preceding week, etc. Or rotate the order of discussion. The key is, over time, to consistently deal with all the issues, for all are essential. Each week the group faces difficulties, secures guidance, makes commitments, and prays. This enables the following week's progress reports and challenges to be always new and current, not stagnant.

✦Repeat this meeting after meeting.

Note: It is valuable to gradually let other group members lead this meeting in order to help equip them to lead meetings, both for disciples and for disciple-makers.

Spend as much time as possible with your disciples informally—meals, out after church, activities, trips, and ministry times (like evangelism calls or "pastoral" calls). The more you "live" together, the more the model approximates Jesus' method. When together, it is paramount to demonstrate likeness to Jesus, and to be honest and open about any unChristlikeness.

When disciples of Jesus are committed and genuinely accountable to the lifestyle described above, by God's grace something very special has been achieved in disciple-making. This lifestyle will work for the ongoing growth and maturity of their hearts and lives. There is always much heart work to be done, but they are now capable of being increasingly discipled (pastored) directly by Jesus, through His Word and Spirit. Their involvement in discipling others will also be used by God to strengthen their own hearts. If you will give yourself for the long term to helping your family and 5 or 10 disciple-makers to make disciples who make disciples, great will be your reward as the multiplication of disciple-makers unfolds. If you have 10 authentic disciples of Jesus each of whom make 10 authentic disciples who make 10 authentic disciples, there are 1000 leaders whose Kingdom influence—informally and formally—is much, much greater than many of the huge congregations whose members live lives that are show little difference than the lives of our culture's unchurched.

⁺**Support structures for disciple-makers**—In addition to the groups for disciples and disciple-makers, other support structures are helpful to strengthen the disciple-makers in the church:

+ Lay Seminary—The systematic teaching (perhaps a one-year cycle) where young converts can gain an essential overview of Christian essentials. It probably can and should be offered by you, the pastor, until associate pastors or gifted lay teachers are adequately prepared to teach the essentials of Christian truth and practice as a foundation for all the disciple-makers of the church—especially the parents. A person could go through the class several times and continue to gain help.

+ Disciple-making events (retreats, conferences, celebrations, seminars, etc.) that encourage and equip disciple-makers as need arises.

+ Disciple-making books, DVD's, tapes, and other well thought through resources.

+ The greatest human resource: A possible lifelong adoption and commitment by you the disciple-maker to your disciple-makers as long as they make disciples who make disciples who make disciples

What about the rest of the church? This works only for the 8 to 10 involved in your group, right? Never forget: Jesus was a very good pastor—the good Pastor (John 10:11). He knew that in addition to pastoring His flock (of 6,000-15,000 at some of the very credible, authentic seeker services) He had to disciple a few. His answer to "What about the rest of the church," (maybe the world-wide church) was to *pray and make disciples*. I am urging you to be a disciple of Jesus—to lead a lifestyle of prayer, to discipe your family, to love your neighbor—and to give a few hours per week to help a few others in the church to live this way. This is not your job. You don't get paid to do this—this is called being a Christ-ian, a follower of Jesus. You are going to urge lay persons to live this way and still work 40 or 50 hours a week at their jobs. This will require that we give more—all—of our hearts and lives to Jesus. We want nothing less than loving God wholeheartedly, with all our strength, right? Do you want to give Him anything less than truly loving Him with all your heart?

---

*His answer to "What about the rest of the church,"*
*(maybe the world-wide church) was to pray and*
*make disciples.*

---

But we pastors really want to be good pastors. We really do want God's best for His whole flock under our care. Like Jesus, we are broken-hearted for all the lost sheep not yet in the fold. Is there not something fast and big we can do to get disciple-making going for the whole church? Not really. Disciple-making is like having and raising children. It happens one at a time, and is best done through caring, sensitive relationships—which takes time. But there are some important steps that can help:

•If necessary, you can start more than one group. I lead six per week—four early mornings and two evening—plus several monthly meetings. Don't forget: You are adding, hopefully multiplying, small groups—but that takes time.

•You certainly have people in your church who have been sufficiently discipled by Jesus—through their devotional life, through thousands of good sermons and classes, through positive relationships in the church—so that they are now able and ready to lead. They don't need a lot of heart re-training, life healing, and skill development. They just need a vision and a track to run on. I am assuming that hundreds of thousands of authentic disciples of Jesus exist in our culture—any one of whom could read a book like this and commit to purposeful disciple-making. Give them this book or something better and see what God does.

    ♦You could plan, promote, and produce a workshop for families or parents. Use this book or something better for your material. You could thus teach disciple-making in the context of the family unit. This is the location of greatest interest, need, and potential. You could offer a group for everyone wanting help with the workshop information. If 100 sign up, you would need 10 leaders. From the 100 who signed up, you could prayerfully select 10-12 to meet with you in a small group. (This is starting to sound familiar.) You ask these to meet with you for an extended time to thoroughly discuss what they would need to become to facilitate a group of people committed to the workshop information. You would give yourself to discipling and coaching them in a weekly group and personally as needed. This could be your first group and your way of establishing a serious, reproducing, discipling ministry. My confidence is this: If the disciple-making ball ever gets rolling with Holy Spirit energy, the benefits and testimonies will create a whirlwind of life, of church-wide momentum, and of community impact. I am asking and believing God to empower the church I pastor to gain a reputation as a place where families get healed through healed and equipped parents. Everyone, especially Jesus, wants this for his/her family.

    ♦You could strategically disciple your Children's Director or Pastor to start a disciple-making group for parents of children. You could help your Youth Director or Pastor to start a disciple-making group for parents of youth—or a disciple-making group for youth. A disciple-making group for youth could have the most long range potential, if done well, of any disciple-making group in the church. Well-formed hearts and lives (like your staff or lay leaders) can take a tool like this book and, by generally following a track toward God's high calling, have a powerful ministry.

    ♦You might pray about the small group structure of your church being the household—the family unit. In other words, if you have 200 family units in your church, you pray to have at least 200 small groups—every family being a small group led by one or both adults of the family. You would sensitively include singles, gently encouraging them to use their home and time to invite friends and neighbors to their home for a small group meeting—or seeing to it that they are very welcomed into a family setting. You could announce your dream that every household and family become one of the church's small groups that meet together weekly to encourage one another, to love one another, to pray for one another, to bear one another's burdens, to speak the truth in love to one another, etc. Your small group roster would be very much like your church directory. Your dream includes every parent being a small group leader, and small group training is available for every leader. (Remember, parents are influencing, leading, discipling their families now—for better or worse.) Use whatever structures you presently use for leaders, or adapt them as necessary, for parents.

---

## *Christians really are aliens—not to follow earthlings but to lead them to their King.*

---

♦You could imagine that many of your adult groups (or all of them) are leadership groups. The leaders (parents) of your small groups (families) could gather regularly to help each other with the things that the small group leaders (parents) need. Remember, every Christian is called to leadership. Every Christian is a disciple of Jesus (Acts 11:26). Every disciple of Jesus follows Him and fishes for men (Matthew 4:19). Christians really are aliens—not to follow earthlings but to lead them to their King. We are to go into our world and live so differently that pre-Christians see our good lives and actually celebrate our Father in heaven. What they need is to be discipled by Jesus, to learn how to disciple their family, to honestly love their neighbor, and to help each other in these areas.

♦Your teaching, preaching, and total educational delivery system can be very helpful for vision-creating, passion-generating, and strategy-adopting. Books and tapes to strengthen basic biblical truths, theological issues, morality and practical issues are wonderful assets. Important learning can happen adequately in very large groups, via CDs and DVDs, seminars, etc. Godly information is our ally.

But we want and need to have our hearts formed—not just informed (Galatians 4:19). We have had too few doers of the Word, with too many sincere, well-intentioned, frustrated, discouraged hearers only. We can co-operate with the Holy Spirit in forming hearts through commitment to the highest truth in the context of gracious, honest, open, caring relationships. These relationships are usually initiated, established, and made successful by Word-formed, Spirit-led persons. We call them pastors ... leaders ... mentors ... coaches ... friends ... parents. Jesus called them disciple-makers.

Let's roll.